Revenue Statistics in Asian and Pacific Economies

OECD
dev
DEVELOPMENT CENTRE

Please cite this publication as:
OECD (2018), *Revenue Statistics in Asian and Pacific Economies*, OECD Publishing, Paris.
https://doi.org/10.1787/9789264308091-en

ISBN 978-92-64-30800-8 (print)
ISBN 978-92-64-30809-1 (PDF)
ISBN 978-92-64-30846-6 (ePub)

Corrigenda to OECD publications may be found on line at: *www.oecd.org/about/publishing/corrigenda.htm.*

Foreword

Revenue Statistics in Asian and Pacific Economies *is a joint publication by the OECD Centre for Tax Policy and Administration, the OECD Development Centre with the co-operation of the Asian Development Bank (ADB), the Pacific Island Tax Administrators Association (PITAA), and the Pacific Community (SPC) and the financial support of the European Union and the Government of Japan. It presents detailed, internationally comparable data on tax revenues for 16 Asian and Pacific economies (Australia, the Cook Islands, Fiji, Indonesia, Japan, Kazakhstan, Korea, Malaysia, New Zealand, Papua New Guinea, the Philippines, Samoa, Singapore, the Solomon Islands, Thailand and Tokelau) and on non-tax revenues for 4 Pacific economies (the Cook Islands, Papua New Guinea, Samoa and Tokelau). Four of these economies are OECD members (Australia, Korea, Japan and New Zealand). The approach used in* Revenue Statistics in Asian and Pacific Economies *is based on the well-established methodology of the* OECD Revenue Statistics *(OECD, 2018), which has become an essential reference source for OECD member countries. Comparisons are also made with the averages for OECD economies, Latin American and Caribbean (LAC) countries and 21 African countries.*

In this publication, the term "taxes" is confined to compulsory, unrequited payments to general government. As outlined in the Interpretative Guide to the Revenue Statistics, taxes are "unrequited" in the sense that benefits provided by government to taxpayers are not normally in proportion to their payments. The OECD methodology classifies a tax according to its base: income, profits and capital gains (classified under heading 1000), payroll (heading 3000), property (heading 4000), goods and services (heading 5000) and other taxes (heading 6000). Compulsory social security contributions paid to general government are treated as taxes, and are classified under heading 2000. Greater detail on the tax concept, the classification of taxes and the accrual basis of reporting is set out in the Interpretative Guide in Annex A.

Information is also presented on non-tax revenues in four Pacific economies. The term "non-tax revenue" includes all general government revenue that does not meet the OECD definition of tax revenues. Non-tax revenues include grants (e.g. foreign aid), returns on government market investments, rents on the extraction of resources from public lands, sales of government-produced goods and services, and the collection of fines and forfeits. More details on the definition of these revenues are available in Annex B.

Chapter 1 of this report provides an overview of the main tax revenue trends in the 16 economies and non-tax revenue trends in the 4 relevant Pacific economies from 2007 to 2016. A special feature on managing taxpayer compliance is found in Chapter 2, while Chapter 3 contains comparative tables on the level and structure of taxation in the 16 economies since 1990. Chapter 4 contains detailed information on tax revenues on a country-by-country basis. Chapter 5 includes information on the level and structure of non-tax revenues in selected Pacific economies.

Acknowledgements

Revenue Statistics in Asian and Pacific Economies is jointly produced by the Organisation for Economic Co-operation and Development (OECD)'s Centre for Tax Policy and Administration (CTP) and the OECD Development Centre (DEV) with the co-operation of the Asian Development Bank (ADB), the Pacific Island Tax Administrators Association (PITAA), and the Pacific Community (SPC) and the financial support of the European Union and the government of Japan. The partners would like to thank PITAA and the ADB for co-organising with the OECD a technical workshop in Nadi, Fiji on 7-8 December 2017, with financial support from the European Union. PITAA and SPC have also provided invaluable support and advice in expanding the coverage of this publication to the Pacific region.

The staff with responsibility for producing the publication were: Kensuke Tanaka, Head of Asia Desk, Jingjing Xia, Statistician, Prasiwi Ibrahim, Economist, and Alexander Pick, Coordinator at the OECD Development Centre under the supervision of the Director of the Development Centre and Special Advisor to the OECD Secretary-General on Development Mario Pezzini; Michelle Harding, Head, Tax Data and Statistical Analysis, Emmanuelle Modica, Statistician/Analyst, Leonie Beisemann, Statistician, Talita Yamashiro Fordelone, Advisor and Osamu Yoshida, Deputy Head, Global Relations of the OECD Centre for Tax Policy and Administration under the supervision of the Director Pascal Saint-Amans, Deputy Director Grace Perez-Navarro and the Head of the Tax Policy and Tax Statistics Division David Bradbury. The special feature benefited from useful inputs, based on "*A Comparative Analysis of Tax Administration in Asia and the Pacific 2018 Edition*" from the Asian Development Bank (ADB), provided by Donghyun Park, Principal Economist, Yasushi Suzuki, Public Management Specialist, and Yuji Miyaki, Public Management Specialist. Inputs were also provided by Sybrand Brekelmans, Intern at the Asia Desk, OECD Development Centre. Elizabeth Nash, Delphine Grandrieux, at DEV and Marie-Aurélie Elkurd at CTP assisted with the production and publication of this report and Stephanie Coic produced the cover.

The authors would like to thank other officials for their invaluable help in completing this publication. Support was also provided by Piera Tortora, Economist/Policy Analyst at the OECD Development Co-operation Directorate; Policy Officer Vincent Bigot, Head of Domestic Revenue Mobilisation Sector Stefan Agne, Head of Budget Support, Public Finance Management, Domestic Revenue Mobilisation Unit Erica Gerretsen at the European Commission; Team leader Economic Cooperation and Agriculture Section Emmanuelle Guiheneuf, Programme Manager Budget Support Marga Peeters, and Programme Manager Economic Cooperation and Agriculture Section Shaleshni Prasad at the Delegation of the European Union for the Pacific; Regional Economic Adviser Guillaume Barraut at the Delegation of the European Union to Thailand; Nilima Lal, Economic Statistics Advisor at the Pacific Community (SPC); Koni Ravono, Head of Secretariat, and Petero Maivucevuce, Training Coordinator at PITAA; as well as Koichoro Aritoshi, Rokiah Bakar, Assel Baltabayeva, Dariya Bissengaliyeva, Gil Beltran, Rowena Sta Clara, Meirbekov Daniyar, Kenneth Lee, Zhi Wei Lim, Datuk Haji Mohd Esa Abd Manaf, Mohammad Reezal Ahmad, Brian McAuley, Teresa Mendoza, Amir Abdul

Mutalib Shaari, Rena Nagayama, Hui Li Ng, Kunta Nugraha, Kumara Candra, Ratri Raden, Punjung Raras, Jiehui Shen, Hiroto Sugano, Adzhar Sulaiman, Joanne Tan, Mui Choo Teng, Suryani Widarta, Zarina Yerkebayeva, Dauren Zakumbayev, Marsidi Zelika, Shaun Bayne, Siva Gounder, Fraser Hawkins, Xavier Mitchell, Shiri Gounder, Shavindra Nath, Rhoda Karl, Hiyemute Waine, Jeannie Chadwick, Ian Filemu, Andrew Bryan Tafua Stratton, Eric D Saelea, Gibson Sanau, Sarah Wickham, Ajchara Chidkrue, Inthu-on Whangprasert, Iapi Japerse, Alan Shaw. The authors are also very grateful to all participants at the technical workshop in Nadi, Fiji in December 2017 as well as to colleagues working in national governments with whom they consulted regularly. These institutions include the finance ministries of Australia, the Cook Islands, Fiji, Indonesia, Japan, Kazakhstan, Korea, New Zealand, Papua New Guinea, the Philippines, Samoa, Singapore, the Solomon Islands, Thailand and Tokelau's National Statistics Office and the Inland Revenue Board of Malaysia.

This document was produced with financial support from the European Union. The views expressed herein can in no way be taken to reflect the official opinion of the European Union or of its member countries.

Table of contents

Figures

Executive summary

In light of the United Nation's 2030 Agenda for Sustainable Development, awareness of the need to mobilise government revenue in developing countries to fund public goods and services is increasing. *Revenue Statistics in Asian and Pacific Economies* presents key indicators to track progress on domestic resource mobilisation and to inform tax policy and reform.

Revenue Statistics in Asian and Pacific Economies presents detailed, internationally comparable data on tax revenues for 16 Asian and Pacific economies (Australia, the Cook Islands, Fiji, Indonesia, Japan, Kazakhstan, Korea, Malaysia, New Zealand, Papua New Guinea, the Philippines, Samoa, Singapore, the Solomon Islands, Thailand and Tokelau) and on non-tax revenues for 4 Pacific economies (the Cook Islands, Papua New Guinea, Samoa and Tokelau). The report also includes a special feature on managing taxpayer compliance.

Tax-to-GDP ratios in Asian and Pacific economies

In 2016, tax-to-GDP ratios in the Asia and Pacific region ranged from 11.6% in Indonesia to 31.6% in New Zealand. The tax-to-GDP ratio refers to total tax revenue, including social security contributions, as a percentage of gross domestic product (GDP). All countries in this publication had lower ratios in 2016 than the OECD average of 34.0% and half of the economies included in this publication had tax-to-GDP ratios above the Latin American and the Caribbean (LAC) average of 22.7%.

Six of the eight Asian countries covered in this publication had a tax-to-GDP ratio below 20% (the exceptions being Japan and Korea) whereas six of the eight Pacific economies had a tax-to-GDP ratio above 24% (the exceptions being Papua New Guinea and Tokelau).

Since 2015, nearly two-thirds of the economies included in this publication experienced decreases in their tax-to-GDP ratios and three countries registered no change in 2016. Only three economies (the Cook Islands, Korea and Singapore) had higher tax-to-GDP ratios in 2016 than in 2015. Since 2015, the largest changes in tax-to-GDP ratios were recorded in Papua New Guinea and the Solomon Islands (both decreases, of 2.2 and 2.1 percentage points, respectively) and in the Cook Islands and Korea (both increases, of 1.5 and 1.1 percentage points, respectively).

Most economies included in the publication have increased their tax-to-GDP ratios since 2007, with the exception of Australia, Indonesia, Kazakhstan, Malaysia, New Zealand and Papua New Guinea. The highest increases between 2007 and 2016 were observed in the Cook Islands and Samoa (5.6 and 3.9 percentage points, respectively), primarily explained by increases in value-added tax (VAT) and other taxes on goods and services in both countries. Across the same period, Kazakhstan and Papua New Guinea experienced the largest decreases in their tax-to-GDP ratios (11.2 and 8.6 percentage points, respectively), driven in both cases by decreases in corporate income tax (CIT) revenues. These were explained by the impact of declining prices of natural resources on the profitability of companies in the mining and oil sector in both countries, as well as by a reduction of CIT rates in Kazakhstan.

Tax structures in Asian and Pacific economies

Economies in Asia and the Pacific rely predominantly on goods and services taxes and on income taxes. In six economies in this publication (the Cook Islands, Fiji, Kazakhstan, Samoa, the Solomon Islands and Thailand), taxes on goods and services accounted for the largest share of tax revenues in 2016. Within goods and services, VAT is an important and increasing source of revenues in most economies. In 2016, VAT revenue ranged from 12.9% of total tax revenue in Australia to 46.1% of total tax revenue in the Cook Islands (the Solomon Islands and Tokelau do not impose VAT) and was higher as a share of total taxes in the Pacific compared to Asian economies. In the Pacific economies that apply a VAT, VAT accounted for more than 25% of revenues in 2016 except in Australia and Papua New Guinea. In contrast, VAT revenue generated less than 25% of total tax revenue in 2016 in all Asian countries except Indonesia.

Income taxes provided the main share of tax revenues in the nine remaining countries with the exception of Japan, where social security contributions (40.4% of total tax revenue) represented the principal source. Across all countries, revenues from CIT varied between 9.4% of total tax revenue in Samoa and 41.1% of total tax revenue in Malaysia in 2016. The three countries – Kazakhstan, Papua New Guinea and Malaysia – with the highest share of revenue from CIT (over 27% of total tax revenue) are highly reliant on revenues from natural resource companies in the oil and mining sector. All Asian countries except Indonesia, Japan and Korea had a greater share of CIT relative to personal income tax in 2016, whereas the reverse was observed for the Pacific economies (with the exception of Fiji).

Non-tax revenues in selected Pacific economies in 2016

This publication also includes non-tax revenues for four Pacific economies (the Cook Islands, Papua New Guinea, Samoa and Tokelau). In 2016, non-tax revenues as a percentage of GDP were significant for the Cook Islands and Tokelau but lower than 5% in Papua New Guinea and Samoa.

The sources of non-tax revenues varied between countries in 2016. Property-related income was the main source of non-tax revenues for the Cook Islands in 2016 (44.2% of non-tax revenues) and Tokelau (64.4%); in both countries, the majority of this income was from fishing rents. Grants were also an important source of revenues for all four economies in 2016, exceeding 30% of total non-tax revenues.

Special feature: Managing taxpayer compliance

A special feature explores important topics in the management of taxpayer compliance in Asian and Pacific economies. The level of taxpayer compliance and government enforcement is one of the factors that influence the level of tax revenues in an economy. In the management of taxpayer compliance, it is important to pay attention to a number of issues such as ensuring effective compliance risk management – including tax gap research, managing the compliance of large taxpayers, addressing international tax avoidance and evasion, optimising the use of tax withholding at source and third party reporting requirements, as well as appropriately calibrated voluntary disclosures policies and programmes. In Asia and the Pacific, the management of taxpayer compliance varies widely. For example, tax gap research has been implemented in a few larger economies – Australia and the Philippines, for instance – while almost all tax administrations in the region have in place an organisational division or unit managing the tax affairs of large taxpayers.

Chapter 1

Tax revenue trends in Asian and Pacific economies

In light of the United Nations 2030 Agenda for Sustainable Development, awareness of the need to mobilise government revenue in developing countries to fund public goods and services is increasing. Taxation provides a predictable and sustainable source of government revenue, in contrast with official development assistance and the volatility of non-tax revenues with respect to commodity prices.

This report presents detailed and internationally comparable data on tax revenues in 16 Asian and Pacific economies (Australia, the Cook Islands, Fiji, Indonesia, Japan, Kazakhstan, Korea, Malaysia, New Zealand, Papua New Guinea, the Philippines, Samoa, Singapore, the Solomon Islands, Thailand and Tokelau) and on non-tax revenues for 4 Pacific economies (the Cook Islands, Papua New Guinea, Samoa and Tokelau). This chapter discusses the key tax indicators for this group of economies: the tax-to-GDP ratio; the tax structure and the share of tax revenue by level of government; and non-tax revenue for selected Pacific economies. The discussion supplements detailed revenue information in Chapters 4 and 5.

1.1. Tax ratios

Tax-to-GDP ratios in 2016

In 2016, tax-to-GDP ratios in the Asia and Pacific region ranged from 11.6% in Indonesia to 31.6% in New Zealand. Eight of the 16 economies covered in this report had tax-to-GDP ratios above the Latin American and the Caribbean (LAC) average of 22.7% in 2016, and all economies in the publication had lower ratios than the OECD average of 34.0%. All of the Asian countries in this publication had a tax-to-GDP ratio below 20% with the exception of Japan and Korea, at 30.6% and 26.2% respectively. Among the Pacific economies, six of the eight economies included in this publication had a tax-to-GDP ratio above 24%. The exceptions in the Pacific are Papua New Guinea and Tokelau, with ratios of 12.2% and 14.7% respectively.

Indonesia had the lowest tax-to-GDP ratio among the Asian and Pacific economies included in this publication in 2016, at 11.6%. A relatively high share of agriculture in the economy (above 10% of GDP) compared to the other Asian countries in this publication as well as a low openness to trade contribute to this low tax-to-GDP ratio, together with high levels of informality (estimated to amount to 70% of employment), tax evasion and narrow tax bases (OECD, 2012[2]). Indonesia has undertaken reforms since 2002 to address these issues and increase tax revenues. These have focused on strengthening its tax administration through modernising processes and systems, building human capacity and enhancing the tax administration's integrity (OECD, 2018[3]). The Economic Survey for Indonesia (OECD, 2018[3]) explains that Indonesia aims to reach tax revenues amounting to 17% of GDP by 2019. The extra revenues will contribute to increasing financial capacity to fund government priorities and will reduce dependence on oil revenues (OECD, 2018[3]).

Structural economic factors are a key determinant of tax-to-GDP ratios across economies. These include the importance of agriculture in the economy, openness to trade and the size of the informal economy, as seen in Indonesia. Agriculture, for example is a challenging sector to tax: most people in the agriculture sector in developing economies are on low incomes and many are not registered for tax purposes (PEAKS, 2013[4]). In addition, agriculture benefits from numerous tax exemptions. For example, Malaysia allows an agriculture allowance to be deducted from profits of eligible businesses (Inland Revenue Board of Malaysia, 2016[5]) and goods and services related to the agriculture sector are exempt from import duty and excise duty (Ministry of International Trade and Industry, 2016[6]).

Figure 1.1. **Tax-to-GDP ratios (total tax revenue as % of GDP), 2016**

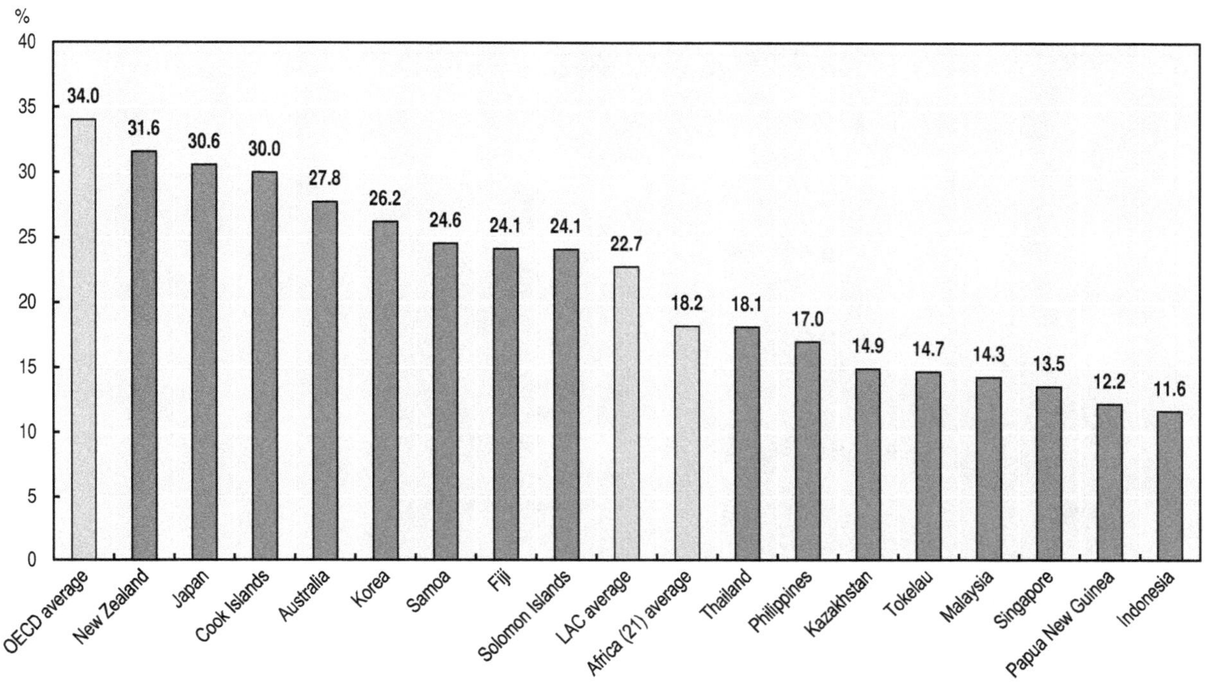

Note: The data do not include sub-national tax revenue for the Cook Islands, Fiji, Malaysia, Papua New Guinea, Samoa and the Solomon Islands as well as social security contributions for Indonesia.

The averages for Africa (21 countries), for LAC (25 Latin American and Caribbean countries) and the OECD (36 countries) are unweighted. Australia, Japan, Korea and New Zealand are part of the OECD (36) group. Data for Australia, Japan, Korea, New Zealand and the OECD average are taken from OECD (2018[1]), *Revenue Statistics 2018*, *https://doi.org/10.1787/2522770x*.

Source: Table 3.1.

StatLink *https://doi.org/10.1787/888933853471*

In addition to structural economic factors, tax policy and tax administration settings also strongly influence the level of tax revenues. These include the power of tax administrations, the levels of corruption within these administrations and tax morale (i.e. willingness of people to pay taxes) (OECD, 2014[7]). For example, Aizenman (2015[8]) found that in Asia, government effectiveness and institution quality are positively correlated with the level of tax-to-GDP ratio. Finally, in general, GDP per capita is also related to tax-to-GDP ratios. Tax-to-GDP ratios tend to be higher in high-income economies, although the relationship is not direct and is less pronounced at lower levels of income due to the influence of other factors.

The relationship between GDP-per-capita and tax levels across the Asian and Pacific economies in this publication is more varied and less direct than seen across the groups of LAC or OECD countries. Five Asian and Pacific economies have broadly similar GDP per capita and tax-to-GDP ratios as the majority of LAC countries. Papua New Guinea and the Solomon Islands have lower, and similar, per capita levels of income, but their tax-to-GDP ratios differ markedly. In contrast, Australia, Japan, Korea and New Zealand have higher per capita income and tax-to-GDP ratios. Finally, Singapore has the highest GDP per-capita of the 16 economies and one of the lowest tax-to-GDP ratios. The high GDP per capita in Singapore results from significant inward flows of foreign direct investment (FDI) due to its attractive business climate and stable political environment (UNCTAD, 2012[15]); whereas the tax-to-GDP ratio is explained by lower income tax rates (particularly on corporate income) and VAT rates, compared to other Asian and Pacific economies (UNESCAP, 2014[16]).

Figure 1.2. **Tax-to-GDP ratios and GDP per capita (in PPP) in Asian and Pacific economies, Latin America and the Caribbean, OECD and African countries, 2016**

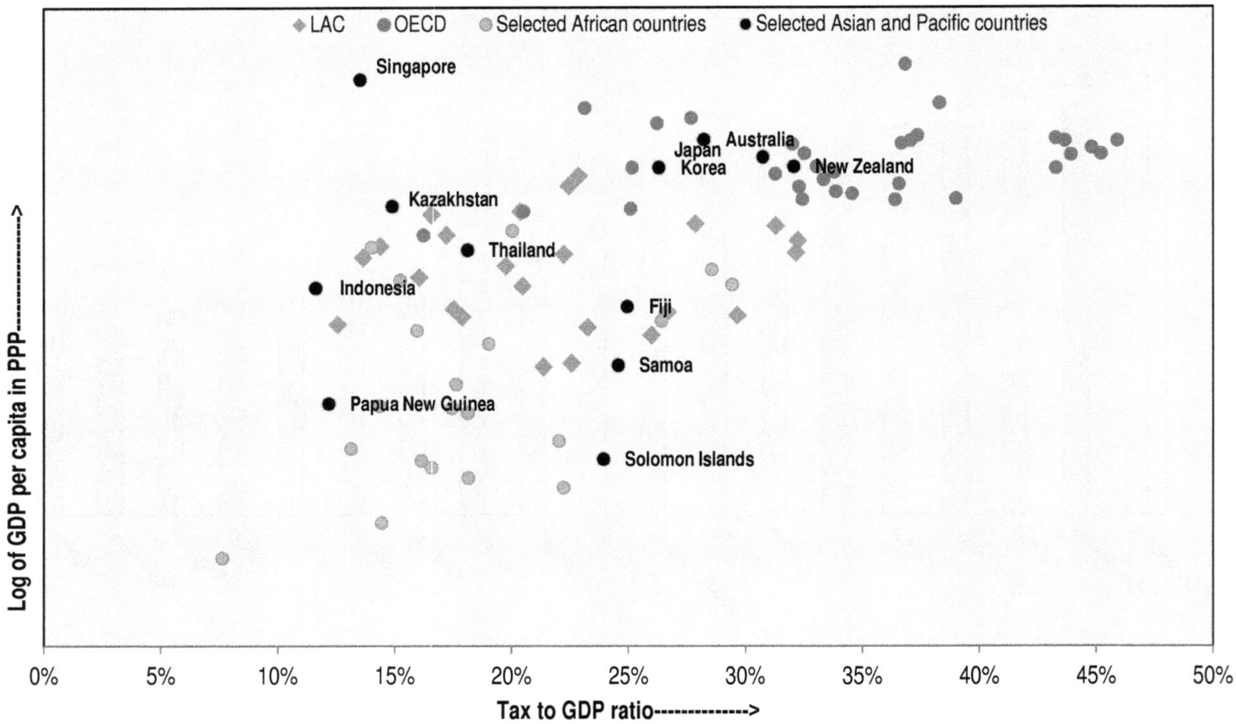

Note: The y-axis is on a logarithmic scale. The Cook Islands and Tokelau are excluded as GDP per capita data were unavailable for these countries. The purchasing-power-parity (PPP) between two countries is the rate at which the currency of one country needs to be converted into that of a second country to ensure that a given amount of the first country's currency will purchase the same volume of goods and services in the second country as it does in the first. The implied PPP conversion rate is expressed as national currency per current international dollar. An international dollar has the same purchasing power as the US dollar has in the United States. An international dollar is a hypothetical currency that is used as a means of translating and comparing costs from one country to the other using a common reference point, the US dollar [definitions derived from IMF (2016[9]) and WHO (2015[10])].

Source: IMF (2018[11]) *World Economic Outlook*, April 2018, International Monetary Fund for figures of GDP per capita. Tax-to-GDP ratios are sourced from the OECD (2018[1]) database (*www.oecd.org/tax/tax-policy/global-revenue-statistics-database.htm*).

StatLink https://doi.org/10.1787/888933853490

Box 1.1. **Enhancing domestic resource mobilisation in small island developing states through revenue statistics**

Small island developing states (SIDS) comprise a diverse group of the smallest and most remote economies in the world. They are located across the African, Asian, Latin American and the Caribbean, and Pacific regions. They share a common and unique set of development challenges, owing to their small populations and landmasses, spatial dispersion and remoteness from major markets, and exposure to severe climate-related events and natural disasters. With small and undiversified economies, SIDS are highly vulnerable to external shocks, as they rely strongly on the global economy for financial services, tourism, remittances and concessional finance.

Box 1.1. **Enhancing domestic resource mobilisation in small island developing states through revenue statistics** *(cont.)*

Common challenges faced by SIDS are the achievement of adequate domestic resource mobilisation and debt sustainability. Domestic revenues are often erratic due to narrow economic productive bases, often concentrated in sectors that are exposed to external fluctuations, such as natural resources or tourism. At the same time, SIDS typically have large current expenditures, as the high unit costs of providing services to small and scattered populations increase public sector spending above the average levels of other developing countries [29% of GDP in SIDS, compared to 22% in other developing countries in 2014 (Horscroft, 2014[12])]. Severe climate events and natural disasters also tend to have heavy fiscal and economic impacts. These combined factors lead to high levels of public debt for many SIDS (57% of GDP compared to 47% for all developing countries in 2015) and reduce the fiscal space to invest in development.

Taxes are an important and stable source of revenues in many SIDS economies, although their ability to raise domestic revenues varies significantly. The *Global Revenue Statistics* publications and database (OECD, 2018[13]) shows that among the Pacific SIDS, tax-to-GDP ratios ranged from 12.2% in Papua New Guinea to 30% in the Cook Islands in 2016. Among African SIDS, Cabo Verde had a tax-to-GDP ratio of 19% and Mauritius of 20% in 2016. Finally, SIDS in Latin America and the Caribbean displayed the biggest variation, from Dominican Republic's tax-to-GDP ratio of 13.7% to Cuba's ratio of 41.7%.

Tangible opportunities exist in many SIDS to expand domestic resource mobilisation and improve the stability of domestic revenues through enhanced management of key sectors, including fisheries, tourism and natural resource extraction. Policies to reduce "leakages" from these sectors – especially tourism – and to support backward and forward linkages with other domestic sectors (e.g. food and agriculture, consumer goods and construction) could expand the taxable production base.

Improving the efficiency of revenue collection, enlarging the tax base and employing efficient tax policies are also essential to increase the resources required to sustain development. The *Global Revenue Statistics* project supports 16 SIDS[1] in these efforts by providing accurate, comparable and detailed data on their tax revenues. This information is essential for tax policy making and administrative reforms, and forms a common evidence base for mutual learning across SIDS on how to scale up domestic resource mobilisation. This will be an important area for dialogue and collaboration across SIDS going forward.

1. SIDS in *Global Revenue Statistics* in 2018 are: Bahamas, Barbados, Belize, Cabo Verde, the Cook Islands, Cuba, the Dominican Republic, Fiji, Guyana, Jamaica, Mauritius, Papua New Guinea, Samoa, Singapore, the Solomon Islands, and Trinidad and Tobago.

Source: By Piera Tortora and Talita Yamashiro Fordelone, based on Making Development Cooperation Work for Small Island Developing States (OECD, 2018[14])

Changes in tax-to-GDP ratios in 2016

Since 2015, nearly two-thirds of the economies in this publication have experienced decreases in their tax-to-GDP ratios (Figure 1.3). Ten economies had lower tax-to-GDP ratios in 2016, relative to 2015, whereas only three economies (the Cook Islands, Korea and Singapore) had higher ratios in 2016. The ratios in the three remaining countries (Japan, New Zealand and the Philippines) remained stable. The scale of the changes in tax-to-GDP ratios, and in particular of the decreases in these ratios, was more pronounced in the Pacific economies covered in this publication; the three economies that experienced the largest decreases were all Pacific economies.

Although most economies saw decreases in their tax-to-GDP ratios between 2015 and 2016, all but four economies experienced changes that were comparatively small, at less than one percentage point of GDP. Changes larger than one percentage point were observed in the Cook Islands and Korea (both of which increased their tax-to-GDP ratios) and Papua New Guinea and the Solomon Islands (both of which decreased tax-to-GDP ratios).

Figure 1.3. **Annual changes in tax-to-GDP ratios (p.p.), 2016**

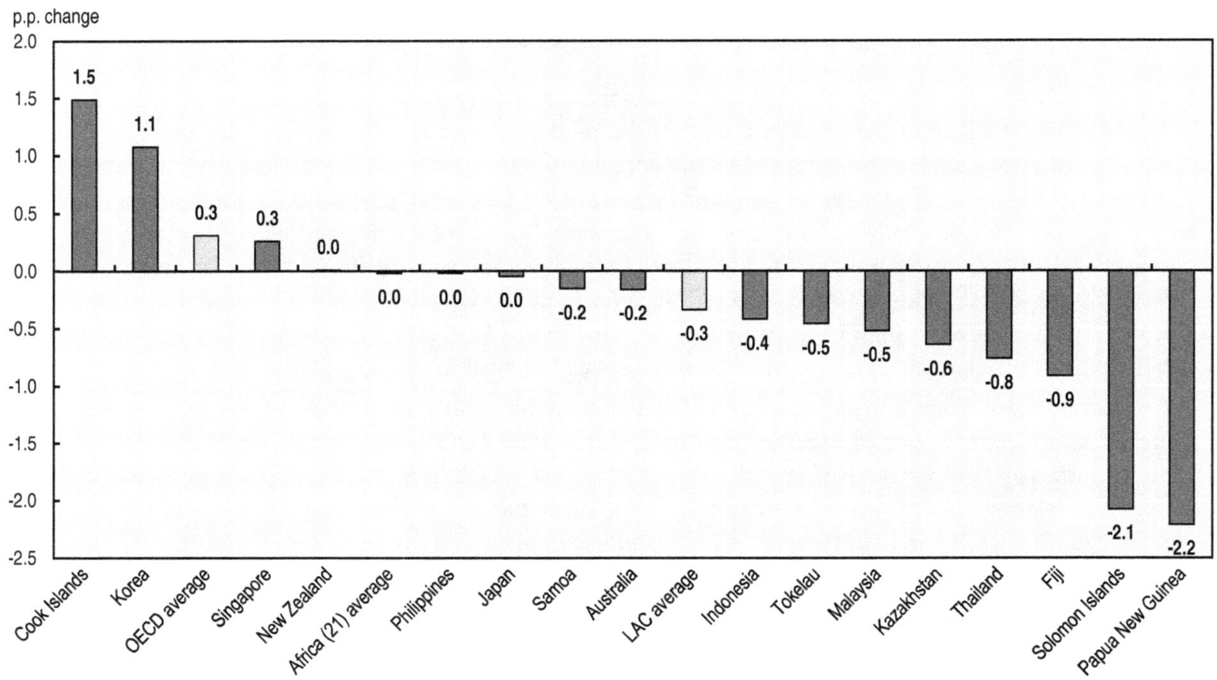

Note: The figures do not include sub-national tax revenue for the Cook Islands, Fiji, Malaysia, Papua New Guinea, Samoa and the Solomon Islands as well as social security contributions for Indonesia.

The averages for Africa (21 countries), for LAC (25 Latin American and Caribbean countries) and the OECD (36 countries) are unweighted. Australia, Japan, Korea and New Zealand are part of the OECD (36) group. Data for Australia, Japan, Korea, New Zealand and the OECD average are taken from OECD (2018[1]), *Revenue Statistics 2018, https://doi.org/10.1787/2522770x.*

Source: Authors' calculations based on Table 3.1.

StatLink *https://doi.org/10.1787/888933853509*

The Cook Islands and Korea had the highest increases of tax-to-GDP ratios between 2015 and 2016, at 1.5 percentage points (p.p.) and 1.1 p.p., respectively. The increase of the tax-to-GDP ratio in Korea was primarily the result of higher revenues from corporate income taxes (CIT) due to higher business activity, and of an increase in revenues from value-added tax (VAT) due to higher consumption (Reuters, 2017[17]). The increase of the tax-to-GDP ratio of the Cook Islands was the result of greater revenues from custom and import duties and from the departure tax, the latter reflecting increased activity in the tourism sector (ADB, 2017[18]).

The Solomon Islands and Papua New Guinea recorded the largest decreases among Asian and Pacific economies, at 2.1 p.p. and 2.2 p.p. between 2015 and 2016. These are also the only two economies that recorded a decrease in nominal tax revenues (1.3% and 7.9% respectively) between 2015 and 2016, in contrast to their GDP, which increased.

The decrease of the tax-to-GDP ratio in Papua New Guinea was the result of lower revenue from income taxes. Between 2015 and 2016, personal income taxes (PIT) decreased by 0.8 p.p. and CIT by 1.1 p.p., in both cases due to a general decline in business activity. As the economy of Papua New Guinea depends highly on natural resources, such as gold, liquefied natural gas (LNG), copper and oil, the global decline of prices for natural resources affected the business activity in the country in 2016 (ADB, 2017[18]). As a result, low business profitability contributed to the decline in CIT revenue while an unforeseen reduction in employment led to the decline in PIT revenues (Deloitte, 2018[19]; ADB, 2017[18]).

By contrast, the decline in the tax-to-GDP ratio in the Solomon Islands resulted from a decrease in revenues from non-VAT taxes on goods and services of 1.2 p.p. In addition, revenues from PIT decreased by 0.6 p.p. and from CIT by 0.3 p.p. between 2015 and 2016.

In addition to the decreases observed in the Solomon Islands and Papua New Guinea, Fiji also experienced a smaller decrease in its tax-to-GDP ratio, of 0.9 p.p., between 2015 and 2016. This was accompanied by a change in tax structure, as Fiji shifted away from revenues from VAT towards revenues from direct taxes and from other goods and services taxes. The large decrease in VAT revenues (3.1 p.p. of GDP) resulted from a decrease in the VAT rate from 16% in 2015 to 9% in 2016 (VAT Life, 2015[20]). This fall in revenues was partially offset by higher revenue from income taxes (0.9 p.p.) and other taxes on goods and services (1.2 p.p.). The latter can be partially explained by an increase of the service turnover tax rate from 5% to 10% in 2016, increasing total tax revenue by 0.5% of GDP, and by the introduction of a new environmental levy for service providers, which generated revenues equivalent to 0.7% of GDP (FRCS, 2018[21]).

Across all the Asian and Pacific economies in this publication, one of the main drivers of change in the tax-to-GDP ratio between 2015 and 2016 was revenue from taxes on goods and services, including both VAT (which mostly recorded increases) and other taxes on goods and services (mostly decreases). Income taxes were also an important cause of decreases observed between 2015 and 2016 (Figure 1.4). Taken together, the Asian and Pacific economies have, as a group, tended to shift toward revenues from value-added taxes and away from revenues from other goods and services taxes, as well as away from income taxes.

Figure 1.4. **Net changes in tax-to-GDP ratios between 2015 and 2016 by main type of taxes (p.p.)**

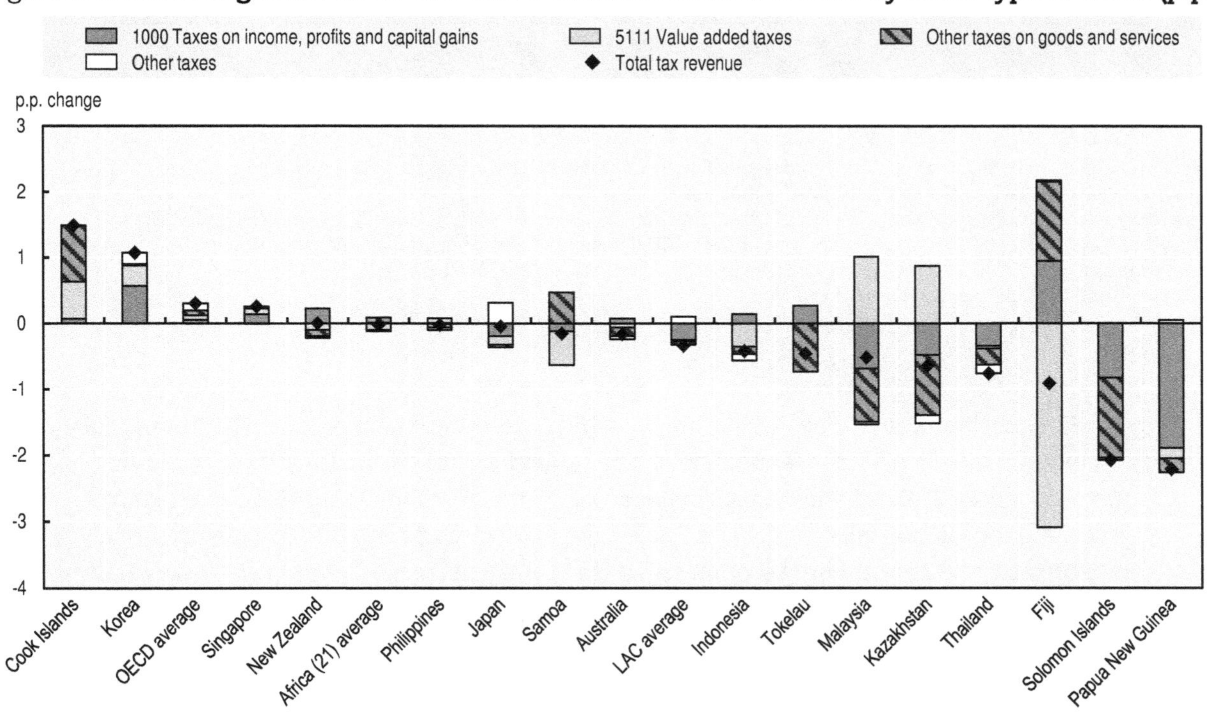

Note: The data do not include sub-national tax revenue for the Cook Islands, Fiji, Malaysia, Papua New Guinea, Samoa and the Solomon Islands as well as social security contributions for Indonesia.

The averages for Africa (21 countries), for LAC (25 Latin American and Caribbean countries) and the OECD (36 countries) are unweighted.

Australia, Japan, Korea and New Zealand are part of the OECD (36) group. Data for Australia, Japan, Korea, New Zealand and the OECD average are taken from OECD (2018[1]), *Revenue Statistics 2018, https://doi.org/10.1787/2522770x.*

Source: Authors' calculations based on OECD (2018[22]) "Revenue Statistics - Asian and Pacific economies: Comparative tables", OECD Tax statistics (database).

StatLink *https://doi.org/10.1787/888933853528*

Evolution of tax-to-GDP ratios since 2007

Across a longer time horizon, most economies in the publication have increased their tax-to-GDP ratios since 2007, with six exceptions (Australia, Indonesia, Kazakhstan, Malaysia, New Zealand and Papua New Guinea).

Figure 1.5. **Changes in tax-to-GDP ratios (p.p.), 2007-16 and 2012-16**

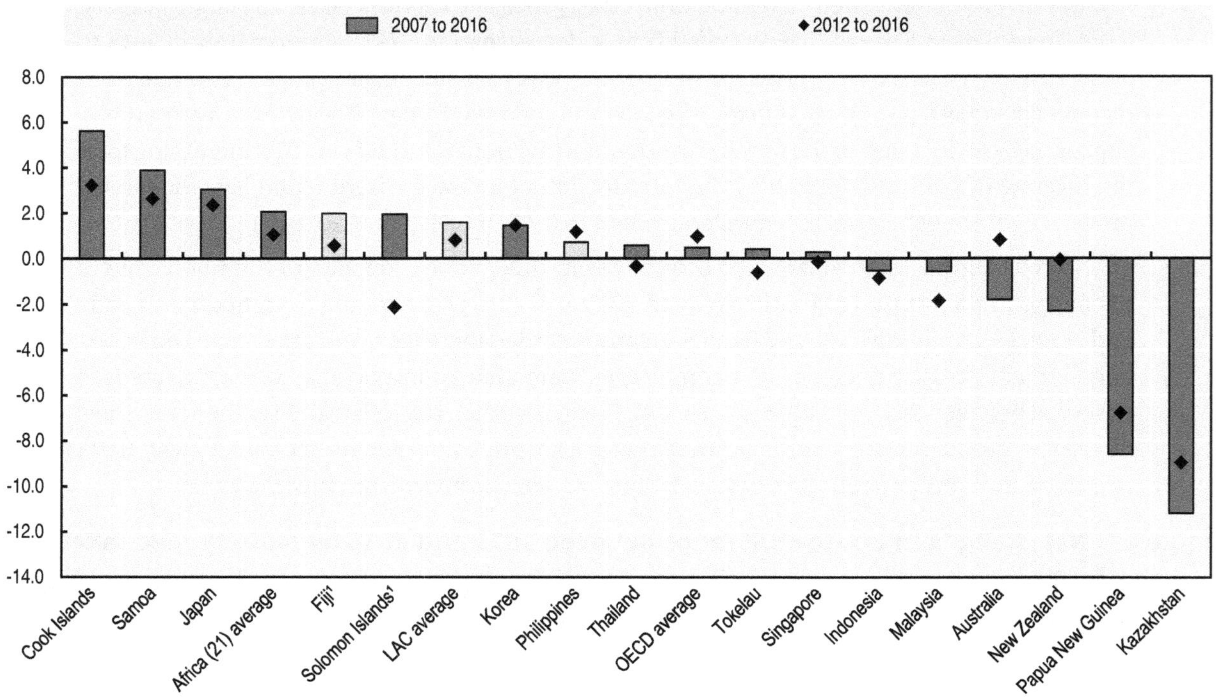

Note: The data do not include sub-national tax revenue for the Cook Islands, Fiji, Malaysia, Papua New Guinea, Samoa and the Solomon Islands as well as social security contributions for Indonesia.
The averages for Africa (21 countries), for LAC (25 Latin American and Caribbean countries) and the OECD (36 countries) are unweighted. Australia, Japan, Korea and New Zealand are part of the OECD (36) group. Data for Australia, Japan, Korea, New Zealand and the OECD average are taken from OECD (2018[1]), *Revenue Statistics 2018, https://doi.org/10.1787/2522770x.*
Data for Fiji and the Solomon Islands start in 2008.
Source: Authors' calculations based on Table 3.1

StatLink https://doi.org/10.1787/888933853547

Kazakhstan and Papua New Guinea, which were both affected by the recent fall in mineral resource prices, experienced the largest decreases in their tax-to-GDP ratio (respectively by 11.2 p.p. and 8.6 p.p.) between 2007 and 2016. The tax-to-GDP ratio of Samoa and the Cook Islands grew by 3.9 and 5.6 p.p. over the same period. The change in the tax-to-GDP ratio for the remaining economies ranged from a decrease of 1.8 p.p. in New Zealand to an increase of 3.0 p.p. in Japan.

Across the Asian countries included in the publication, the change in tax-to-GDP ratios ranged from -11.2 p.p. in Kazakhstan to 3.0 p.p. in Japan, with half of the Asian countries covered in this publication decreasing and the other half increasing. Across the Pacific economies in this publication, tax-to-GDP ratio changes ranged from -8.6 p.p. in Papua New Guinea and 5.6 p.p. in the Cook Islands.

Most economies maintained a consistent trajectory of change throughout the decade from 2007-2016, although in four economies trends differed in the first and second five-year periods. In the Solomon Islands, Tokelau and Singapore, tax-to-GDP ratios increased between 2007 and 2012 but declined (by 2.1, 0.6 and 0.1 p.p., respectively) between 2012 and 2016. In Australia, the tax-to-GDP ratio decreased between 2007 and 2012 but increased by 1.3 p.p. in the period up to 2016.

Changes in tax-to-GDP ratios from 2007 to 2016 by tax category

Between 2007 and 2016, CIT revenues were the driver for the major decreases observed in tax-to-GDP ratios experienced in many economies, whereas VAT contributed to several of the increases, although to a lesser extent. These changes reflect a diverse range of policy measures and economic developments in Asian and Pacific economies.

Of the six economies where tax-to-GDP ratios declined between 2007 and 2016, decreasing CIT revenues contributed to the decline in five of them (the exception being New Zealand). The declines in the tax-to-GDP ratio in Papua New Guinea (8.6 p.p.) and Kazakhstan (11.2 p.p.) both resulted from lower CIT revenues, which declined by around 8 p.p. in both. As noted, both economies were strongly affected by declines in natural resource prices. Kazakhstan also reduced its corporate tax rate from 30% in 2008 to 20% in 2009.

Figure 1.6. **Net changes in tax-to-GDP ratios between 2007 and 2016 by main type of taxes (p.p.)**

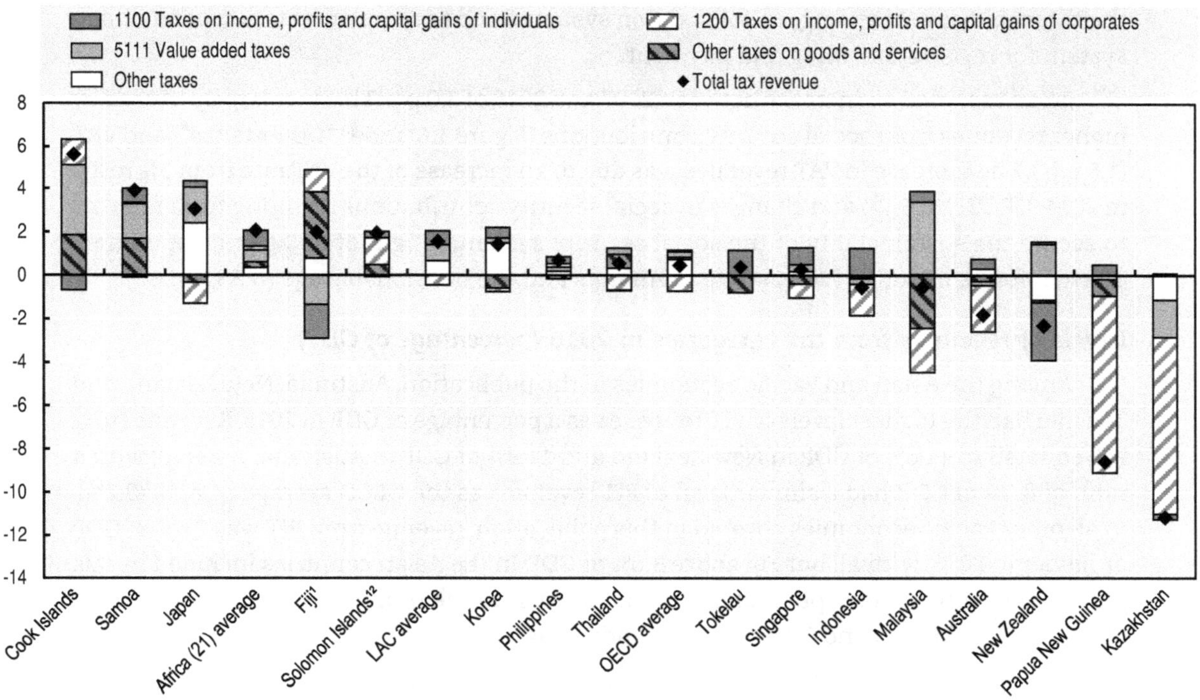

Note: The data do not include sub-national tax revenue for the Cook Islands, Fiji, Malaysia, Papua New Guinea, Samoa and the Solomon Islands as well as social security contributions for Indonesia.

The averages for Africa (21 countries), for LAC (25 Latin American and Caribbean countries) and the OECD (36 countries) are unweighted. Australia, Japan, Korea and New Zealand are part of the OECD (36) group. Data for Australia, Japan, Korea, New Zealand and the OECD average are taken from OECD (2018[1]), *Revenue Statistics 2018, https://doi.org/10.1787/2522770x*.

1. Data for Fiji and the Solomon Islands start in 2008.
2. Data on import duties for the Solomon Islands are estimated for 2008.

Source: Authors' calculations based on OECD (2018[22]), "Revenue Statistics - Asian and Pacific economies: Comparative tables", OECD Tax statistics (database).

StatLink *https://doi.org/10.1787/888933853566*

Malaysia's overall tax-to-GDP ratio declined by 0.6 p.p. between 2007 and 2016 due to a decrease in income tax revenues over that period caused by a fall in petroleum prices and the sustained decrease of the CIT rate over several years, which has come down from 27% in 2007 to 24% in 2016 (World Bank, 2016[23]). Between 2015 and 2016, the structure of Malaysia's revenues from goods and services taxes changed due to the introduction of the VAT system; however, this has subsequently been reversed by the new government.[1]

Ten economies recorded increases in their tax-to-GDP ratios between 2007 and 2016. The highest increases were seen in the Cook Islands and Samoa, where VAT and other taxes on goods and services were the main contributor. Higher VAT revenues in the Cook Islands (by 3.2 p.p.) are partially explained by an increase of the VAT rate from 12.5% to 15% in April 2014 (Cook Islands News, 2013[24]) and were supplemented with higher revenues from the departure tax (1.5 p.p.) following an increase in tourism (Ministry of Finance of the Cook Islands, 2017[25]).

The increase of 3.9 p.p. in the tax-to-GDP ratio for Samoa was mainly driven by increases in VAT (1.6 p.p.) and other taxes from goods and services (1.7 p.p.). These increases followed major tax policy and administrative reforms, including: a review of the principal taxation acts; the creation of new units for effective administration and improved services for responding to taxpayers in a timely manner; an increase of excise tax rates; an increase in the threshold of VAT; an upgrade of taxation systems; and the implementation of an online system for registration, filing and payment.

Japan recorded an increase between 2007 and 2016 of 3.0 p.p. This was largely caused by higher revenues from social security contributions (Figure 1.6 under "Other taxes") and VAT (1.8 p.p.). The increase in VAT revenues was due to an increase of the VAT rate from 5% to 8% in 2014 (OECD, 2016[26]) and changes in social security contributions resulting from reforms to secure the sustainability of the social security system in light of an ageing population. These reforms included increases to premiums and the pensionable age (IPSS, 2014[27]).

Levels of revenues from tax categories in 2016 (percentage of GDP)

Among the Asian and Pacific economies in the publication, Australia, New Zealand and Tokelau had the highest levels of PIT revenues as a percentage of GDP in 2016. Revenue from PIT equated to 11.6% of GDP in New Zealand and 11.3% of GDP in Australia. Tokelau, with a ratio of 8.0% of GDP, had a similar level of PIT revenues as the OECD average in 2016 (8.2%). In all other Pacific economies covered in this publication, revenue from PIT was 2.0% of GDP or higher in 2016, with all but Fiji above 3.0% of GDP. In the Asian countries included in this publication, with the exception of Japan and Korea, revenue from PIT ranged between 1.5% of GDP in Kazakhstan and 3.1% of GDP in Indonesia in 2016.

Revenues from CIT were lower than revenues from PIT in almost all economies included in this publication. In 2016, CIT revenues ranged from 2.3% of GDP in Indonesia to 5.9% of GDP in Malaysia (excluding Tokelau, which does not have a corporate tax). Only Fiji and Malaysia had corporate tax revenues that amounted to more than 5% of GDP.

Social security contributions play a small role in the tax revenues of Asian and Pacific economies. Ten of the economies in this publication, and all of the Pacific economies, do not levy social security contributions. In the remaining economies, revenue from social security contributions are relatively low in Malaysia (0.3% of GDP), Kazakhstan (0.5% of GDP) and Thailand (1.0% of GDP), the Philippines (2.4% of GDP), significantly below the LAC and OECD averages (3.7% and 9.2% of GDP, respectively). Among of the Asian and Pacific economies in this publication, only Korea and Japan have high shares of revenue from social security contributions (6.9% and 12.4% of GDP, respectively).

Figure 1.7. **Tax structures as percentage of GDP, 2016**

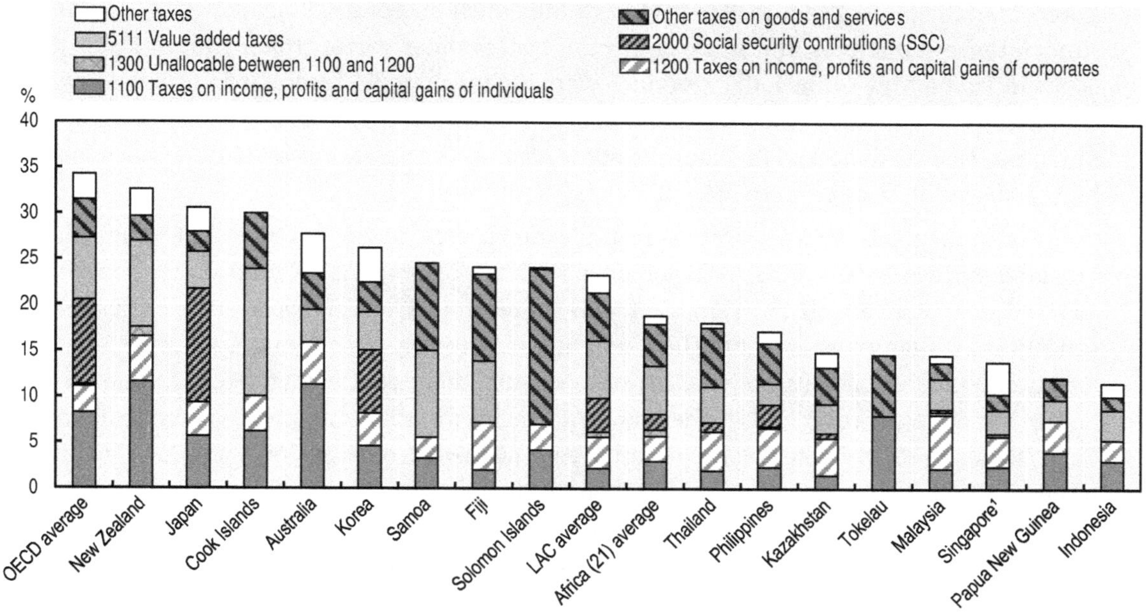

Note: The data do not include sub-national tax revenue for the Cook Islands, Fiji, Malaysia, Papua New Guinea, Samoa and the Solomon Islands as well as social security contributions for Indonesia.

The averages for Africa (21 countries), for LAC (25 Latin American and Caribbean countries) and the OECD (36 countries) are unweighted. Australia, Japan, Korea and New Zealand are part of the OECD (36) group. Data for Australia, Japan, Korea, New Zealand and the OECD average are taken from OECD (2018[1]), *Revenue Statistics 2018, https://doi.org/10.1787/2522770x.*

1. Social security contributions in Singapore are estimated for 2016.

Source: OECD (2018[22]), "Revenue Statistics - Asian and Pacific economies: Comparative tables", OECD Tax statistics (database).

StatLink *https://doi.org/10.1787/888933853585*

Revenue from taxes on goods and services is below 8.0% of GDP in most Asian countries in the publication, ranging from 4.3% of GDP in Singapore to 7.4% in Korea. The exception is Thailand, which raises revenues equivalent to 10.3% of GDP. Revenues from taxes on goods and services are therefore lower than in other regions, as represented by the Africa, LAC and OECD averages. By contrast, taxes on goods and services raise higher levels of revenues in most Pacific economies, ranging from 12.1% of GDP (New Zealand) and 20.0% of GDP (the Cook Islands). Among Pacific economies, only Australia (7.5% of GDP) and Tokelau (6.7% of GDP) have revenues from goods and services taxes below 10% of GDP.

1.2. Tax structures

The tax structure, measured as the composition of tax revenues of different types, is the second key indicator in *Revenue Statistics*, since different taxes have different economic and social effects. Across the 16 economies in this publication, the composition of taxes varies widely, reflecting their different policy choices, economic structures and conditions, tax administration capabilities and historical factors.

Tax structures in 2016 and evolution since 2007

The tax structure of the economies covered in this publication varied greatly in 2016: in nine economies, the main source of tax revenue was income taxes, while six economies mainly obtained tax revenues from taxes on goods and services. Japan is the only country in this group in which the greatest share of revenues was derived from social security contributions.

In 2016, income taxes were the predominant source of revenue for Australia, Indonesia. Korea, Malaysia, New Zealand, Papua New Guinea, the Philippines, Singapore and Tokelau. Among these economies, the share of income tax revenues varied from 31.2% in Korea to 61.5% in Papua New Guinea. CIT revenues were higher than PIT revenues in several Asian countries (Malaysia, the Philippines and Singapore), while the Pacific economies in this group (Australia, New Zealand and Tokelau) and some Asian countries (Korea and Indonesia) raised higher shares of revenue from PIT.

Taxes on goods and services were the main source of tax revenue in Kazakhstan, Thailand, Fiji, the Cook Islands, the Solomon Islands and Samoa in 2016, contributing between 48.2% (Kazakhstan) and 77.2% (Samoa) of total tax revenue. Taxes on goods and services also contributed the largest share for the LAC and the Africa average, amounting to just over 50% of total tax revenue. Within this group, taxes from goods and services other than VAT, such as excises and import duties, were typically higher than VAT, ranging from 20.4% of total tax revenues in the Cook Islands to 70.1% in the Solomon Islands. Among these economies, only the Cook Islands received a larger share of revenue from VAT (46.1% of total tax), while VAT's contribution to total tax revenue (38.5%) was similar to that of other taxes on goods and services (38.7%) in Samoa.

As discussed earlier, social security contributions play a small role in revenues for most Asian and Pacific economies, with a few exceptions. In 2016, Japan derived the largest share of revenues from social security contributions, at 40.4% of total tax revenues. Social security contributions also play a significant role in revenues in Korea (26.2%) and the OECD average (26.2%).

Figure 1.8. **Tax structures as a percentage of total tax revenue, 2016**

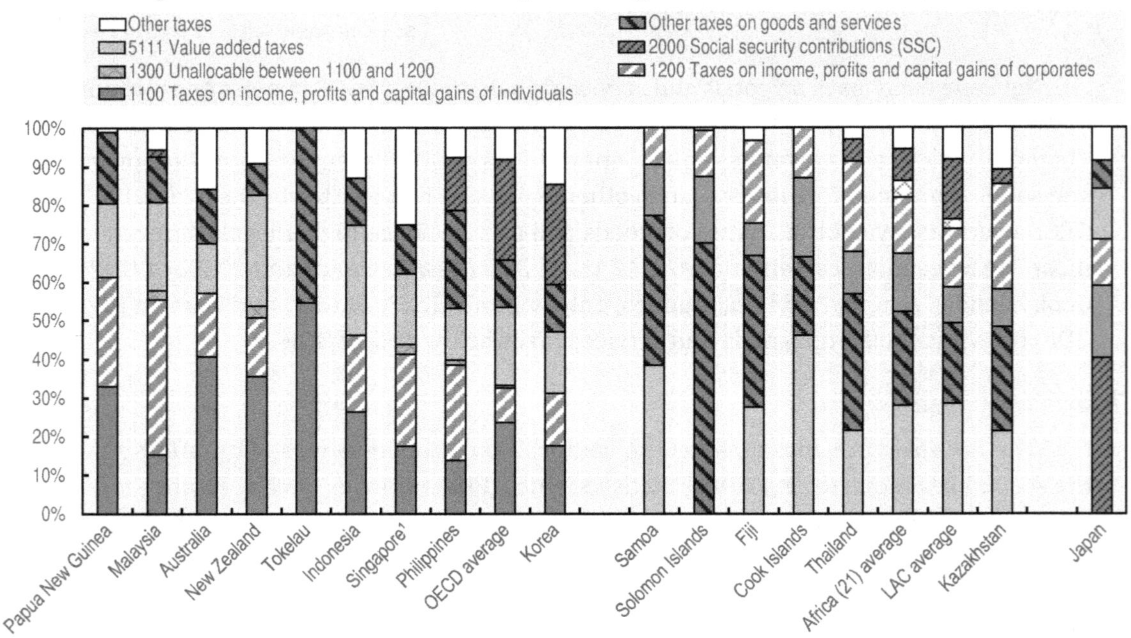

Note: The data do not include sub-national tax revenue for the Cook Islands, Fiji, Malaysia, Papua New Guinea, Samoa and the Solomon Islands as well as social security contributions for Indonesia.

The averages for Africa (21 countries), for LAC (25 Latin American and Caribbean countries) and the OECD (36 countries) are unweighted. Australia, Japan, Korea and New Zealand are part of the OECD (36) group. Data for Australia, Japan, Korea, New Zealand and the OECD average are taken from OECD (2018[1]), *Revenue Statistics 2018, https://doi.org/10.1787/2522770x*.

Social security contributions in Singapore are estimated for 2016.

Source: OECD (2018[22]), "Revenue Statistics - Asian and Pacific economies: Comparative tables", OECD Tax statistics (database).

StatLink https://doi.org/10.1787/888933853604

Across the full group of economies in this publication, VAT is an important and increasing source of revenues in most. In 2016, VAT revenue ranged from 12.9% of total tax revenue in Australia to 46.1% of total tax revenue in the Cook Islands. Tokelau and the Solomon Islands do not have value added taxes. Levels of VAT as a share of total taxes are higher in Pacific than in Asian economies. In the Asian countries, VAT revenue was less than 25% of total tax revenue in 2016 in all countries except Indonesia, ranging from 13.5% in the Philippines to 23.5% in Malaysia. In the Pacific economies that apply a VAT system, only Australia and Papua New Guinea had shares of VAT of less than 25% in 2016 (12.9% and 19.0%, respectively); Samoa and the Cook Islands had the largest shares (38.5% and 46.1% of total tax revenues, respectively).

Figure 1.9. **Revenue from value added tax and other taxes on goods and services as a percentage of total tax revenue, 2016**

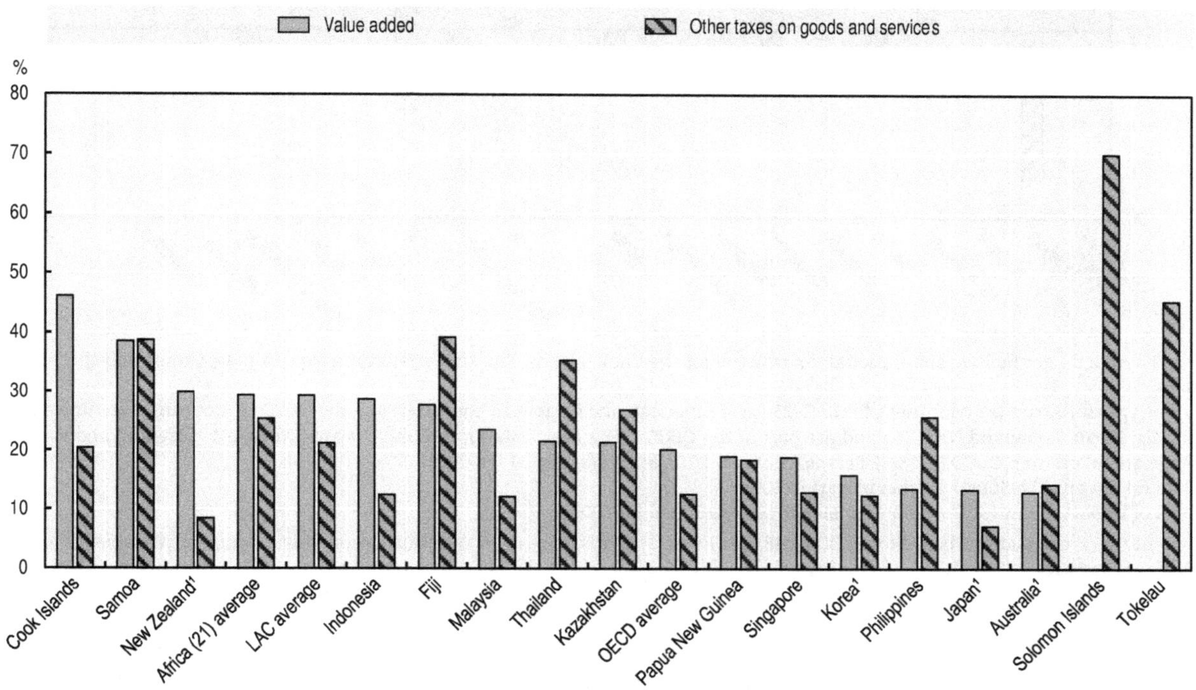

Note: The data do not include sub-national tax revenue for the Cook Islands, Fiji, Malaysia, Papua New Guinea, Samoa and the Solomon Islands.

The averages for Africa (21 countries), for LAC (25 Latin American and Caribbean countries) and the OECD (36 countries) are unweighted. Australia, Japan, Korea and New Zealand are part of the OECD (36) group. Data for Australia, Japan, Korea, New Zealand and the OECD average are taken from OECD (2018[1]), *Revenue Statistics 2018*, *https://doi.org/10.1787/2522770x*.

Source: OECD (2018[22]), "Revenue Statistics - Asian and Pacific economies: Comparative tables", OECD Tax statistics (database).

StatLink *https://doi.org/10.1787/888933853623*

Revenues from other taxes on goods and services contributed between 7.1% of total tax revenue in Japan and 70.0% in the Solomon Islands in 2016. The high share in the Solomon Islands is derived from general taxes on goods and services, such as the goods tax and the sales tax, as the Solomon Islands does not apply a VAT. Shares of non-VAT taxes in total revenue are also comparatively high in Thailand, Fiji, Samoa and Tokelau, where they are larger than 35.0%.

In 2016, revenue from other taxes on goods and services played a more prominent role in the Pacific economies than in Asian countries covered in this publication. Five of the eight Pacific economies generated more revenue from other taxes on goods and services than from VAT, whereas five of the eight Asian countries received more revenue from VAT. For the Africa, LAC and the OECD averages, revenue from VAT contributed a larger share to total tax revenue than other taxes on goods and services.

Figure 1.10. **Changes in revenue from value added tax and other taxes on goods and services as a percentage of total tax revenue between 2007 and 2016**

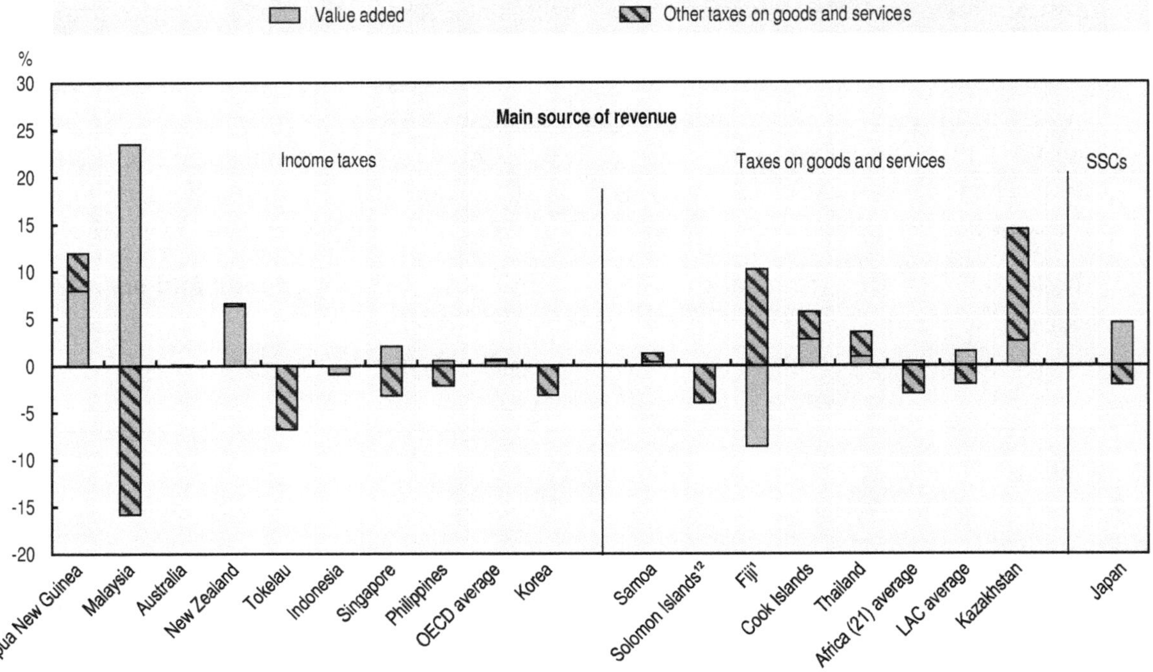

Note: The data do not include sub-national tax revenue for the Cook Islands, Fiji, Malaysia, Papua New Guinea, Samoa and the Solomon Islands.

The averages for Africa (21 countries), for LAC (25 Latin American and Caribbean countries) and the OECD (36 countries) are unweighted. Australia, Japan, Korea and New Zealand are part of the OECD (36) group. Data for Australia, Japan, Korea, New Zealand and the OECD average are taken from OECD (2018[1]), *Revenue Statistics 2018, https://doi.org/10.1787/2522770x*.

1. Data for Fiji and the Solomon Islands start in 2008.

2. Data of import duties for the Solomon Islands are estimated for 2008.

Source: Authors' calculations based on OECD (2018[22]), "Revenue Statistics - Asian and Pacific economies: Comparative tables", OECD Tax statistics (database).

StatLink https://doi.org/10.1787/888933853642

In the period between 2007 and 2016, revenue from other taxes on goods and services was more variable than revenue from VAT in all economies covered in this publication. The change between 2016 and 2007 varied from a decrease of 6.7 p.p. in Tokelau to an increase of 11.8 p.p. in Kazakhstan.

Figure 1.10 shows the change in revenue from value added taxes and other taxes on goods and services between 2007 and 2016. In this figure, countries are ordered by their main source of revenue (i.e. taxes on goods and services, income taxes, social security contributions, as shown in Figure 1.8).

- Out of the six Asian and Pacific economies that obtain the majority of their tax revenues from taxes on goods and services, five experienced an increase in revenue from non-VAT taxes on goods and services over the period 2007 to 2016. This contrasts with the changes between 2007 and 2016 observed for the Africa average and the LAC average, whose revenue from non-VAT taxes on goods and services declined over the same period. It also contrasts with trends observed in the economies whose main share of revenue is derived from income taxes or social security contributions, where revenue from non-VAT taxes also declined in most cases.
- Among the nine economies that received the majority of their tax revenue from taxes on income, changes in the share of VAT revenue were more pronounced than changes in non-VAT goods and services taxes, which can largely be attributed to policy changes.

Four economies introduced VAT or increased their VAT rate between 2007 and 2016: New Zealand, from 12.5% to 15% in 2011 (OECD, 2012[28]); Japan, from 5% to 8% in 2014 (OECD, 2016[26]); the Cook Islands, from 12.5% in to 15% in 2014 (Cook Islands News, 2013[24]); and Malaysia, which replaced its sales tax with a VAT at 10% in 2015 (Bloomberg, 2015[29]). Since the introduction of VAT in 2015, VAT revenues in Malaysia have strongly increased from 15.8% of total taxation to 23.5% in 2016.

The only economies in this publication that experienced a decline in VAT revenues over this period were Fiji and Indonesia. Fiji's VAT revenue declined by 8.6 p.p. in 2016 to 27.6% of total tax revenue, following a decrease of the VAT rate from 15% to 9%. VAT revenues in Indonesia declined more slightly, by 0.8 p.p., between 2007 and 2016.

Figure 1.11. **Revenue from corporate income tax and personal income tax as a percentage of total tax revenue, 2016**

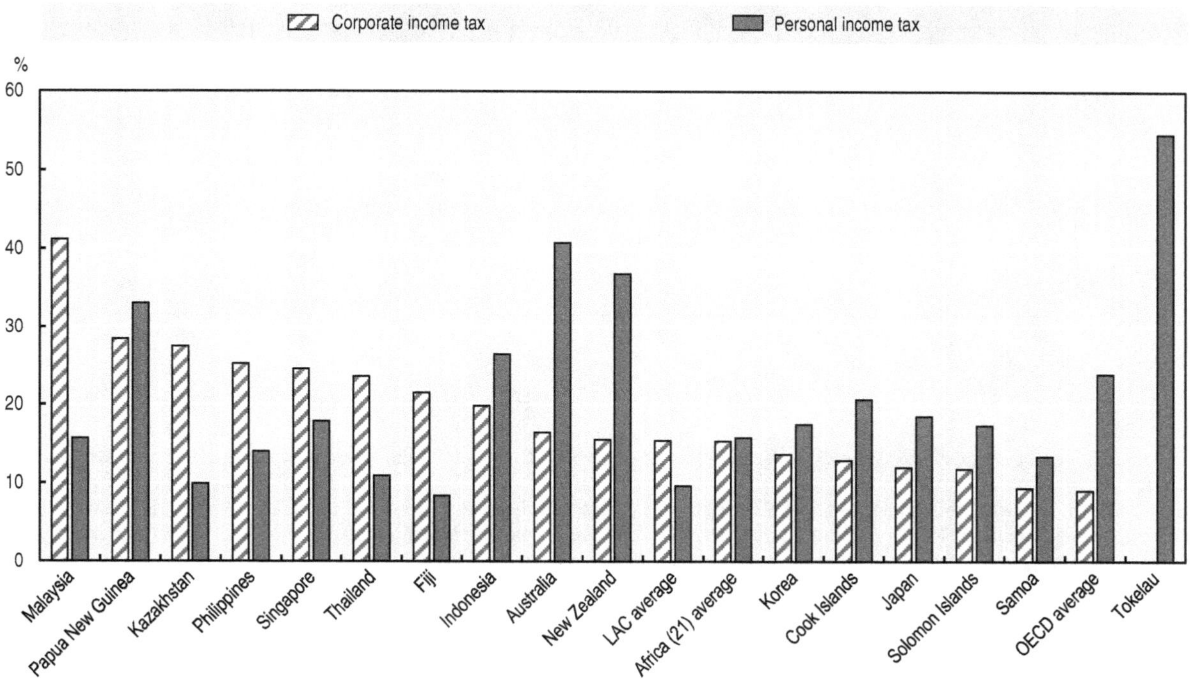

Note: The data do not include sub-national tax revenue for the Cook Islands, Fiji, Malaysia, Papua New Guinea, Samoa and the Solomon Islands.

The averages for Africa (21 countries), for LAC (25 Latin American and Caribbean countries) and the OECD (36 countries) are unweighted. Australia, Japan, Korea and New Zealand are part of the OECD (36) group. Data for Australia, Japan, Korea, New Zealand and the OECD average are taken from OECD (2018[1]), *Revenue Statistics 2018, https://doi.org/10.1787/2522770x.*

A small amount of income tax revenue (less than 5%) cannot be allocated to either personal or corporate tax in Malaysia, New Zealand, the Philippines and Singapore as well as the three regional averages [Africa (21) average, LAC average, OECD average].

Source: Authors' calculations based on OECD (2018[22]), "Revenue Statistics - Asian and Pacific economies: Comparative tables", OECD Tax statistics (database).

StatLink *https://doi.org/10.1787/888933853661*

Within income taxes, differences were observed between trends in corporate and personal income taxes across the period, as shown in Figure 1.11. In 2016, revenues from CIT varied between 9.4% of total tax revenue in Samoa and 41.1% of total tax revenue in Malaysia. The three economies with the highest share of revenue from CIT, Kazakhstan (27.4%), Papua New Guinea (28.4%) and Malaysia, received most CIT revenue from companies in the oil and mining sector. By contrast, revenues from PIT ranged between 8.4% of total tax revenues in Fiji to 40.8% in Australia and 54.6% in Tokelau in 2016. Tokelau does not have a CIT and obtains the majority of its tax revenue from PIT.

All Asian countries except Indonesia, Japan and Korea had a greater share of corporate relative to personal income taxes in 2016. In contrast, all Pacific economies covered in this publication except Fiji had a greater share of PIT than CIT.

Figure 1.12. **Changes in revenue from corporate income tax and personal income tax as a percentage of total tax revenue between 2007 and 2016**

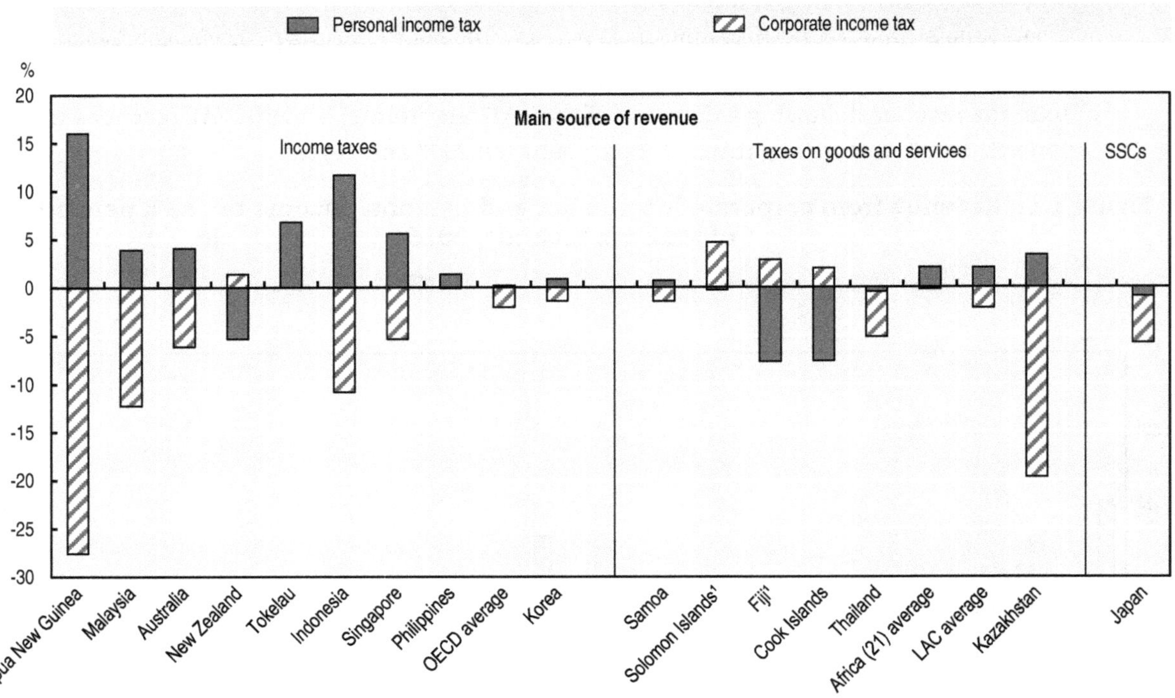

Note: The data do not include sub-national tax revenue for the Cook Islands, Fiji, Malaysia, Papua New Guinea, Samoa and the Solomon Islands.

The averages for Africa (21 countries), for LAC (25 Latin American and Caribbean countries) and the OECD (36 countries) are unweighted. Australia, Japan, Korea and New Zealand are part of the OECD (36) group. Data for Australia, Japan, Korea, New Zealand and the OECD average are taken from OECD (2018[1]), *Revenue Statistics 2018, https://doi.org/10.1787/2522770x.*

Data for Fiji and the Solomon Islands start in 2008.

Source: Authors' calculations based on OECD (2018[22]), "Revenue Statistics - Asian and Pacific economies: Comparative tables", OECD Tax statistics (database).

StatLink https://doi.org/10.1787/888933853680

Between 2007 and 2016, revenues from CIT were more variable as a share of total tax revenues than revenues from PIT in all economies covered in this publication. In most economies, CIT revenues were lower in 2016 than in 2007. Revenue from CIT decreased as a share of total tax revenues in 12 economies, by between 0.1 p.p. in the Philippines and 27.6 p.p. in Papua New Guinea.

The decreases in CIT as a proportion of total revenues were significantly more pronounced in the economies whose main source of revenues were income taxes. In most of these economies, the decreases in CIT revenues were partly offset by increases in PIT revenues. CIT revenues increased as a share of total revenues between 2007 and 2016 in four economies: the Cook Islands (1.9 p.p.), Fiji (2.8 p.p.), New Zealand (1.4 p.p.) and the Solomon Islands (4.6 p.p.).

By contrast, the share of revenues from PIT decreased for only six Asian and Pacific economies between 2007 and 2016, and the scale of the decreases was comparatively small, ranging from 7.7 p.p. in Fiji to 0.3 p.p. in the Solomon Islands. Revenue from PIT increased as a share of total taxation for all other economies in this period, from 0.7 p.p. in Samoa to 16.0 p.p. in Papua New Guinea.

Box 1.2. **VAT revenue ratios in Asian countries**

The VAT revenue ratio (VRR) measures the difference between the VAT revenue collected and what would theoretically be raised if VAT was applied at the standard rate to the entire potential tax base in a "pure" VAT regime and all revenue was collected. A VRR of 1 suggests no loss of VAT revenue as a consequence of exemptions, reduced rates, fraud, evasion or tax planning. This section describes the VRR levels in the Asian countries in this publication.

There was a wide disparity of VRRs in Asian countries in 2016. The Philippines had the lowest VRR ratio at 0.23 and Thailand had the highest at 0.86. Of the countries in this publication, Japan, Korea and Singapore have relatively high VRR (exceeding 0.6), above the OECD average of 0.51. This is partially because of the relatively broad-based VAT in each country: Japan does not have any reduced rates while in Singapore, only international services are zero-rated, with the only exemptions applying to the sales and leases of residential properties and to most financial services (MOF, 2017[39]). Korea has a reduced rate on a number of goods and services. In comparison, many OECD countries have one or more reduced rates (OECD, 2016[26]), which partly explains the lower average VRR in the OECD region.

The VRR needs to be interpreted with caution and can be affected by several factors that inflate it. One reason can be where exemptions on products and services relating to intermediate consumption can lead to a cascading effect that increases VAT revenue (IMF, 2017[38]). For example, in Thailand, excessive exemptions may cause "cascading", which artificially increases the VRR. Another reason the VRR may be inflated is refund processes do not work correctly, which may discourage taxpayers from claiming their VAT refunds, resulting in artificially higher VAT revenue and VRR.

Figure 1.13. **VAT revenue ratio (VRR) in Asian countries, 2016**

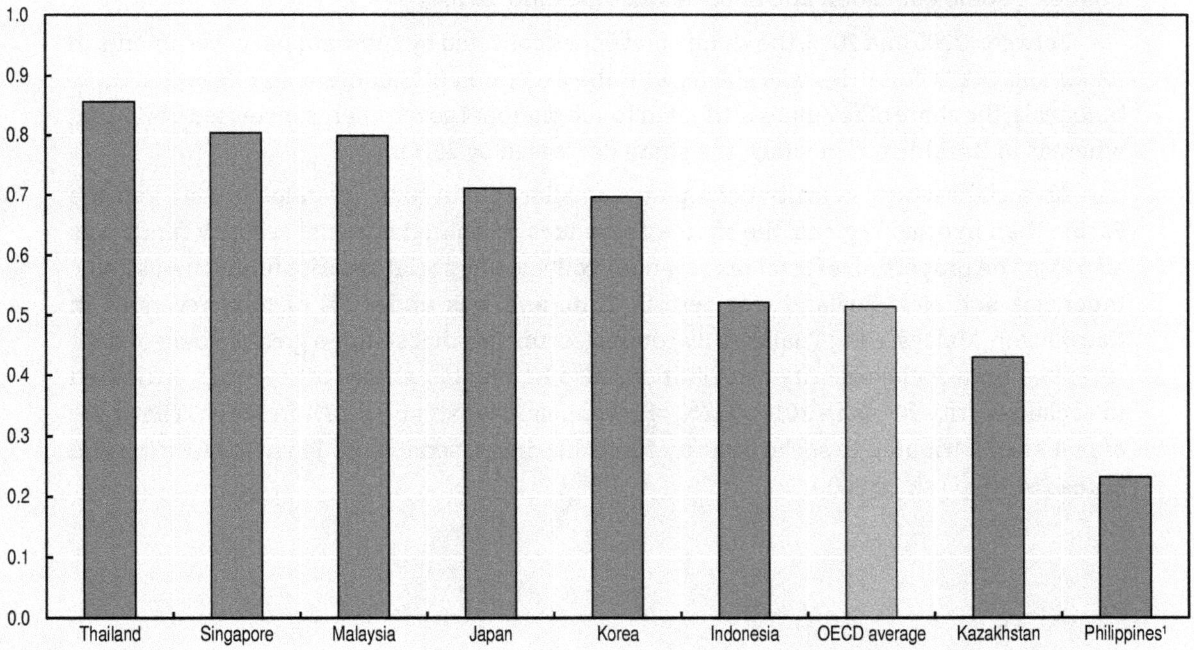

Note: OECD average (36 countries) is unweighted. Data for Singapore and Malaysia are for 2015, data for Thailand are for 2014.
1. The VRR is currently underestimated as the VAT revenue collected at customs is not accounted for in total VAT revenue in this publication [this revenue could not be distinguished from revenue from other import duties and is currently classified under heading 5120 (taxes on specific goods and services)].

Source: VAT rates are sourced from national governments, the Trading Economics and KPMG websites and OECD (2018[30]). The final expenditure consumption figures come from the United Nations Statistics Division website (UN, 2018[31]) and the OECD Annual National Account (OECD, 2018[32]). VAT revenues are sourced from the country tables in Chapter 4.

StatLink https://doi.org/10.1787/888933853699

1.3. Taxes by level of government

This section discusses the relative share of tax revenues attributed to the various subsectors of general government in 2016. The different sub-sectors discussed here are central government, sub-national government (including state government, where relevant) and local government) and social security funds.

In many economies included in this publication, the share of sub-national taxes was comparatively small as a share of total tax revenues in 2016. Shares of sub-national government tax revenue in the Asian countries ranged from 5.2% in the Philippines and 8.0% in Thailand to 17.5% in Korea, 23.9% in Japan and 24.5% in Kazakhstan. In Indonesia, revenues attributed to sub-national governments are rising and were over 10% in 2016, following the shift of property taxation to the local level in 2014. In New Zealand, sub-national government revenues were 6.7%; and in Australia subnational revenues (including both state and local revenues) amounted to 20.5% of total revenues.

The types of taxes levied at local government level vary between countries. Local governments in the Philippines have a narrow range of taxes under their jurisdiction, relying on property taxes and taxes on income and profits. By contrast, Sub-national governments in Japan and Korea raised revenue from taxes on income and profits, property taxes, taxes on goods and services, payroll (Korea only) and other taxes. The share of sub-national government revenue also depends on the range of services which local governments are expected to provide: for example, local revenues are higher in Japan since local governments finance a wide range of goods and services including public welfare and are responsible for financing some education and debt services (Beshho, 2016[33]).

Between 2000 and 2016, the share of revenues collected by sub-national governments in Asian and OECD countries was stable, with the exception of Indonesia and Kazakhstan. In Indonesia, the share of revenues attributed to sub-national governments increased by 7.7 p.p., whereas in Kazakhstan in which the share decreased by 25.4 p.p.

As social security contributions play a smaller role in total revenues in Asia and the Pacific than in other regions, the share of revenues attributed to social security funds was also low. The proportion of total tax revenues collected by social security funds in Australia, Indonesia and New Zealand was zero in 2016, and was under 6% of total revenues in Kazakhstan, Malaysia and Thailand. By contrast, countries that source a greater share of their revenues from social security contributions also had higher shares of revenues attributed to social security funds in 2016: 40.4% of revenues in Japan and 26.2% in Korea. The share of revenues attributed to social security funds has increased in both Japan (by 6.8 p.p.) and Korea (14.1 p.p.) since 2000.

Table 1.1. **Attribution of tax revenues to sub-sectors of general government as a percentage of total tax revenue, 2016**

	Federal or central government				Sub-national government				Social security funds			
	1995	2000	2010	2016	1995	2000	2010	2016	1995	2000	2010	2016
Australia[1]	77.5	81.8	80.2	79.5	22.5	18.2	19.8	20.5	..	..	..	..
Indonesia	..	96.8	92.8	89.1	..	3.2	7.2	10.9	..	..	..	..
Japan	41.2	38.7	33.0	35.7	25.2	26.1	25.9	23.9	33.6	35.2	41.1	40.4
Kazakhstan	..	50.1	81.3	71.8	..	49.9	16.2	24.5	..	..	2.5	3.7
Korea	69.2	68.2	60.0	56.3	18.7	15.1	16.6	17.5	12.1	16.7	23.3	26.2
Malaysia	100.0	98.0	98.2	98.2	..	..	..	..	..	2.0	1.8	1.8
New Zealand	94.7	94.3	92.8	93.3	5.3	5.7	7.2	6.7	..	..	..	..
Philippines	90.8	81.5	82.2	80.9	..	5.3	5.2	5.2	9.2	13.1	12.7	14.0
Thailand	..	88.9	86.3	86.4	..	7.5	6.6	8.0	..	3.7	7.1	5.6

Note: The figures exclude the Cook Islands, Fiji, Papua New Guinea, Samoa, the Solomon Islands as sub-national data are not available. Tokelau and Singapore are also excluded, as they do not have local governments.
Australia, Japan, Korea and New Zealand are part of the OECD (36) group. Data for Australia, Japan, Korea, New Zealand and the OECD average are taken from OECD (2018[1]), *Revenue Statistics 2018, https://doi.org/10.1787/2522770x.*
1. Sub-national figures in Australia include data from state and local governments.
Source: OECD (2018[22]), "Revenue Statistics - Asian and Pacific economies: Comparative tables", OECD Tax statistics (database).

StatLink https://doi.org/10.1787/888933853718

1.4. Non-tax revenues in selected Pacific economies

This publication also includes information on non-tax revenues for selected Pacific economies for which data are available. Non-tax revenues are defined as all revenues received by general government that do not meet the OECD definition of taxes, as set out in the Interpretative Guide (Annex A). They are further divided into five categories according to the definitions set out in Annex B: grants; property income; sales of goods and services; fines, penalties and forfeits; and miscellaneous and unidentified revenues.

Non-tax revenues as a percentage of GDP

Non-tax revenues were equivalent to a significant share of GDP in 2016 for two of the Pacific economies for which data are available: the Cook Islands (11.5% in 2016) and Tokelau (236.5% of GDP in 2016). The very high levels of non-tax revenues in Tokelau, measured as a share of GDP, are due to the fact that they derive primarily from payments from foreign vessels for access to Tokelau fishing waters. In the 2008 System of National Accounts these revenues are recorded as part of GNI, but they do not add to GDP. By contrast, non-tax revenues are comparatively low in Papua New Guinea and Samoa (2.9% and 4.8% of GDP in 2016, respectively).

Further, non-tax revenues have been on an upwards trend since 2007 for the Cook Islands and Tokelau, whereas they have been declining as a share of GDP for the other two economies. The upwards trend for Tokelau has been driven by the increase in revenues from property income, which is entirely sourced from fishery income. Tokelau receives support from New Zealand to strengthen the management of its Exclusive Economic Zone to maximise Tokelau's revenue collection from its international fisheries (New Zealand Foreign Affairs & Trade, 2018[34]). Fisheries income also increased after Tokelau became a partner to the Nauru Agreement, which administers the fishing vessel-day scheme (VDS). The VDS is the system to sustainably manage the world's largest tuna fishery in the Western and Central Pacific Ocean and has increased revenue to participating islands by over 500% in the past six years (Parties to the Nauru Agreement, 2016[35]).

The increase in non-tax revenue for the Cook Islands has been predominantly driven by an increase in grant revenues from New Zealand, Australia and the European Union. This support contributes to upgrading infrastructure, growing sustainable tourism, and supporting initiatives that strengthen the public sector and improve education, health and social services.

Table 1.2. **Non-tax revenue of main headings as a percentage of GDP in selected Pacific economies, 2016**

	2007	2008	2009	2010	2011	2012	2013	2014	2015	2016
Cook Islands	5.5	5.1	9.0	12.8	8.0	8.2	14.1	16.8	9.0	11.5
Papua New Guinea	4.0	4.1	3.5	4.7	3.3	3.1	2.4	3.1	3.1	2.9
Samoa	7.8	10.0	3.6	9.3	5.8	4.6	6.7	4.8	4.9	4.8
Tokelau[1]	149.3	157.6	165.2	154.6	196.4	192.6	246.6	173.4	252.5	236.5

1. Tokelau receives significant revenues from foreign vessels for access to Tokelau fishing waters. In the 2008 SNA, these revenues are recorded as part of GNI, but they do not add to GDP.

Source: OECD (2018[22]), "Revenue Statistics - Asian and Pacific economies: Comparative tables", OECD Tax statistics (database).

StatLink https://doi.org/10.1787/888933853737

Structure of non-tax revenues

As mentioned, non-tax revenues are divided into different categories: grants; property income; sales of goods and services; fines, penalties and forfeits; and miscellaneous and unidentified revenues.

In 2016, the shares of each of these categories in total non-tax revenues varied across the four Pacific economies for which the data are included:

- Grants were an important source of revenues for all economies in 2016, exceeding 30% of total non-tax revenues. They ranged from 33.4% of non-tax revenues in Tokelau to 69.3% of total non-tax revenues in Papua New Guinea and were the main source of non-tax revenues for Papua New Guinea.
- Property income was the main source of non-tax revenues for the Cook Islands in 2016 (44.2% of non-tax revenues) and Tokelau (64.4%), whereas it was relatively small for Samoa (6.4%). Property income in the Cook Islands and Tokelau was derived predominantly from fisheries income (i.e. fishing rents), which represented more than 80% of the total property income in both economies. Fisheries revenues have been increasing in the Cook Islands and were boosted by reforms and new initiatives in the past decade (Bertram, 2016[36]; Roy, 2017[37]).
- Revenues from sales on goods and services and from grants were the main sources of non-tax revenues in Samoa, where both categories amounted to around 40% of non-tax revenues in 2016.

Table 1.3. **Non-tax revenue of main headings as a percentage of total non-tax revenues in selected Pacific economies, 2016**

	Grants	Property income	Sales of goods and services	Fines, penalties and forfeits	Miscellaneous and unidentified revenue
Cook Islands	39.7	44.2	5.0	1.1	10.0
Papua New Guinea	69.3	25.6	0.0	0.0	5.1
Samoa	40.9	6.4	41.4	11.4	0.0
Tokelau	33.4	64.4	2.1	0.0	0.0

Source: OECD (2018[22])"Revenue Statistics - Asian and Pacific economies: Comparative tables", OECD Tax statistics (database).

StatLink https://doi.org/10.1787/888933853756

Note

1. As of 1 September 2018, the new government replaced the GST with the old system of a sales and services tax (SST). For goods, the rate is set to be between 5-10%, while the tax on services is set at a 6% rate. The new measure came into force following a three-month tax break from June 2018.

References

ADB (2017), *Asian Development Outlook (ADO) 2017: Transcending the Middle-Income Challenge*, *http://dx.doi.org/10.22617/FLS178632-3*. [18]

Aizenman, E. (2015), "Tax revenue trends in Asia and Latin America: A comparative analysis", *NBER Working Paper* No.217555, Cambridge, *http://www.nber.org/papers/w21755*. [8]

Bertram, G. (2016), "Implications of the Cook Islands' Graduation from Development Assistance Committee (DAC) Eligibility", *Ministry of Finance & Economic Management Cook Islands*, *http://www.mfem.gov.ck/images/documents/DCD_Docs/Development-Resources/Implications_of_the_CKI_Graduation_from_DAC_Eligibility.pdf*. [36]

Beshho, S. (2016), "Case Study of Central and Local Government Finance in Japan", *ADBI Working Paper* No.599, *https://www.adb.org* /publications/case-study-centraland-centraland-and-local-government-finance-japan/. [33]

Bloomberg (2015), "Malaysia's New GST: A Brief Comparison with its Former Sales Tax and Service Tax Regime", *https://www.bna.com/malaysias-new-gst-b17179925799*. [29]

Cook Islands News (2013), *Changes to the Cook Islands System*, *http://www.cookislandsnews.com/item/42583-changes-to-the-cook-islands-tax-system/*. [24]

Deloitte (2018), *Papua New Guinea Budget 2018*, *https://www2.deloitte.com/content/dam/Deloitte/pg/Documents/financial-services/deloitte-pg-fs-2018-papua-new-guinea-budget-301117.pdf*. [19]

FRCS (2018), *Fiji Revenue & Custom Service: Environment & Climate Adaptation Levy (ECAL)*, *https://www.frcs.org.fj/our-services/taxation/business/environmental-levy/*. [21]

Horscroft, V. (2014), *Public Sectors in the Pacific Islands Are They 'Too Big' and Do They 'Crowd Out' the Private Sector?*, *http://econ.worldbank.org*. [12]

IMF (2018), *World Economic Outlook, April 2018: Cyclical Upswing, Structural Change*, *https://www.imf.org/en/Publications/WEO/Issues/2018/03/20/world-economic-outlook-april-2018*. [11]

IMF (2017), "Indonesia, selected issues", *IMF Country Report* No. 17/48, International Monetary Fund, Washington, DC, *https://www.imf.org/~/media/Files/Publications/CR/2017/cr1748.ashx*. [38]

IMF (2016), *World Economic Outlook – Frequently Asked Questions*, *https://www.imf.org/external/pubs/ft/weo/faq.htm#q4d*. [9]

Inland Revenue Board of Malaysia (2016), "Agriculture allowances public ruling no. 1/2016", *http://www.hasil.gov.my/pdf/pdfam/PR_01_2016.pdf*. [5]

IPSS (2014), *Social Security in Japan 2014*, National Institute of Population and Social Security Research, Tokyo, *http://www.ipss.go.jp/s-info/e/ssj2014/pdf/SSJ2014.pdf*. [27]

Ministry of Finance of the Cook Islands (2017), *Cook Islands government budget estimates 2017/2018 Book 1 Appropriation Bill Appropriations and Commentary*, *http://www.mfem.gov.ck/images/2018_Cook-Islands_Budget-Book-1_Appropriation-Bill_Appropriations-and-Commentary.pdf*. [25]

Ministry of International Trade and Industry, K. (2016), *http://www.miti.gov.my/index.php/pages/view/content5235.html*. [6]

MOF (2017), *www.mof.gov.sg/Policies/Tax-Policies/Goods-and-Services-Tax*. [39]

New Zealand Foreign Affairs & Trade (2018), "Aid partnership with Tokelau", *https://www.mfat.govt.nz/en/aid-and-development/our-work-in-the-pacific/tokelau/*. [34]

OECD (2018), *Consumption Tax Trends 2018.*, OECD Publishing, Paris, *https://doi.org/10.1787/ctt-2018-en*. [30]

OECD (2018), *Global Revenue Statistics Database*, Organisation for Economic Co-operation and Development, *http://www.oecd.org/tax/tax-policy/global-revenue-statistics-database.htm*. [13]

OECD (2018), *Making Development Co-operation Work for Small Island Developing States*, OECD Publishing, Paris, *http://dx.doi.org/10.1787/9789264287648-en*. [14]

OECD (2018), *National Accounts of OECD Countries, Volume 2018 Issue 1 - Main Aggregates.*, OECD Publishing, *https://doi.org/10.1787/na_ma_dt-v2018-1-en.* [32]

OECD (2018), *OECD Economic Surveys: Indonesia 2018*, OECD Publishing, Paris, *http://dx.doi.org/10.1787/eco_surveys-idn-2018-en.* [3]

OECD (2018), *Revenue Statistics - Asian and Pacific Economies : Comparative tables*, Organisation for Economic Co-operation and Development, *https://stats.oecd.org/index.aspx?DataSetCode=RS_ASI* (accessed on 19 October 2018). [22]

OECD (2018), *Revenue Statistics 2018*, Organisation for Economic Co-operation and Development, *http://dx.doi.org/10.1787/rev_stats-2018-en-fr.* [1]

OECD (2014), *Development Co-operation Report 2014 : Mobilising Resources for Sustainable Development.*, OECD Publishing, Paris, *https://doi.org/10.1787/dcr-2014-5-en.* [7]

OECD (2012), *Consumption Tax Trends 2012.*, OECD Publishing, Paris, *https://doi.org/10.1787/ctt-2012-en.* [28]

OECD (2012), *OECD Economic Surveys: Indonesia 2012*, OECD Publishing, Paris, *http://dx.doi.org/10.1787/eco_surveys-idn-2012-en.* [2]

OECD (2016), *Consumption tax trends 2016 : VAT/GST and excise rates, trends and policy issues*, OECD Publishing, Paris, *https://doi.org/10.1787/ctt-2016-en.* [26]

Parties to the Nauru Agreement (2016), "PNA members confirm: Vessel Day Scheme is here to stay", *https://www.pnatuna.com/node/340.* [35]

PEAKS, E. (2013), *Taxation and Developing Countries*, Overseas Development Institute training notes. [4]

Reuters (2017), *South Korea reports second annual budget surplus in 2016*, *https://www.reuters.com/article/southkorea-economy-budget/s-korea-reports-second-annual-budget-surplus-in-2016-will-pay-down-debt-idUSL4N1FU395.* [17]

Roy, E. (2017), "Cook Islands faces its 'worst case scenario', being granted developed country status", *The Guardian*, *https://www.theguardian.com/world/2017/oct/08/cook-islands-faces-its-worst-case-scenario-being-granted-developed-country-status.* [37]

UN (2018), *United Nations Statistics Division database* (indicator), *http://data.un.org/Data.aspx?q=final+consumption+expenditure&d=SNA&f=group_code%3a401%3bitem_code%3a42.* [31]

UNCTAD (2012), *World Investment Report 2012, Towards a new Generation of Investment Policies, New York*, *http://unctad.org/en/PublicationsLibrary/wir2012_embargoed_en.pdf.* [15]

UNESCAP (2014), *Economic and Social Survey of Asia and the Pacific 2014, Regional Connectivity for Shared Prosperity*, UN, *https://www.unescap.org/sites/default/files/Economic20and%20Social%20Survey%20of%20Asia%20and%20the%20Pacific%202014.pdf.* [16]

VAT Life (2015), *Fiji drops VAT to 9%*, *https://www.vatlive.com/vat-news/fiji-drops-vat-rate-to-9/.* [20]

WHO (2015), *Purchasing Power Parity 2005*, *http://www.who.int/choice/costs/ppp/en/.* [10]

World Bank (2016), *Malaysia Economic Monitor: The quest for productivity growth*, *http://documents.worldbank.org/curated/en/773621481895271934/pdf/111103-WP-PUBLIC-MEM-15-December-2016-Final.pdf.* [23]

Chapter 2

SPECIAL FEATURE
Managing taxpayers' compliance

The level of tax revenues in an economy is influenced by many factors, including economic structure and conditions, tax policy and tax administration, as well as the level of taxpayers' compliance and government enforcement, as outlined in Chapter 1. This chapter discusses a number of important issues in the management of taxpayers' compliance: (i) compliance risk management, including the conduct of tax gap research; (ii) managing the compliance of large taxpayers; (iii) international tax avoidance and evasion; (iv) optimising the use of tax withholding at source and third party reporting requirements; and (v) the use of voluntary disclosure policies and programmes.

2.1. Compliance risk management

Effective compliance risk management processes are an integral part of a revenue body's strategy for improving taxpayers' compliance. While most revenue bodies report having a formal compliance risk management process, relatively few publicly report on how this critical area of tax administration is conducted.

A compliance risk management framework encompasses a series of steps that should be undertaken systematically and cyclically. It is a "top-down" process that focuses on the overall compliance environment rather than on individual taxpayers. In practice, many revenue bodies adopt a taxpayer segment-by-segment approach when applying the framework. By identifying and assessing the main compliance risks and their drivers, the compliance risk management process aims to assist revenue bodies to establish overall priorities for their compliance activities across all segments of taxpayers. Importantly, understanding the drivers of non-compliance is essential as treatment of the more complex compliance risks invariably requires a mix of treatments to achieve the desired outcomes.

Important steps in the compliance risk management process concern monitoring and evaluation activities. Monitoring is an ongoing process that should commence shortly after the introduction of compliance treatments and aims to ensure that implementation is proceeding as intended and that any specific objectives set are being met. Evaluation takes place further on in the process and is intended to assess if the treatment is having the desired overall outcomes and/or if further or new treatments are required.

In addition, revenue bodies should look at influencing compliance risk by creating an environment which supports compliant behaviour and reduces opportunities for non-compliant behaviour (OECD, 2012[1]). This can be achieved through moving from reactive activities targeting symptoms to proactive approaches aimed at the causes of non-compliance (OECD, 2017[2]) and by co-operating with providers of tax services (OECD, 2016[3]).

The Field Guide to accompany the Tax Administration Diagnostic Tool (TADAT) of the International Monetary Fund (IMF) also contains guidance on good practice in compliance risk management.

Compliance risk management in Asia and the Pacific

In a survey[1] conducted by the Asian Development Bank (ADB), revenue bodies in Asia and the Pacific were asked a number of questions concerning aspects of compliance risk management. The OECD report Tax Administration 2017, which is based on the ISORA survey, also contains information on revenue bodies in Asia and the Pacific. The following are the key findings and observations from the surveys (Table 2.1):

- Tax administrations were asked to identify the relative priority attached to a number of risk categories in their current compliance strategies. There was a high degree of commonality, with highest priority areas seen as: value added tax (VAT) fraud, aggressive tax avoidance schemes (including those leading to base erosion and profit shifting), the shadow economy and transactions involving zero or near zero tax jurisdictions. Many administrations also identified e-commerce, identity-fraud, and high net wealth individuals (HNWIs) as medium to high priorities.
- The high priority attached to VAT fraud reflects both its importance as a major source of revenue and the continued vulnerability of repayment mechanisms generally to organised fraud. VAT fraud and other refund-based fraud schemes are increasingly taking new and sophisticated forms involving the use of technologies and at times considerable resources on the part of the perpetrators (OECD, 2017[2]).

Table 2.1. **Risk categories and their relative priority for revenue administrations in Asia and the Pacific**

Risk category	(number of revenue administrations ranking as a priority)		
	High	Medium	Low
Base erosion and profit shifting	15	5	4
Aggressive domestic tax avoidance	17	5	1
VAT fraud (including VAT refund fraud)	17	2	4
Identity fraud	10	6	6
Shadow economy	14	5	4
Amortisation of goodwill	3	9	12
Preferential tax regimes	12	7	4
Transactions with tax havens	12	5	6
High net worth individuals	11	7	5
Research and development tax credits	8	6	9
E-commerce	9	12	2

Source: ADB survey responses and OECD (2017[2]), *Tax Administration 2017*, Table A.138.

StatLink https://doi.org/10.1787/888933853775

Tax gap research

The tax gap is an estimate of the difference between the amount of revenue actually collected for a tax in respect of fiscal year and the amount that would have been collected with perfect compliance. It is typically measured on a "tax-by-tax" basis, exclusive of penalties and interest, and the results across all taxes are sometimes aggregated to give a "total tax gap" amount for a tax system. By its nature, tax gap estimation is an imprecise science and the various models and methodologies used in practice by revenue bodies and others for gap estimation purposes are subject to numerous qualifications and assumptions.

Drawing on international experience, tax gap estimation research has a number of potential uses, although its value at the individual tax level depends on the methodology used, the reliability of the information gathered, and the timeliness of research findings.

While relatively few national revenue bodies undertake comprehensive programmes of tax gap research, interest in tax gap estimation, particularly in respect of VAT, has grown considerably in recent years as governments, tax administrators and others have sought to quantify the extent of revenue leakage from their tax systems and/or to better understand the overall impacts of revenue bodies' compliance improvement activities. Australia, Canada and Finland are examples of economies where comprehensive research efforts have been launched in recent years, while countries such as Denmark, Sweden, United Kingdom and the United States have many years of experience. The European Commission arranges regular VAT gap estimation research for all of its 28 member countries and publishes the findings (CASE, 2017[4]).

Only a few larger countries have conducted tax gap research across the Asia–Pacific region, although independent research institutes have looked into industry-specific cases of tax evasion (e.g. a report by the Oakland Institute on large scale tax evasion in the forestry sector in Papua New Guinea (Mousseau and Lau, 2016[5])). Interest for tax gap research appears to have grown over the last five years or so and a number of revenue bodies have explored its use, have ongoing research programmes, or have had some exposure to such research:

- The Australian Taxation Office (ATO) has a comprehensive approach, with a programme of research introduced gradually over the last four years that, in 2018, includes all of the taxes under its responsibility. A programme of random inquiries is a core element of its approach to estimating the tax gap for income taxes. The findings of its research are released progressively, and are published on its website and in its annual performance report (ATO, 2018[6]). At the time of finalising this report, tax gap estimates had been released for a range of taxes, including the goods and services tax (GST),[2] corporate income tax (large taxpayers), the pay-as-you-go withholding regime for the personal income tax and some excises (ATO, 2018[6]). Summary findings include:
  - GST gap – the net GST gap estimate for 2015-16 has trended slightly upwards from previous years to AUD 4.5 billion (7.3%). It is the highest gap among the taxes analysed to date, but compliance levels are quite stable. Australia ranks relatively well among similar nations that have estimated GST/VAT gaps.
  - Large corporate income tax gap – in 2014-15, the net large corporate income tax gap is estimated to be AUD 2.5 billion (5.8%). This figure has been steady for a number of years, and the gap primarily reflects differences in the interpretation of complex areas of tax law.
  - Tobacco tax gap – for the 2015-16 year, the net tobacco tax gap is estimated to be AUD 594 million (5.6%). ATO analysis indicates that sea and air cargo is the most significant source of detected illicit tobacco entering Australia.
- China's State Administration of Taxation (SAT) has a comprehensive programme. SAT's representative noted that the knowledge gained from its tax gap research efforts (i) assists in the development of uniform tax payment arrangements, (ii) improves the efficiency of tax collection, (iii) improves targeting of revenue management, and (iv) supports tax reform. SAT employs both the "top down" methodology to estimate the tax gap for indirect taxes and the "bottom up" methodology for direct taxes. Concerning the VAT, findings from 2001 to 2009 had revealed progressively improving tax compliance, with the estimated VAT tax gap declining from around 40% to 25% across China over the period studied (Zhong, 2016[7]).

- The Philippines' Bureau of Internal Revenue (BIR) also has experience with tax gap research. As part of a technical assistance agreement between the governments of the United States and the Philippines, the BIR participated with the IMF from 2011 to 2015 to produce a series of gap estimates for the VAT making use of the IMF's Revenue Administration Gap Analysis Program (RA-GAP) assistance. In a presentation made in December 2017, the BIR's representative reported that its findings from 2008 to 2015 reveal a marginally declining trend in the gap which is estimated at 38% for the 2015 fiscal year (ADB, 2018[8]).
- Indonesia's Directorate General of Tax (DGT) at the Ministry of Finance regularly conducts assessments of the income tax coverage ratio. Since 2005, the agency has given sectoral estimates for the potential tax revenues, to detect weaknesses in its compliance system. The publication of these results is irregular, and the latest official figures date back to 2011 when the tax gap was 29.20% (APBN, 2014[9]).
- Nepal's Inland Revenue Department (IRD) has collected statistics on tax compliance for VAT in 2015 with the support of the Fiscal Affairs Department of the IMF (IMF, 2017[10]). The IRD has also systematised its income tax gap measurement to a yearly basis (IRD, 2016[11]).

2.2. Managing the compliance of large taxpayers

There has been a trend in the Asia-Pacific region to organise revenue bodies' compliance programmes around "taxpayer segments", in particular, for large corporate taxpayers. Almost all tax administrations in Asia and the Pacific report having in place an organisational division or unit that manages the tax affairs of designated large taxpayers. This reflects the importance of large business in terms of its contribution to the tax base and also the complexity of large business tax affairs. One country that has implemented a separate organisational division for larger taxpayers is Myanmar, where the revenue body introduced a large taxpayer unit (LTU) in 2015. Exceptions to this practice include revenue bodies in Brunei Darussalam; Hong Kong, China; Korea; and Papua New Guinea. Officials from Papua New Guinea recently reported that their new medium term development strategy for 2018-22 includes provision for commencement of work in 2018 to establish an LTU (IRC, 2017[12]).

In contrast to the practice in many advanced economies where the functions of LTUs tend to be limited to service and verification, many LTUs in the region perform a broader range of functions, for many including returns processing, service, audit, debt collection, and disputes processing. Most LTUs administer all of the major taxes for which large taxpayers are responsible.

The criteria used to identify taxpayers for the LTU vary to a fair degree in Asian and Pacific economies and include, singularly or in combination, turnover level, tax paid, assets, number of employees, capital invested, and specific economic sectors. For ease of identification, many revenue bodies use a single criterion, generally turnover level, to identify taxpayers for the LTU's supervision. Furthermore, being classified as a large taxpayer can lead to more stringent reporting standards, as is the case in the Philippines and Myanmar.

As mentioned above, most Asia-Pacific region tax organisations have LTUs. Examples include:

- The Inland Revenue Board of Malaysia (IRBM) created in 2015 a Large Taxpayer Branch (LTB) that will handle large and high profile taxpayers based on the following criteria: i) corporate taxpayers with turnover exceeding MYR 30 million, ii) non-corporate taxpayers with aggregate income greater or equal to MYR 1 million (IRBM, 2015[13]). It will also manage the income tax files of taxpayers within the special sectors of construction, real property, finance and insurance.

- The BIR of the Philippines has a criterion based on size for each type of tax it collects, being above the indicated threshold implies being serviced by the LTU. For instance, having a yearly income greater than or equal to 1 million PHP or a net VAT payable of 100 000 PHP per quarter implies being classified as a large taxpayer (Udaundo, 2016[14]). The LTU of the Philippines was staffed by 564 agents in 2017, and covered 2 320 large taxpayers. The current administration has the ambition to expand the size and scope of the unit to service all taxpayers that should fall under its jurisdiction (DOF, 2017[15]). The main contributors to the LTU of the BIR are banks, tobacco, wholesale and retail trade.
- The Fiji Revenue and Customs Service (FRCS) has a High Wealth Individual (HWI) database. This allows FRCS to place more emphasis on understanding the complexity of high net worth individuals' tax affairs, the amounts of tax revenue potentially at stack through aggressive tax planning and the effect of the compliance behaviour on the overall integrity of the tax system (FRCS, 2017[16]).

2.3. International tax avoidance and evasion

Over the last nine years, the OECD, along with many advanced and developing economies and regional tax bodies, has been working to develop new rules and processes to strengthen the international tax system. These efforts have been strongly supported by G20 leaders.[3] These developments were set out in some detail in an ADB governance brief issued in early 2017 and the key points made are summarised below, along with details of some further developments over the last year (ADB, 2017[17]).

Global developments to reform the international tax system

International efforts to address weaknesses in the international tax system rely on two building blocks: (i) promoting transparency and exchange of information among jurisdictions for tax purposes and (ii) tackling tax avoidance with the OECD/G20's Base Erosion and Profit Shifting (BEPS) project. With considerable progress made over recent years to develop comprehensive proposals for reform in both areas, the focus of these international efforts has shifted to their global implementation.

Promoting transparency and exchange of information for tax purposes

The work of tax transparency has been at the heart of the OECD's role in the international tax area. With its peer reviews of the standard for exchange of information on request (EOIR) and its monitoring of the implementation of the standard for automatic exchange of financial account information (AEOI), the Global Forum on Transparency and Exchange of Information for Tax Purposes has played a crucial role in establishing and maintaining a level playing field and in ensuring that the voices of all relevant jurisdictions are heard (OECD, 2018[18]).

Exchange of information on request

The impetus for major changes to address the tax compliance problems presented by the practices of some jurisdictions came in 2009 when G20 leaders declared that bank secrecy would no longer be tolerated and committed to take action against non-cooperative jurisdictions, including tax havens. In line with this commitment, many countries agreed to fight cross-border tax evasion together by committing to the international standard for exchange of tax information on request (EOIR) developed by the OECD, and by joining a restructured Global Forum on Transparency and Exchange of Information for Tax Purposes.

Automatic exchange of information

Further steps to strengthen tax transparency were taken in 2013 when G20 leaders committed to the OECD proposal for Automatic Exchange of Information (AEOI) to be the new international standard, and fully supported further work by member countries of the OECD and G20 to present a single global standard in 2014. This work culminated in the development of the Common Reporting Standard (CRS) for automatic exchange of tax information. The CRS, which deals with the automatic exchange of financial account information, is designed to meet the requirements of multiple jurisdictions and minimise the compliance burden on financial institutions that must report to multiple jurisdictions.

Implications of implementing automatic exchange of information for developing economies

Implementing the CRS for automatic exchanges requires considerable effort and costs on the part of individual participating jurisdictions. However, these more immediate imposts need to be assessed against the potential ongoing benefits from CRS adoption and implementation, in particular: (i) the detection of tax evasion and concealed offshore assets, (ii) the deterrence of future non-compliance, (iii) supporting domestic synergies, and (iv) enhancing an economy's reputation.

In addition to translating the CRS into domestic law, a key element of its successful implementation is putting in place an international framework that allows the automatic exchange of CRS information between jurisdictions. International bodies, the Global Forum on Transparency and Exchange of Information for Tax Purposes, regional tax bodies, and advanced economies are providing considerable support to assist developing economies. The establishment of a Common Transmission System to be used globally for the automatic exchange of bulk taxpayer information is expected to significantly simplify exchanges for participating jurisdictions and minimise their operational costs.

AEOI Reform in Asia and the Pacific

Good progress has been made by many economies, including by a number of jurisdictions that operate as major financial centres in the region (i.e., Hong Kong, China; and Singapore) (Table 2.2). However, considerably more work is required by a number of economies within the region to take advantage of the new AEOI reforms. While many participating revenue bodies have taken steps to make provision for AEOI reforms in their strategic plans, further work appears necessary in quite a few economies, including: (i) the establishment of a dedicated organisational unit to manage AEOI matters, (ii) developing working arrangements for AEOI with treaty partners, (iii) the initiation of actions to have the CRS fully implemented by financial bodies, (iv) determining policies and practices for effective use of AEOI received from partners, and (v) devising strategies to promote awareness among citizens, and (vi) measuring the effectiveness of AEOI.

The OECD's base erosion and profit shifting project

The past two to three decades have seen dramatic changes in many economies as a result of globalisation. Technological advancements, increased mobility of capital and labour, the shift in manufacturing bases from high to low cost jurisdictions, and the gradual lifting of trade barriers, are some of the many developments that have boosted foreign direct investment in many economies. However, there have been a number of downsides, including in the area of taxation, where it is widely agreed that international tax rules have not kept up with the pace of change. A major consequence of this deficiency has been revenue leakage; from research conducted in 2013, global revenue losses from BEPS were conservatively estimated at USD 100 billion to 240 billion annually, which is equivalent to between 4% and 10% of global revenues from corporate income tax. Developing countries' higher reliance on corporate income tax means they suffer from BEPS disproportionately (OECD, 2015[19]). More broadly, BEPS weakens tax system integrity and undermine citizens' trust in government.

The goal of the BEPS project is to realign the international tax rules with developments in the world economy, to restore trust and ensure profits are taxed where economic activities are carried out and value is created, while maintaining the ability to eliminate double taxation. In September 2013, G20 leaders endorsed a comprehensive action plan developed by the OECD to address BEPS. This action plan on BEPS identified a series of domestic and international actions to address the problem and set timelines for their further development. After considerable consultation over the ensuing two years, the BEPS project delivered outputs for all elements of the action plan to G20 Finance Ministers in October 2015. In November 2015, G20 leaders endorsed the measures and expressly called for an implementation framework that would be open to all interested countries and jurisdictions, including developing economies. The BEPS measures aim to close gaps in international tax rules that allow multinational enterprises to legally, but artificially, shift profits to low or no-tax jurisdictions. The measures seek to achieve this by improving the coherence of tax rules across borders, tightening substance requirements, and ensuring increased transparency and certainty.

Implementing the BEPS measures – The Inclusive Framework

The member countries of the OECD and G20 have developed an inclusive framework that enables interested countries and jurisdictions to work with them on an equal footing in developing standards on BEPS-related issues, and to review and monitor the implementation of the BEPS package across jurisdictions. The Inclusive Framework on BEPS currently brings together 118 jurisdictions, including many developing countries, to collaborate on the implementation of the OECD-G20 BEPS Package.

Many economies in the Asian and Pacific region are members of the Inclusive Framework (Table 2.2). Also, tax administrations in a number of non-participating economies have highlighted BEPS and domestic tax avoidance schemes as high risk areas for tax compliance, while at the same time having weaknesses in their corporate tax regimes that limit their ability to properly deal with such risks.

Table 2.2. **Engagement and participation of ADB members in international tax reform efforts**

Region/member	Commitments to International Tax Reform Efforts			
	Tax evasion: transparency and exchange of information			
	Member of Global Forum on Transparency and EOI[1]	Signatory to Multilateral Convention on Mutual Assistance[2]	Signatory to Introduction of New AEOI Standard (year)	Tax avoidance: member of BEPS Inclusive Framework[3]
Central and West Asia				
Afghanistan	x	x	x	x
Kazakhstan	✓	✓	x	✓
Kyrgyzstan	x	x	x	x
Tajikistan	x	x	x	x
East Asia				
China, People's Republic	✓	✓	✓ (2018)	✓
Hong Kong, China	✓	x	✓ (2018)	✓
Japan	✓	✓	✓ (2018)	✓
Korea	✓	✓	✓ (2017)	✓
Mongolia	✓	x	x	✓
Pacific				
Australia	✓	✓	✓ (2018)	✓
Cook Islands	✓	✓	✓ (2018)	x
Fiji	x	x		x
Kiribati	x	x		x
Marshall Islands	✓	✓	✓ (2018)	x
Nauru	✓	✓	✓ (2018)	x
New Zealand	✓	✓	✓ (2018)	✓
Papua New Guinea	✓	✓		✓
Samoa	✓	✓	✓ (2018)	x
Timor-Leste	x	x		x
Tonga	x	x		x
Tuvalu	x	x		x
Vanuatu	✓	✓	✓ (2018)	x
South Asia				
Bangladesh	x	x	x	x
Bhutan	x	x	x	x
India	✓	✓	✓ (2017)	✓
Maldives	✓	x		✓
Nepal	x	x	x	x
Southeast Asia				
Brunei Darussalam	✓	✓	✓ (2018)	✓
Cambodia	✓	x		x
Indonesia	✓	✓	✓ (2018)	✓
Lao PDR	x	x	x	x
Malaysia	✓	✓	✓ (2018)	✓
Myanmar	x	x	x	x
Philippines	✓	✓		x
Singapore	✓	✓		✓
Thailand	✓	x	x	✓
Viet Nam	x	x	x	✓

Note: ✓ = relevant, x = not relevant, AEOI = automatic exchange of information, BEPS = base erosion and profit shifting, EOI = exchange of information, Lao PDR = Lao People's Democratic Republic.

1. Global Forum on Transparency and Exchange of Information for Tax Purposes (154 members as of October 2018).
2. Multilateral Convention on Mutual Administrative Assistance in Tax Matters (September 2018).
3. Inclusive Framework on Base Erosion and Profit Shifting (119 members as of October 2018).

Source: OECD (2018[20]), "Members of the inclusive framework on BEPS", *http://www.oecd.org/tax/beps/inclusive-framework-on-beps-composition.pdf*; OECD (2018[21]), "Status of convention", *http://www.oecd.org/tax/exchange-of-tax-information/Status_of_convention.pdf*; OECD (2018[22]), "Global Forum members & observers", *http://www.oecd.org/tax/transparency/about-the-global-forum/members/* (all accessed 17 October 2018).

StatLink https://doi.org/10.1787/888933853794

2.4. Optimising the use of withholding at source and third-party reporting

Withholding at source arrangements are generally regarded as the cornerstone of an effective personal income tax system. Imposing the obligation on intermediaries such as employers and financial institutions to withhold tax from payments of income generally ensures that the vast bulk of tax due on such income is paid to government in a timely manner, and that taxpayers generally meet their tax obligations in respect of such income. The benefits of withholding mechanisms are particularly important to developing and emerging economies where the level of tax morale and understanding may be low, and most taxpayers are not required to file annual tax returns.

In practice, withholding regimes vary considerably in their design to take account of a variety of tax policy choices (e.g., the tax rate structure in place, final or creditable withholdings, residency, and annual assessment requirements). These factors, coupled with the fact that some intermediaries will be tempted to avoid their tax withholding obligations, mean that revenue bodies must be prepared to provide adequate education and support services, as well as be vigilant to non-compliance behaviour that requires an administrative response.

Withholding regimes are also often accompanied by systems of third party reporting to the revenue body. This is particularly important where the tax withheld at source is creditable (i.e., not final) and is intended to be applied in a tax assessment process. Third party reporting regimes are also often used in the absence of withholding, in particular for categories of self-employment and professional income that are paid by contracting parties. Such reporting generally provides the revenue body with relevant payee identity and income information that can be used to detect non-compliance (e.g., non-filers deriving income and filers who omit income from their tax returns).

Some key points of information reported by revenue bodies on the nature and use of withholding and reporting regimes in place in Asia and the Pacific are set out below.

Employment income

Cumulative withholding regimes are widely used in developing economies, limiting the numbers of employees who are required to file annual tax returns or undergo some other form of reconciliation (e.g., Japan). In Viet Nam for instance, employers must withhold the income taxes of their employees and deposit them with the State Treasury before the 20th of the following month, employers also fill in the personal income tax declarations on behalf of their employees if they are their sole source of revenues and submit them before the end of the year (KPMG, 2018[23]). Similar systems exist in smaller economies such as Nauru where tax payments by the employer need to be made 15 days after the end of the month of withholding. In a few economies [i.e., Hong Kong, China; and Singapore], tax withholding at source is not applied and employees must make their own advance payments and file returns.

Other categories of income

Some revenue bodies report that withholding provisions apply to prescribed categories of interest and dividend incomes, for both resident and non-resident taxpayers. Revenue bodies in Bangladesh, China, Indonesia, Kazakhstan, Mongolia, the Philippines, and Thailand report extensive use of withholding across the main categories of incomes surveyed – i.e. employment income (wage and salary), dividends, interest, rents, specified business income, royalties and patents, share sales and purchases, real estates sales and purchases, and other income – for both resident and non-resident taxpayers. In the Philippines, revenues are withheld from passive incomes such as interest and dividends at levels of 20 and 10% respectively (BIR, 2018[24]). Lao PDR has a similar system but at a flat rate of 10% (Lao PDR Government, 2018[25]). Revenue bodies in Australia, Hong Kong, China, Malaysia, Maldives, New Zealand and Singapore report they make relatively limited use of tax withholding across the main categories of personal income, although relaying on reporting regimes to gather data on taxpayers' incomes. Countries also target very specific forms of income using withholding taxes, for example the Solomon Islands which target goods such as marine products or cocoa.

Computer processing of third party income reports

There are many benefits of using third party data in enhancing tax compliance and service delivery. These data include wage and salary information from employers as well as data from financial institutions, property sales, other government agencies, and information exchanged with other jurisdictions.

Many revenue bodies (e.g., Australia, Korea, Malaysia, New Zealand, Singapore, and Thailand) reported having computerised processes for the bulk capture and processing of large volumes of taxpayer income data reported by third parties. Papua New Guinea has indicated that as part of its reform plan for its taxation authority it wishes to make much greater use of third party information sources; as such, it intends to use data from the national Investment Promotion Authority (IPA) to cross check businesses' compliance (TRC, 2015[26]). Similarly, the tax authorities of the Solomon Islands, Samoa and Fiji indicate that they use many information streams to detect misconducts. For instance, the Samoa tax authorities use data from different ministries, the Samoa National Provident Fund (SNPF), the central bank and commercial banks (MFRS, 2017[27]).

2.5. The use of voluntary disclosure policies and programmes

Voluntary disclosure mechanisms can be an important part of compliance programmes when used as part of a broad approach to facilitating compliance outcomes. Such programmes offer non-compliant taxpayers the opportunity and incentive to proactively put their tax affairs in order. As well as being less resource-intensive than investigations, they can also potentially generate significant insights into the reasons for evasion (including accidental) and the structures used to facilitate deliberate evasion (OECD, 2017[2]).

The international tax environment has changed dramatically towards greater transparency and exchange of information for tax purposes. All financial centres have now committed to the OECD standard on transparency and exchange of information. This will provide greater insight into the undisclosed income and assets of high net worth individuals (HNWIs) and other taxpayers. The time required for exchange of information agreements or other mechanisms to come into force offers a unique opportunity for these taxpayers to voluntarily disclose their income and assets. Tax administrations may also seize this opportunity to facilitate such voluntary disclosures (OECD, 2009[28]).

At the same time, a number of countries have implemented initiatives to encourage taxpayers to disclose past non-compliance, including administrative measures such as the recent voluntary compliance initiatives in Ireland and the United Kingdom. Canada has had a voluntary disclosure programme for many years. In economies where these policies are regularly applied, the tax laws typically contain provisions that give some discretion to revenue bodies to frame the terms of their voluntary disclosure policy. While the terms offered under such programmes vary from economy to economy they generally include incentives in the form of: (i) reduced penalties, (ii) no audit providing a full disclosure is made, (iii) a commitment to no prosecution, and (iv) a commitment to no publicity where it is normal practice to publish details of detected tax evaders, (e.g., Cook Islands).

For instance in Singapore, where the Inland Revenue Authority of Singapore (IRAS) has a permanent programme for voluntary disclosures, in lieu of possible legal charges and a 400% fine on unpaid taxes in case of willful tax evasion, the sanctions are reduced to a 200% fine for those that voluntarily report to the authorities (IRAS, 2018[29]).

Voluntary disclosure policies and programmes are fairly limited across economies in the region (Table 2.3). These policies and programmes have been known to deliver benefits in economies such as Australia and New Zealand.

Table 2.3. **The use of voluntary disclosure policies and programmes**

Feature	Economies reporting this feature for 2015
Revenue bodies empowered to offer reduced penalties for voluntary disclosures	Australia; Bhutan; Hong Kong, China; Indonesia; Japan; Korea; Malaysia; New Zealand; Singapore; Thailand
Revenue bodies empowered to offer reduced interest for voluntary disclosures	Australia; Bhutan; Hong Kong, China; Indonesia; New Zealand; Thailand
Revenue bodies reporting the use of voluntary disclosure programme in 2015	Afghanistan; Australia; Bhutan; Hong Kong, China; Indonesia; Japan; Korea; Malaysia; New Zealand; Singapore; Thailand

Source: ADB survey responses and OECD (2017[2]), Tax Administration 2017, Table A.136.

StatLink https://doi.org/10.1787/888933853813

Voluntary disclosure programmes can be distinguished from what are sometimes referred to as tax amnesty programmes, although the terms are often used interchangeably. Unlike a voluntary disclosure, a tax amnesty typically includes an incentive in the form of a reduction or waiver in a taxpayer's primary tax liability, along with other conditions and concessions. Tax amnesties have already been implemented in some countries in the region (Box 2.1).

Box 2.1. **Tax amnesty programmes**

Some countries in the region have been implementing tax amnesty programme as part of their efforts to increase tax revenues. The results of such programmes have, however, been mixed.

- Indonesia's amnesty programme, launched in 2016, was running until end of March 2017. It has brought in IDR 4 882.2 trillion worth of assets and involved more than 745 000 participants (MOF, 2017[30]). The country imposed a redemption levy on the declared assets, ranging from 2 to 10% depending on the localisation of the assets and in which phase of the scheme the disclosure was made.
- Fiji implemented in the end of 2017 two tax amnesty programmes, one for the regularisation of undeclared foreign assets, the other offering a waiver of penalties related to overdue tax returns and payments (FRCS, 2017[31]; 2017[32]).
- Papua New Guinea's Inland Revenue Commission (IRC) offered an amnesty programme in late 2017, whereby penalties related to late payments or non-filing of returns for a broad array of taxes would be lifted. Taxes covered include: income tax, interest withholding tax and business income payment tax (IRC, 2017[33]).
- India's Income Declaration Scheme was launched in June 2016 and lasted for four months. It attracted 64 275 non-compliant taxpayers for a total of INR 652.5 billion of regularised assets (CBDT, 2016[34]). The scheme's participating taxpayers faced a charge of 45% on the declared assets, which may have contributed to the lower uptake compared to similar initiatives in the region.

Notes

1. In 2016, the OECD, the Inter-American Center of Tax Administration (CIAT), the Intra-European Organisation of Tax Administrations (IOTA), and the International Monetary Fund (IMF) agreed to collect revenue administration data through a joint web-based survey, the International Survey on Revenue Administration (ISORA). The survey that was conducted by the ADB was a shortened paper-version of ISORA.
2. The Goods and Services Tax (GST) in Australia is a value-added tax under the OECD classification of taxes set out in the Interpretative Guide.
3. The G20 (or G-20 or Group of Twenty) is an international forum for the governments and central bank governors from 20 major economies. It was founded in 1999 with the aim of studying, reviewing, and promoting high-level discussion of policy issues pertaining to the promotion of international financial stability.

References

ADB (2018), *Comparative Analysis of Tax Administration in Asia and the Pacific 2018 Edition*, Asian Development Bank, Manila, *http://dx.doi.org/10.22617/TCS189264.* [8]

ADB (2017), *Adopting the new international tax rules and standards*, Asian Development Bank, Manila, *https://www.adb.org/sites/default/files/publication/225216/governance-brief-29.pdf.* [17]

APBN (2014), *Study of potential tax revenue based on macro approach*, APBN Policy Center Fiscal Policy Agency, Jakarta. [9]

ATO (2018), *Australian tax gap overview*, Government of Australia Taxation Office, *https://www.ato.gov.au/About-TO/Researchand-statistics/In-detail/Tax-gap/Australian-tax-gaps-overview/.* [6]

BIR (2018), *Withholding tax*, Philippine Bureau of Internal Revenue, Manila, *https://www.bir.gov.ph/index.php/tax-information/withholding-tax/10-tax-information.html.* [24]

CASE (2017), *Study and reports on the VAT gap in the EU-28 member states: the final report*, Centre for Social and Economic Research. [4]

CBDT (2016), *Income declaration scheme 2016 unearths Rs.65250 crore of hitherto undeclared income and assets*, Central Board of Direct Taxes of India, *http://pib.nic.in/newsite/PrintRelease.aspx?relid=151330.* [34]

DOF (2017), *Expanding large taxpayers unit part of tax system overhaul*, Philippine Department of Finance, Manila, *https://www.dof.gov.ph/index.php/expanding-large-taxpayers-unit-part-of-tax-system-overhaul/.* [15]

FRCS (2017), *2017 Tax Amnesty - Waiver of penalties on tax returns and payments that were overdue on or before 1 July 2017*, Fiji Revenue and Customs Service, *https://www.frcs.org.fj/wp-content/uploads/2017/01/FINAL-PS-62-General-Tax-Amnesty-27Oct2017.pdf.* [32]

FRCS (2017), *2017 Tax Amnesty - Waiver of tax payable in respect of foreign assets, including related penalties for any tax period prior to 1 January 2018*, Fiji Revenue and Customs Service, *https://www.frcs.org.fj/wp-content/uploads/2017/01/FINAL-PS-63-Foreign-Assets-Tax-Amnesty-18Oct2017.pdf.* [31]

FRCS (2017), *Compliance Improvement Strategy 2017-2018*, Fiji Revenue and Customs Service, *https://www.frcs.org.fj/wp-content/uploads/2018/01/CIS-2017-2018.-E-Version.pdf.* [16]

IMF (2017), *Article IV consultation: Nepal*, International Monetary Fund, Washington DC. [10]

IRAS (2018), *IRAS' voluntary disclosure programme*, Inland Revenue Authority of Singapore, *https://www.iras.gov.sg/irashome/About-Us/Taxes-in-Singapore/Helping-and-Encouraging-Compliance/IRAS--Voluntary-Disclosure-Programme/.* [29]

IRBM (2015), *Press release: Decentralization of income tax files subsequent to the setting up of large taxpayer branch (LTB) and large taxpayer unit (LTU)*, Inland Revenue Board of Malaysia, *http://lampiran1.hasil.gov.my/pdf/pdfam/DECENTRALISATION_OF_INCOME_TAX.pdf.* [13]

IRC (2017), *Papua New Guinea's medium term revenue strategy the roadmap for reforming Papua New Guinea's taxation system.* [12]

IRC (2017), *Press statement – IRC Tax Amnesty*, Internal Revenue Commission of Papua New Guinea, *http://irc.gov.pg/wp-content/uploads/2017/11/Press-Statemen_IRC-Tax-Amnesty-_2017-1.pdf.* [33]

IRD (2016), *Reform plan*, Nepal Inland Revenue Department, Kathmandu, *https://ird.gov.np/Content/ContentAttachment/4/ReformPlanIRD8122016114507AM.pdf.* [11]

KPMG (2018), *Viet Nam income tax: taxation of international executives*, KPMG International Cooperative, *https://home.kpmg.com/xx/en/home/insights/2011/12/vietnam-income-tax.html.* [23]

Lao PDR Government (2018), *Tax information*, Tax Department of Lao PDR, *http://www.tax.gov.la/Eng_WebPages/IncomeTax.aspx.* [25]

MFRS (2017), *Samoa 2017: background paper*, Ministry for Revenue Samoa, *http://www.cata38.gov.gh/media/attachments/2017/09/14/samoa---leveraging-technology-to-enhance-revenue-administration.pdf.* [27]

MOF (2017), *Economic, financial and fiscal review edition IV*, Ministry of Finance of Indonesia, Jakarta, *http://www.fiskal.kemenkeu.go.id/publikasi/tekf/2017/tekf4/files/bimonthly_iv.pdf.* [30]

Mousseau, F. and P. Lau (2016), *The great timber heist the logging industry in Papua New Guinea*, The Oakland Institute, Oakland, *https://www.oaklandinstitute.org/great-timber-heist-logging-industry-papua-new-guinea.* [5]

OECD (2018), *Global Forum members and observers*, OECD Publishing, Paris, *http://www.oecd.org/tax/transparency/about-the-global-forum/members/.* [22]

OECD (2018), *Members of the inclusive framework on BEPS*, OECD Publishing, Paris, *http://www.oecd.org/tax/beps/inclusive-framework-on-beps-composition.pdf.* [20]

OECD (2018), *OECD Secretary-General report to G20 finance ministers and central bank governors*, OECD Publishing, Paris, *http://www.oecd.org/tax/OECD-Secretary-General-tax-report-G20-Finance-Ministers-Argentina-March-2018.pdf.* [18]

OECD (2018), *Status of convention*, OECD Publishing, Paris, *http://www.oecd.org/tax/exchange-of-tax-information/Status_of_convention.pdf.* [21]

OECD (2017), *Tax Administration 2017: Comparative Information on OECD and Other Advanced and Emerging Economies*, OECD Publishing, Paris, *http://dx.doi.org/10.1787/tax_admin-2017-en.* [2]

OECD (2016), *Rethinking Tax Services: The Changing Role of Tax Service Providers in SME Tax Compliance*, OECD Publishing, Paris, *http://dx.doi.org/10.1787/9789264256200-en.* [3]

OECD (2015), *Taxing multinational enterprises*, OECD Publishing, Paris, *http://www.oecd.org/policy-briefs/PB-Base-Erosion-Profit-Shifting-(BEPS-III)-Oct-2015.pdf.* [19]

OECD (2012), *Right from the start: influencing the compliance environment for small and medium enterprises*, OECD Publishing, Paris, *https://www.oecd.org/tax/administration/right-from-the-start-influencing-the-compliance-environment-for-smes.pdf.* [1]

OECD (2009), *Engaging with High Net Worth Individuals on Tax Compliance*, OECD Publishing, Paris, *http://dx.doi.org/10.1787/9789264068872-en.* [28]

TRC (2015), *Report to the treasurer part 2 of 2: detailed analysis*, Tax Review Committee of Papua New Guinea, *http://taxreview.gov.pg/wpcontent/uploads/2015/11/15.10.22_taxreview.final_.report_vol.2.pdf.* [26]

Udaundo, E. (2016), "Revenue performance of the BIR large taxpayers service: 2006-2015", *NTRC Tax Research Journal*, Vol. 27. [14]

Zhong, S. (2016), *China's practice of tax gap analysis*, *https://www.imf.org/external/np/seminars/eng/2016/asiatax/pdf/sz24.pdf.* [7]

Revenue Statistics in Asian and Pacific Economies

Chapter 3

Tax levels and tax structure, 1990-2016

Table 3.1. **Total tax revenue as percentage of GDP, 1990-2016**

	1990	1998	1999	2000	2001	2002	2003	2004	2005	2006
Australia[1]	28.1	29.4	29.8	30.5	28.9	29.8	30.0	30.3	30.0	29.4
Cook Islands	..	..	..	..	..	..	..	..	..	26.9
Fiji	..	..	..	..	..	..	..	..	..	..
Indonesia[2]	..	6.2	7.8	7.9	10.9	11.3	11.8	12.1	12.4	11.9
Japan[1]	28.2	25.7	25.2	25.8	25.9	24.9	24.5	25.2	26.2	27.0
Kazakhstan[3]	..	12.3	15.9	19.8	22.2	20.5	22.7	21.7	25.5	26.1
Korea[1]	18.8	19.4	19.7	21.5	21.8	21.9	22.7	22.0	22.5	23.6
Malaysia[4]	18.5	16.6	15.7	14.1	18.3	18.3	16.3	15.9	15.5	15.1
New Zealand[1]	36.2	32.3	32.3	32.5	31.9	33.3	33.2	34.2	36.1	35.3
Papua New Guinea[5]	..	..	..	..	..	13.3	13.5	16.1	17.1	20.1
Philippines	..	15.5	15.8	15.8	15.6	15.0	15.0	14.6	15.2	16.5
Samoa	..	..	..	..	..	..	..	..	20.4	23.1
Singapore	..	..	..	15.2	15.2	12.9	12.4	12.1	11.8	11.9
Solomon Islands[6]	..	..	..	..	..	..	..	..	..	..
Thailand	..	..	..	14.8	14.9	15.6	16.9	17.6	18.8	17.9
Tokelau	..	..	..	..	..	..	..	..	..	13.3
Africa (21) average[7]	..	..	..	13.1	13.8	14.3	14.6	15.1	15.4	15.6
LAC average[8]	16.0	17.5	17.7	18.0	18.2	18.2	18.6	19.0	19.8	20.9
OECD average[1,9]	31.9	33.6	33.8	33.8	33.3	33.0	32.9	32.9	33.4	33.5
	2007	**2008**	**2009**	**2010**	**2011**	**2012**	**2013**	**2014**	**2015**	**2016**
Australia[1]	29.6	26.9	25.6	25.3	25.9	27.0	27.2	27.3	27.9	27.8
Cook Islands	24.4	23.7	26.0	25.4	24.0	26.8	24.7	22.9	28.5	30.0
Fiji	..	22.2	21.6	21.6	22.7	23.6	23.5	24.1	25.1	24.1
Indonesia[2]	12.2	13.0	11.1	11.4	12.2	12.5	12.5	12.2	12.0	11.6
Japan[1]	27.5	27.4	26.0	26.5	27.5	28.2	28.9	30.3	30.6	30.6
Kazakhstan[3]	26.1	27.6	21.2	23.8	24.5	23.9	22.6	21.1	15.5	14.9
Korea[1]	24.8	24.6	23.8	23.4	24.2	24.8	24.3	24.6	25.2	26.2
Malaysia[4]	14.8	15.1	15.5	13.8	15.3	16.1	15.8	15.3	14.8	14.3
New Zealand[1]	33.9	32.9	30.2	30.3	30.1	31.6	30.5	31.2	31.6	31.6
Papua New Guinea[5]	20.8	18.6	15.9	17.0	20.0	18.9	18.4	18.2	14.4	12.2
Philippines	16.3	16.2	15.0	14.8	15.1	15.8	16.2	16.7	17.0	17.0
Samoa	20.7	19.3	21.4	20.1	19.9	21.9	23.1	23.0	24.7	24.6
Singapore	13.3	14.1	12.5	12.6	13.1	13.7	13.3	13.5	13.3	13.5
Solomon Islands[6]	..	22.2	21.9	25.1	25.4	26.2	26.5	26.2	26.2	24.1
Thailand	17.6	17.1	16.6	17.6	18.5	18.5	19.3	18.4	18.9	18.1
Tokelau	14.3	16.1	15.5	17.7	15.6	15.3	16.2	17.1	15.1	14.7
Africa (21) average[7]	16.1	16.6	16.3	16.3	16.8	17.1	17.7	17.7	18.2	18.2
LAC average[8]	21.2	21.3	20.8	20.9	21.4	21.9	21.9	22.4	23.1	22.7
OECD average[1,9]	33.6	32.9	32.2	32.3	32.6	33.1	33.4	33.6	33.7	34.0

.. Not available

1. Australia, Japan, Korea and New Zealand are part of the OECD (36) group. Data for Australia, Japan, Korea, New Zealand and the OECD average are taken from OECD (2018), *Revenue Statistics*, https://doi.org/10.1787/2522770x.
2. The figures exclude social security contributions. The figures for social security contributions (heading 2000) are not available but they are thought to be negligible as they relate only to the "Asuransi Kesehatan" — a health insurance programme for employees in for-profit state-owned enterprises.
3. The data are estimated for 2016 (social security contributions).
4. Figures do not include tax revenues from local governments (Quit Rent and Assessment tax), which are unavailable.
5. Total revenues are not calculated for 2000 and 2001 as the data are incomplete and do not include customs revenues for these two years.
6. The social security contributions in the Solomon Islands are null as they do not meet social security criteria of the OECD classification set in Annex A of the Interpretative Guide. The data are estimated for 2008 (import duties).
7. Represents an unweighted average for the 21 African countries included in the publication *Revenue Statistics in Africa 2018*.
8. Represents an unweighted average for the 25 Latin American and Caribbean (LAC) countries included in the publication *Revenue Statistics in Latin America and the Caribbean 2018*.
9. Represents an unweighted average for the 36 OECD member countries included in the publication *Revenue Statistics 2018*.

StatLink https://doi.org/10.1787/888933853832

Table 3.2. **Tax revenue of main headings as percentage of GDP, 2016**

	1000 Income & profits	2000 Social security	3000 Payroll	4000 Property	5000 Goods & services	6000 Other
Australia[1]	15.9	0.0	1.4	3.0	7.5	0.0
Cook Islands	10.1	0.0	0.0	0.0	20.0	0.0
Fiji	7.2	0.0	0.0	0.8	16.1	0.0
Indonesia[2]	5.4	..	0.0	0.2	4.8	1.3
Japan[1]	9.4	12.4	0.0	2.6	6.3	0.1
Kazakhstan[3]	5.6	0.5	1.1	0.5	7.2	0.0
Korea[1]	8.2	6.9	0.1	3.0	7.4	0.7
Malaysia[4]	8.5	0.3	0.0	0.0	5.1	0.5
New Zealand[1]	17.6	0.0	0.0	1.9	12.1	0.0
Papua New Guinea	7.5	0.0	0.0	0.1	4.6	0.0
Philippines	6.9	2.4	0.0	0.5	6.6	0.6
Samoa	5.6	0.0	0.0	0.0	19.0	0.0
Singapore	6.1	0.0	0.0	1.8	4.3	1.4
Solomon Islands[5]	7.0	0.0	0.0	0.2	16.9	0.0
Thailand	6.2	1.0	0.0	0.4	10.3	0.1
Tokelau	8.0	0.0	0.0	0.0	6.7	0.0
Africa (21) average[6]	6.2	1.7	0.2	0.4	9.8	0.2
LAC average[7]	6.0	3.7	0.2	0.8	11.4	0.5
OECD average[1,8]	11.3	9.2	0.4	1.9	11.0	0.2

.. Not available

1. Australia, Japan, Korea and New Zealand are part of the OECD (36) group. Data for Australia, Japan, Korea, New Zealand and the OECD average are taken from OECD (2018), *Revenue Statistics*, https://doi.org/10.1787/2522770x.
2. The figures exclude social security contributions. The figures for social security contributions (heading 2000) are not available but they are thought to be negligible as they relate only to the "Asuransi Kesehatan" — a health insurance programme for employees in for-profit state-owned enterprises.
3. The data are estimated for 2016 (social security contributions).
4. Figures do not include tax revenues from local governments (Quit Rent and Assessment tax), which are unavailable.
5. The social security contributions in the Solomon Islands are null as they do not meet social security criteria of the OECD classification set in Annex A of the Interpretative Guide. The data are estimated for 2008 (import duties).
6. Represents an unweighted average for the 21 African countries included in the publication *Revenue Statistics in Africa 2018*.
7. Represents an unweighted average for the 25 Latin American and Caribbean (LAC) countries included in the publication *Revenue Statistics in Latin America and the Caribbean 2018*.
8. Represents an unweighted average for the 36 OECD member countries included in the publication *Revenue Statistics 2018*.

StatLink https://doi.org/10.1787/888933853851

Table 3.3. **Tax revenue of main headings as percentage of total taxation, 2016**

	1000 Income & profits	2000 Social security	3000 Payroll	4000 Property	5000 Goods & services	6000 Other
Australia[1]	57.2	0.0	4.9	10.8	27.1	0.0
Cook Islands	33.5	0.0	0.0	0.0	66.5	0.0
Fiji	29.9	0.0	0.0	3.3	66.8	0.0
Indonesia[2]	46.2	..	0.0	1.3	41.0	11.5
Japan[1]	30.6	40.4	0.0	8.3	20.4	0.3
Kazakhstan[3]	37.3	3.7	7.6	3.3	48.2	0.0
Korea[1]	31.2	26.2	0.3	11.6	28.1	2.6
Malaysia[4]	59.3	1.8	0.0	0.0	35.6	3.3
New Zealand[1]	55.6	0.0	0.0	6.1	38.3	0.0
Papua New Guinea	61.4	0.0	0.2	0.9	37.5	0.0
Philippines	40.4	14.0	0.0	2.7	39.1	3.8
Samoa	22.8	0.0	0.0	0.0	77.2	0.0
Singapore	44.9	0.0	0.0	13.0	31.8	10.3
Solomon Islands[5]	29.2	0.0	0.0	0.7	70.1	0.0
Thailand	34.4	5.6	0.0	2.3	56.9	0.7
Tokelau	54.6	0.0	0.0	0.0	45.4	0.0
Africa (21) average[6]	34.3	8.4	1.2	2.0	54.6	0.9
LAC average[7]	27.3	15.9	0.8	3.4	50.5	2.1
OECD average[1,8]	33.6	26.2	1.1	5.7	32.7	0.5

.. Not available

1. Australia, Japan, Korea and New Zealand are part of the OECD (36) group. Data for Australia, Japan, Korea, New Zealand and the OECD average are taken from OECD (2018), *Revenue Statistics*, https://doi.org/10.1787/2522770x.
2. The figures exclude social security contributions. The figures for social security contributions (heading 2000) are not available but they are thought to be negligible as they relate only to the "Asuransi Kesehatan" — a health insurance programme for employees in for-profit state-owned enterprises.
3. The data are estimated for 2016 (social security contributions).
4. Figures do not include tax revenues from local governments (Quit Rent and Assessment tax), which are unavailable.
5. The social security contributions in the Solomon Islands are null as they do not meet social security criteria of the OECD classification set in Annex A of the Interpretative Guide. The data are estimated for 2008 (import duties).
6. Represents an unweighted average for the 21 African countries included in the publication *Revenue Statistics in Africa 2018.*
7. Represents an unweighted average for the 25 Latin American and Caribbean (LAC) countries included in the publication *Revenue Statistics in Latin America and the Caribbean 2018.*
8. Represents an unweighted average for the 36 OECD member countries included in the publication *Revenue Statistics 2018.*

StatLink *https://doi.org/10.1787/888933853870*

Table 3.4. **Taxes on income and profits (1000) as percentage of GDP**

	1997	2000	2007	2010	2011	2012	2013	2014	2015	2016
Australia[1]	16.2	17.7	17.5	14.3	15.2	15.6	15.4	15.8	15.8	15.9
Cook Islands	..	..	9.6	10.0	9.5	10.8	8.0	5.9	10.0	10.1
Fiji	..	..	..	7.1	6.8	6.4	5.5	5.6	6.3	7.2
Indonesia	3.6	3.8	5.5	5.2	5.5	5.4	5.3	5.2	5.2	5.4
Japan[1]	9.7	9.0	10.0	8.0	8.3	8.8	9.4	9.6	9.5	9.4
Kazakhstan	..	8.3	14.0	9.5	9.4	9.1	8.1	7.8	6.0	5.6
Korea[1]	5.1	6.2	7.9	6.6	7.3	7.4	7.1	7.2	7.6	8.2
Malaysia	9.8	7.7	9.9	9.1	10.8	11.5	11.2	10.9	9.1	8.5
New Zealand[1]	20.3	19.5	21.3	16.3	15.9	17.4	16.6	17.0	17.3	17.6
Papua New Guinea	..	6.4	15.1	11.8	14.0	12.7	12.3	12.2	9.4	7.5
Philippines	6.1	6.1	6.6	5.8	6.3	6.5	6.7	6.7	6.8	6.9
Samoa	..	..	4.9	5.0	5.1	5.5	5.6	5.6	5.7	5.6
Singapore	..	8.0	6.0	5.6	5.9	6.1	5.7	6.0	5.9	6.1
Solomon Islands	..	..	..	7.6	6.6	7.2	7.8	7.2	7.9	7.0
Thailand	..	4.7	7.0	6.4	7.5	7.3	7.3	6.7	6.6	6.2
Tokelau	..	..	6.8	9.0	8.4	8.5	9.4	8.2	7.7	8.0
Africa (21) average[2]	..	3.6	5.3	5.4	5.7	5.8	6.3	6.2	6.2	6.2
LAC average[3]	4.1	4.3	6.0	5.7	6.0	6.1	6.1	6.3	6.3	6.0
OECD average[1,4]	11.5	11.9	12.1	10.6	10.8	11.0	11.1	11.2	11.3	11.3

.. Not available

1. Australia, Japan, Korea and New Zealand are part of the OECD (36) group. Data for Australia, Japan, Korea, New Zealand and the OECD average are taken from OECD (2018), *Revenue Statistics*, https://doi.org/10.1787/2522770x.
2. Represents an unweighted average for the 21 African countries included in the publication *Revenue Statistics in Africa 2018*.
3. Represents an unweighted average for the 25 Latin American and Caribbean (LAC) countries included in the publication *Revenue Statistics in Latin America and the Caribbean 2018*.
4. Represents an unweighted average for the 36 OECD member countries included in the publication *Revenue Statistics 2018*.

StatLink https://doi.org/10.1787/888933853889

Table 3.5. **Taxes on income and profits (1000) as percentage of total taxation**

	1997	2000	2007	2010	2011	2012	2013	2014	2015	2016
Australia[1]	56.6	57.9	59.3	56.5	58.7	57.8	56.8	57.8	56.6	57.2
Cook Islands	..	..	39.2	39.4	39.6	40.3	32.3	25.6	35.0	33.5
Fiji	..	..	..	32.7	30.1	27.1	23.3	23.1	25.0	29.9
Indonesia	47.2	47.7	45.3	45.8	45.2	43.2	42.5	42.5	43.4	46.2
Japan[1]	37.0	34.8	36.4	30.2	30.2	31.1	32.5	31.8	31.2	30.6
Kazakhstan	..	41.7	53.7	40.0	38.5	38.2	36.0	37.2	38.8	37.3
Korea[1]	26.2	28.8	31.8	28.0	30.1	29.9	29.3	29.1	30.3	31.2
Malaysia	49.8	54.6	66.6	66.1	70.4	71.5	70.9	71.0	61.9	59.3
New Zealand[1]	59.8	60.0	62.9	53.8	53.0	54.9	54.6	54.6	54.9	55.6
Papua New Guinea	..	..	73.0	69.4	69.8	67.0	67.0	67.0	65.2	61.4
Philippines	36.6	38.6	40.4	39.2	41.7	41.4	41.1	39.8	40.3	40.4
Samoa	..	..	23.6	24.7	25.5	25.1	24.2	24.4	23.1	22.8
Singapore	..	52.8	45.4	44.7	44.7	44.7	43.1	44.2	44.7	44.9
Solomon Islands	..	..	..	30.3	25.8	27.5	29.3	27.4	30.1	29.2
Thailand	..	31.8	39.6	36.5	40.5	39.7	38.0	36.6	34.9	34.4
Tokelau	..	..	47.8	51.1	53.7	55.6	57.7	48.1	51.1	54.6
Africa (21) average[2]	..	28.1	32.3	32.9	33.7	33.9	36.3	35.4	34.4	34.3
LAC average[3]	23.0	23.2	28.2	27.1	28.1	28.0	28.0	28.3	27.4	27.3
OECD average[1,4]	34.0	34.8	35.9	32.8	33.1	33.3	33.4	33.3	33.6	33.6

.. Not available

1. Australia, Japan, Korea and New Zealand are part of the OECD (36) group. Data for Australia, Japan, Korea, New Zealand and the OECD average are taken from OECD (2018), *Revenue Statistics*, https://doi.org/10.1787/2522770x.
2. Represents an unweighted average for the 21 African countries included in the publication *Revenue Statistics in Africa 2018*.
3. Represents an unweighted average for the 25 Latin American and Caribbean (LAC) countries included in the publication *Revenue Statistics in Latin America and the Caribbean 2018*.
4. Represents an unweighted average for the 36 OECD member countries included in the publication *Revenue Statistics 2018*.

StatLink https://doi.org/10.1787/888933853908

Table 3.6. **Social security contributions (2000) as percentage of GDP**

	1997	2000	2007	2010	2011	2012	2013	2014	2015	2016
Australia[1]	0.0	0.0	0.0	0.0	0.0	0.0	0.0	0.0	0.0	0.0
Cook Islands	..	..	0.0	0.0	0.0	0.0	0.0	0.0	0.0	0.0
Fiji	..	..	..	0.0	0.0	0.0	0.0	0.0	0.0	0.0
Indonesia[2]	..	..	..	..	..	..	..	..	..	..
Japan[1]	9.0	9.1	10.0	10.9	11.4	11.7	11.8	12.0	12.1	12.4
Kazakhstan[3]	..	0.0	0.4	0.6	0.5	0.6	0.6	0.6	0.6	0.5
Korea[1]	2.7	3.6	5.1	5.5	5.8	6.1	6.4	6.6	6.7	6.9
Malaysia	0.0	0.3	0.3	0.2	0.2	0.2	0.2	0.2	0.2	0.3
New Zealand[1]	0.0	0.0	0.0	0.0	0.0	0.0	0.0	0.0	0.0	0.0
Papua New Guinea	..	0.0	0.0	0.0	0.0	0.0	0.0	0.0	0.0	0.0
Philippines	1.4	2.1	1.9	1.9	1.9	2.0	2.1	2.3	2.4	2.4
Samoa	..	..	0.0	0.0	0.0	0.0	0.0	0.0	0.0	0.0
Singapore	..	0.0	0.0	0.0	0.0	0.0	0.0	0.0	0.0	0.0
Solomon Islands[4]	..	..	..	0.0	0.0	0.0	0.0	0.0	0.0	0.0
Thailand	..	0.5	0.9	1.2	0.9	0.9	0.8	1.0	1.1	1.0
Tokelau	..	..	0.0	0.0	0.0	0.0	0.0	0.0	0.0	0.0
Africa (21) average[5]	..	1.3	1.4	1.6	1.6	1.6	1.7	1.6	1.7	1.7
LAC average[6]	2.4	2.6	2.8	3.2	3.2	3.4	3.5	3.6	3.7	3.7
OECD average[1,7]	8.7	8.6	8.4	8.9	8.9	9.0	9.0	9.0	9.0	9.2

.. Not available

1. Australia, Japan, Korea and New Zealand are part of the OECD (36) group. Data for Australia, Japan, Korea, New Zealand and the OECD average are taken from OECD (2018), *Revenue Statistics*, https://doi.org/10.1787/2522770x.
2. The figures exclude social security contributions. The figures for social security contributions (heading 2000) are not available but they are thought to be negligible as they relate only to the "Asuransi Kesehatan" — a health insurance programme for employees in for-profit state-owned enterprises.
3. The data are estimated for 2016.
4. The social security contributions in the Solomon Islands are null as they do not meet social security criteria of the OECD classification set in Annex A of the Interpretative Guide. The data are estimated for 2008 (import duties).
5. Represents an unweighted average for the 21 African countries included in the publication *Revenue Statistics in Africa 2018*.
6. Represents an unweighted average for the 25 Latin American and Caribbean (LAC) countries included in the publication *Revenue Statistics in Latin America and the Caribbean 2018*.
7. Represents an unweighted average for the 36 OECD member countries included in the publication *Revenue Statistics 2018*.

StatLink https://doi.org/10.1787/888933853927

Table 3.7. **Social security contributions (2000) as percentage of total taxation**

	1997	2000	2007	2010	2011	2012	2013	2014	2015	2016
Australia[1]	0.0	0.0	0.0	0.0	0.0	0.0	0.0	0.0	0.0	0.0
Cook Islands	..	..	0.0	0.0	0.0	0.0	0.0	0.0	0.0	0.0
Fiji	..	..	..	0.0	0.0	0.0	0.0	0.0	0.0	0.0
Indonesia[2]	..	..	..	..	..	..	..	..	..	..
Japan[1]	34.3	35.2	36.5	41.1	41.5	41.6	40.8	39.7	39.4	40.4
Kazakhstan[3]	..	0.0	1.5	2.5	2.2	2.5	2.5	2.7	3.8	3.7
Korea[1]	14.2	16.7	20.7	23.3	24.0	24.7	26.4	26.9	26.6	26.2
Malaysia	0.0	2.0	1.7	1.8	1.6	1.5	1.6	1.6	1.7	1.8
New Zealand[1]	0.0	0.0	0.0	0.0	0.0	0.0	0.0	0.0	0.0	0.0
Papua New Guinea	..	..	0.0	0.0	0.0	0.0	0.0	0.0	0.0	0.0
Philippines	8.1	13.1	11.8	12.7	12.7	12.9	12.7	13.5	14.1	14.0
Samoa	..	..	0.0	0.0	0.0	0.0	0.0	0.0	0.0	0.0
Singapore	..	0.0	0.0	0.0	0.0	0.0	0.0	0.0	0.0	0.0
Solomon Islands[4]	..	..	..	0.0	0.0	0.0	0.0	0.0	0.0	0.0
Thailand	..	3.7	5.1	7.1	4.7	4.7	4.2	5.3	5.6	5.6
Tokelau	..	..	0.0	0.0	0.0	0.0	0.0	0.0	0.0	0.0
Africa (21) average[5]	..	8.3	7.7	8.2	8.0	8.0	8.2	8.2	8.2	8.4
LAC average[6]	13.6	14.5	13.7	14.9	14.8	15.4	15.8	15.9	16.0	15.9
OECD average[1,7]	25.1	25.0	24.8	26.8	26.7	26.6	26.5	26.4	26.2	26.2

.. Not available

1. Australia, Japan, Korea and New Zealand are part of the OECD (36) group. Data for Australia, Japan, Korea, New Zealand and the OECD average are taken from OECD (2018), *Revenue Statistics*, https://doi.org/10.1787/2522770x.
2. The figures exclude social security contributions. The figures for social security contributions (heading 2000) are not available but they are thought to be negligible as they relate only to the "Asuransi Kesehatan" — a health insurance programme for employees in for-profit state-owned enterprises.
3. The data are estimated for 2016.
4. The social security contributions in the Solomon Islands are null as they do not meet social security criteria of the OECD classification set in Annex A of the Interpretative Guide. The data are estimated for 2008 (import duties).
5. Represents an unweighted average for the 21 African countries included in the publication *Revenue Statistics in Africa 2018*.
6. Represents an unweighted average for the 25 Latin American and Caribbean (LAC) countries included in the publication *Revenue Statistics in Latin America and the Caribbean 2018*.
7. Represents an unweighted average for the 36 OECD member countries included in the publication *Revenue Statistics 2018*.

StatLink https://doi.org/10.1787/888933853946

Table 3.8. **Taxes on property (4000) as percentage of GDP**

	1997	2000	2007	2010	2011	2012	2013	2014	2015	2016
Australia[1]	2.6	2.7	2.6	2.4	2.2	2.3	2.6	2.8	3.0	3.0
Cook Islands	..	..	0.0	0.0	0.0	0.0	0.0	0.0	0.0	0.0
Fiji	..	..	..	0.0	0.2	0.3	0.6	0.8	0.8	0.8
Indonesia	0.3	0.3	0.7	0.5	0.4	0.3	0.3	0.2	0.3	0.2
Japan[1]	2.9	2.7	2.5	2.6	2.7	2.6	2.6	2.6	2.5	2.6
Kazakhstan	..	0.8	0.6	0.6	0.5	0.5	0.4	0.5	0.6	0.5
Korea[1]	2.5	2.7	3.2	2.6	2.7	2.6	2.5	2.7	3.1	3.0
Malaysia[2]	0.0	0.0	..	..	..	0.0	0.0	0.0	0.0	0.0
New Zealand[1]	1.8	1.7	1.8	2.0	2.0	2.0	1.9	2.0	2.0	1.9
Papua New Guinea	..	0.3	0.3	0.2	0.1	0.2	0.1	0.2	0.1	0.1
Philippines	0.2	0.5	0.5	0.4	0.5	0.5	0.5	0.5	0.5	0.5
Samoa	..	..	0.1	0.0	0.0	0.0	0.0	0.0	0.0	0.0
Singapore	..	1.7	2.3	1.8	2.0	2.2	2.1	1.8	1.7	1.8
Solomon Islands	..	..	..	0.1	0.3	0.1	0.1	0.2	0.2	0.2
Thailand	..	0.3	0.2	0.2	0.4	0.4	0.4	0.5	0.5	0.4
Tokelau	..	..	0.0	0.0	0.0	0.0	0.0	0.0	0.0	0.0
Africa (21) average[3]	..	0.4	0.4	0.4	0.4	0.4	0.4	0.4	0.4	0.4
LAC average[4]	0.5	0.6	0.8	0.7	0.7	0.7	0.8	0.7	0.8	0.8
OECD average[1,5]	1.7	1.8	1.8	1.7	1.7	1.8	1.8	1.9	1.9	1.9

.. Not available

1. Australia, Japan, Korea and New Zealand are part of the OECD (36) group. Data for Australia, Japan, Korea, New Zealand and the OECD average are taken from OECD (2018), *Revenue Statistics*, https://doi.org/10.1787/2522770x.
2. Figures do not include tax revenues from local governments (Quit Rent and Assessment tax), which are unavailable.
3. Represents an unweighted average for the 21 African countries included in the publication *Revenue Statistics in Africa 2018*.
4. Represents an unweighted average for the 25 Latin American and Caribbean (LAC) countries included in the publication *Revenue Statistics in Latin America and the Caribbean 2018*.
5. Represents an unweighted average for the 36 OECD member countries included in the publication *Revenue Statistics 2018*.

StatLink https://doi.org/10.1787/888933853965

Table 3.9. **Taxes on property (4000) as percentage of total taxation**

	1997	2000	2007	2010	2011	2012	2013	2014	2015	2016
Australia[1]	9.2	8.8	9.0	9.4	8.7	8.7	9.5	10.2	10.7	10.8
Cook Islands	..	..	0.0	0.0	0.0	0.0	0.0	0.0	0.0	0.0
Fiji	..	..	..	0.0	0.9	1.3	2.4	3.3	3.1	3.3
Indonesia	4.2	3.7	5.6	4.7	3.1	2.7	2.1	1.8	2.1	1.3
Japan[1]	11.2	10.5	9.0	9.7	9.7	9.1	8.8	8.5	8.2	8.3
Kazakhstan	..	4.1	2.2	2.4	1.9	2.0	2.0	2.3	3.6	3.3
Korea[1]	12.7	12.4	12.8	11.3	11.4	10.6	10.3	11.0	12.4	11.6
Malaysia[2]	0.0	0.0	..	..	..	0.0	0.0	0.0	0.0	0.0
New Zealand[1]	5.4	5.3	5.3	6.6	6.6	6.3	6.4	6.3	6.2	6.1
Papua New Guinea	..	..	1.4	1.0	0.7	0.8	0.8	1.3	0.6	0.9
Philippines	0.9	3.1	2.9	2.9	3.0	3.1	3.0	2.8	2.8	2.7
Samoa	..	..	0.5	0.0	0.0	0.0	0.0	0.0	0.0	0.0
Singapore	..	11.2	17.1	14.5	15.4	16.1	15.9	13.2	13.0	13.0
Solomon Islands	..	..	..	0.6	1.0	0.4	0.5	0.6	0.8	0.7
Thailand	..	2.2	1.2	1.3	2.0	2.2	2.3	2.6	2.7	2.3
Tokelau	..	..	0.0	0.0	0.0	0.0	0.0	0.0	0.0	0.0
Africa (21) average[3]	..	2.3	2.2	2.0	1.9	1.9	1.9	2.0	1.9	2.0
LAC average[4]	2.6	2.8	3.5	3.2	3.1	3.2	3.4	3.2	3.4	3.4
OECD average[1,5]	5.2	5.4	5.5	5.4	5.4	5.4	5.5	5.6	5.7	5.7

.. Not available

1. Australia, Japan, Korea and New Zealand are part of the OECD (36) group. Data for Australia, Japan, Korea, New Zealand and the OECD average are taken from OECD (2018), *Revenue Statistics*, https://doi.org/10.1787/2522770x.
2. Figures do not include tax revenues from local governments (Quit Rent and Assessment tax), which are unavailable.
3. Represents an unweighted average for the 21 African countries included in the publication *Revenue Statistics in Africa 2018*.
4. Represents an unweighted average for the 25 Latin American and Caribbean (LAC) countries included in the publication *Revenue Statistics in Latin America and the Caribbean 2018*.
5. Represents an unweighted average for the 36 OECD member countries included in the publication *Revenue Statistics 2018*.

StatLink https://doi.org/10.1787/888933853984

Table 3.10. Taxes on goods and services (5000) as percentage of GDP

	1997	2000	2007	2010	2011	2012	2013	2014	2015	2016
Australia[1]	7.9	8.8	8.0	7.3	7.1	7.6	7.8	7.3	7.7	7.5
Cook Islands	..	..	14.8	15.4	14.5	16.0	16.7	17.0	18.5	20.0
Fiji	..	..	..	14.6	15.6	16.9	17.4	17.7	18.0	16.1
Indonesia	3.6	3.5	5.1	4.7	5.2	5.6	5.7	5.4	5.2	4.8
Japan[1]	4.5	5.0	4.9	5.0	5.1	5.1	5.1	6.0	6.4	6.3
Kazakhstan	..	6.9	8.8	11.9	13.1	12.6	12.4	11.1	7.2	7.2
Korea[1]	8.3	8.2	7.8	7.9	7.5	7.7	7.5	7.4	7.1	7.4
Malaysia	8.9	5.6	4.1	3.9	3.7	3.8	3.7	3.6	4.9	5.1
New Zealand[1]	11.8	11.3	10.7	12.0	12.1	12.3	11.9	12.2	12.3	12.1
Papua New Guinea[2]	..	2.2	5.3	5.0	5.9	6.1	5.9	5.7	4.9	4.6
Philippines	8.4	6.6	6.6	6.1	5.9	6.1	6.4	6.7	6.6	6.6
Samoa	..	..	15.7	15.2	14.8	16.4	17.5	17.4	19.0	19.0
Singapore	..	4.7	4.4	4.3	4.3	4.2	4.1	4.2	4.2	4.3
Solomon Islands[3]	..	..	..	17.3	18.6	18.9	18.6	18.9	18.1	16.9
Thailand	..	9.2	9.4	9.6	9.6	9.7	10.6	10.1	10.6	10.3
Tokelau	..	..	7.4	8.6	7.2	6.8	6.9	8.8	7.4	6.7
Africa (21) average[4]	..	7.9	9.0	8.9	9.1	9.3	9.2	9.3	9.8	9.8
LAC average[5]	9.9	9.9	10.7	10.4	10.6	10.9	10.8	10.9	11.5	11.4
OECD average[1,6]	11.0	10.9	10.6	10.6	10.6	10.7	10.7	10.8	10.8	11.0

.. Not available

1. Australia, Japan, Korea and New Zealand are part of the OECD (36) group. Data for Australia, Japan, Korea, New Zealand and the OECD average are taken from OECD (2018), *Revenue Statistics*, https://doi.org/10.1787/2522770x.
2. Total revenues are not calculated for 2000 and 2001 as the data are incomplete and do not include customs revenues for these two years.
3. The data are estimated for 2008 (import duties).
4. Represents an unweighted average for the 21 African countries included in the publication *Revenue Statistics in Africa 2018*.
5. Represents an unweighted average for the 25 Latin American and Caribbean (LAC) countries included in the publication *Revenue Statistics in Latin America and the Caribbean 2018*.
6. Represents an unweighted average for the 36 OECD member countries included in the publication *Revenue Statistics 2018*.

StatLink https://doi.org/10.1787/888933854003

Table 3.11. Taxes on goods and services (5000) as percentage of total taxation

	1997	2000	2007	2010	2011	2012	2013	2014	2015	2016
Australia[1]	27.5	28.8	27.0	29.0	27.4	28.3	28.6	26.9	27.6	27.1
Cook Islands	..	..	60.8	60.6	60.4	59.7	67.7	74.4	65.0	66.5
Fiji	..	..	..	67.3	69.1	71.6	74.3	73.5	71.9	66.8
Indonesia	47.6	44.7	41.9	41.8	42.9	44.8	45.3	44.4	43.5	41.0
Japan[1]	17.2	19.3	18.0	18.7	18.4	17.9	17.6	19.8	21.0	20.4
Kazakhstan	..	34.9	33.8	50.2	53.4	52.8	54.8	52.7	46.5	48.2
Korea[1]	42.7	38.4	31.3	33.7	31.2	31.2	30.7	30.0	28.0	28.1
Malaysia	45.2	39.8	27.9	28.4	24.5	23.4	23.5	23.6	33.0	35.6
New Zealand[1]	34.8	34.7	31.7	39.6	40.3	38.8	39.0	39.2	38.9	38.3
Papua New Guinea[2]	..	..	25.5	29.6	29.4	32.1	32.2	31.5	34.3	37.5
Philippines	50.2	42.0	40.7	41.3	38.7	38.8	39.4	40.0	39.0	39.1
Samoa	..	..	76.0	75.3	74.5	74.9	75.8	75.6	76.9	77.2
Singapore	..	31.1	32.9	34.4	32.8	30.5	30.8	31.3	31.7	31.8
Solomon Islands[3]	..	..	..	69.1	73.2	72.1	70.2	72.0	69.1	70.1
Thailand	..	61.9	53.4	54.4	52.1	52.7	54.9	54.9	56.1	56.9
Tokelau	..	..	52.2	48.9	46.3	44.4	42.3	51.9	48.9	45.4
Africa (21) average[4]	..	61.2	57.2	56.4	55.8	55.2	52.7	53.4	54.5	54.6
LAC average[5]	57.2	56.2	51.0	51.0	50.3	50.2	49.6	49.5	50.3	50.5
OECD average[1,6]	33.7	33.1	32.0	33.2	33.0	32.8	32.7	32.7	32.6	32.7

.. Not available

1. Australia, Japan, Korea and New Zealand are part of the OECD (36) group. Data for Australia, Japan, Korea, New Zealand and the OECD average are taken from OECD (2018), *Revenue Statistics*, https://doi.org/10.1787/2522770x.
2. Total revenues are not calculated for 2000 and 2001 as the data are incomplete and do not include customs revenues for these two years.
3. The data are estimated for 2008 (import duties).
4. Represents an unweighted average for the 21 African countries included in the publication *Revenue Statistics in Africa 2018*.
5. Represents an unweighted average for the 25 Latin American and Caribbean (LAC) countries included in the publication *Revenue Statistics in Latin America and the Caribbean 2018*.
6. Represents an unweighted average for the 36 OECD member countries included in the publication *Revenue Statistics 2018*.

StatLink https://doi.org/10.1787/888933854022

Table 3.12. **Taxes on general consumption (5110) as percentage of GDP**

	1997	2000	2007	2010	2011	2012	2013	2014	2015	2016
Australia[1]	2.4	3.7	3.9	3.5	3.3	3.4	3.6	3.6	3.7	3.7
Cook Islands	..	..	10.6	10.4	9.5	9.9	11.1	12.0	13.3	13.8
Fiji	..	..	..	8.7	9.7	10.2	10.4	10.1	10.5	7.9
Indonesia	2.7	2.3	3.6	3.4	3.5	3.9	4.0	3.9	3.7	3.3
Japan[1]	1.9	2.3	2.4	2.5	2.6	2.6	2.7	3.7	4.2	4.1
Kazakhstan	..	4.4	4.9	3.1	2.9	2.9	3.7	3.0	2.3	3.2
Korea[1]	3.7	3.7	3.9	4.1	4.1	4.3	4.1	4.2	3.8	4.2
Malaysia	2.2	1.7	1.0	1.0	0.9	1.0	1.0	1.0	2.8	3.4
New Zealand[1]	8.3	8.1	8.0	9.3	9.4	9.6	9.3	9.5	9.5	9.4
Papua New Guinea	..	2.2	2.3	2.3	2.7	2.9	2.9	2.9	2.6	2.3
Philippines[2]	1.8	1.5	2.1	1.9	1.9	2.2	2.2	2.2	2.2	2.3
Samoa	..	..	7.9	7.1	7.6	8.9	9.2	9.3	10.0	9.5
Singapore	..	1.3	2.2	2.5	2.5	2.5	2.5	2.5	2.5	2.6
Solomon Islands	..	..	..	8.3	8.7	8.9	8.9	8.6	7.9	7.0
Thailand	..	3.4	3.6	3.7	3.9	4.3	4.0	4.0	3.9	3.9
Tokelau	..	..	0.0	0.0	0.0	0.0	0.0	0.0	0.0	0.0
Africa (21) average[3]	..	3.4	5.0	5.1	5.2	5.3	5.2	5.2	5.5	5.4
LAC average[4]	5.4	5.8	6.9	6.7	6.8	7.1	7.1	7.2	7.5	7.5
OECD average[1,5]	6.7	6.7	6.8	6.7	6.7	6.8	6.8	6.9	6.9	7.0

.. Not available

1. Australia, Japan, Korea and New Zealand are part of the OECD (36) group. Data for Australia, Japan, Korea, New Zealand and the OECD average are taken from OECD (2018), *Revenue Statistics*, https://doi.org/10.1787/2522770x.
2. The data exclude revenue from VAT on imports. This revenue could not be distinguished from revenue from other import duties and is currently classified under heading 5120 (taxes on specific goods and services).
3. Represents an unweighted average for the 21 African countries included in the publication *Revenue Statistics in Africa 2018*.
4. Represents an unweighted average for the 25 Latin American and Caribbean (LAC) countries included in the publication *Revenue Statistics in Latin America and the Caribbean 2018*.
5. Represents an unweighted average for the 36 OECD member countries included in the publication *Revenue Statistics 2018*.

StatLink https://doi.org/10.1787/888933854041

Table 3.13. **Taxes on general consumption (5110) as percentage of total taxation**

	1997	2000	2007	2010	2011	2012	2013	2014	2015	2016
Australia[1]	8.4	12.0	13.1	13.8	12.9	12.4	13.1	13.1	13.3	13.2
Cook Islands	..	..	43.4	41.0	39.5	37.1	45.1	52.4	46.6	46.1
Fiji	..	..	..	40.4	42.7	43.3	44.3	41.9	41.8	32.8
Indonesia	35.5	29.4	29.4	29.6	29.2	31.4	32.3	31.8	30.5	28.6
Japan[1]	7.2	9.1	8.8	9.6	9.4	9.2	9.2	12.2	13.7	13.3
Kazakhstan	..	22.4	18.8	13.1	12.0	12.4	16.3	14.3	14.8	21.4
Korea[1]	18.9	17.0	15.8	17.5	17.0	17.2	17.0	17.2	15.3	15.8
Malaysia	11.1	11.9	6.7	7.2	6.2	6.1	6.3	6.5	18.9	23.6
New Zealand[1]	24.5	24.9	23.5	30.7	31.4	30.3	30.6	30.4	30.2	29.8
Papua New Guinea[2]	..	..	11.1	13.3	13.6	15.5	15.8	15.9	17.9	19.1
Philippines[3]	10.6	9.5	12.9	13.0	12.5	13.8	13.4	13.2	13.0	13.5
Samoa	..	..	38.2	35.0	38.4	40.6	39.8	40.3	40.4	38.5
Singapore	..	8.3	16.8	19.6	18.9	18.0	18.6	18.9	18.6	18.9
Solomon Islands	..	..	..	33.2	34.2	33.9	33.5	32.9	30.1	28.9
Thailand	..	23.1	20.6	20.8	20.9	23.0	20.5	21.9	20.9	21.5
Tokelau	..	..	0.0	0.0	0.0	0.0	0.0	0.0	0.0	0.0
Africa (21) average[4]	..	27.0	32.1	31.8	31.7	31.7	29.8	29.9	30.1	29.8
LAC average[5]	30.4	31.2	31.7	31.9	31.8	31.9	31.9	31.9	32.3	32.9
OECD average[1,6]	20.4	20.1	20.4	20.9	20.9	20.8	20.7	21.0	20.8	20.8

.. Not available

1. Australia, Japan, Korea and New Zealand are part of the OECD (36) group. Data for Australia, Japan, Korea, New Zealand and the OECD average are taken from OECD (2018), *Revenue Statistics*, https://doi.org/10.1787/2522770x.
2. Total revenues are not calculated for 2000 and 2001 as the data are incomplete and do not include customs revenues for these two years.
3. The data exclude revenue from VAT on imports. This revenue could not be distinguished from revenue from other import duties and is currently classified under heading 5120 (taxes on specific goods and services).
4. Represents an unweighted average for the 21 African countries included in the publication *Revenue Statistics in Africa 2018*.
5. Represents an unweighted average for the 25 Latin American and Caribbean (LAC) countries included in the publication *Revenue Statistics in Latin America and the Caribbean 2018*.
6. Represents an unweighted average for the 36 OECD member countries included in the publication *Revenue Statistics 2018*.

StatLink https://doi.org/10.1787/888933854060

Table 3.14. **Taxes on specific goods and services (5120) as percentage of GDP**

	1997	2000	2007	2010	2011	2012	2013	2014	2015	2016
Australia[1]	4.0	4.3	3.3	3.0	3.0	3.0	2.9	2.9	2.9	2.8
Cook Islands	..	..	4.0	4.7	4.8	5.8	5.3	4.7	5.1	5.9
Fiji	..	..	..	5.8	5.9	6.7	7.0	7.6	7.5	8.2
Indonesia	0.9	1.2	1.5	1.4	1.7	1.7	1.6	1.5	1.6	1.4
Japan[1]	2.1	2.0	2.0	1.9	2.0	2.0	1.9	1.8	1.8	1.7
Kazakhstan	..	2.1	3.1	8.3	9.8	9.2	8.3	7.7	4.6	3.7
Korea[1]	4.2	4.2	3.6	3.5	2.9	3.0	2.9	2.7	2.8	2.8
Malaysia	5.4	2.9	2.5	2.4	2.3	2.3	2.2	2.2	1.6	1.3
New Zealand[1]	2.8	2.5	2.0	1.9	1.9	1.9	1.8	1.9	1.9	1.9
Papua New Guinea[2]	..	..	3.0	2.8	3.2	3.1	3.0	2.8	2.4	2.2
Philippines[3]	6.5	5.0	4.4	4.1	3.9	3.9	4.1	4.4	4.3	4.3
Samoa	..	..	7.8	8.1	7.2	7.5	8.3	8.1	9.0	9.5
Singapore	..	2.0	1.3	1.3	1.3	1.2	1.2	1.3	1.3	1.2
Solomon Islands	..	..	..	8.9	9.8	9.9	9.6	10.1	10.0	9.8
Thailand	..	5.5	5.5	5.7	5.5	5.2	5.6	5.0	5.4	5.3
Tokelau	..	..	7.4	8.6	7.2	6.8	6.9	8.8	7.4	6.7
Africa (21) average[4]	..	4.3	3.7	3.6	3.7	3.7	3.8	3.8	4.2	4.2
LAC average[5]	4.2	3.8	3.5	3.4	3.4	3.4	3.3	3.4	3.6	3.6
OECD average[1,6]	3.7	3.6	3.2	3.3	3.3	3.3	3.3	3.2	3.2	3.3

.. Not available

1. Australia, Japan, Korea and New Zealand are part of the OECD (36) group. Data for Australia, Japan, Korea, New Zealand and the OECD average are taken from OECD (2018), *Revenue Statistics*, https://doi.org/10.1787/2522770x.
2. Total revenues are not calculated for 2000 and 2001 as the data are incomplete and do not include customs revenues for these two years.
3. The data include revenues from VAT on imports, usually classified under heading 5110 (taxes on general consumption). This revenue could not be distinguished from revenue from other import duties.
4. Represents an unweighted average for the 21 African countries included in the publication *Revenue Statistics in Africa 2018*.
5. Represents an unweighted average for the 25 Latin American and Caribbean (LAC) countries included in the publication *Revenue Statistics in Latin America and the Caribbean 2018*.
6. Represents an unweighted average for the 36 OECD member countries included in the publication *Revenue Statistics 2018*.

StatLink https://doi.org/10.1787/888933854079

Table 3.15. **Taxes on specific goods and services (5120) as percentage of total taxation**

	1997	2000	2007	2010	2011	2012	2013	2014	2015	2016
Australia[1]	13.8	14.1	11.3	11.9	11.4	11.1	10.8	10.5	10.4	10.0
Cook Islands	..	..	16.3	18.6	20.0	21.6	21.5	20.6	17.7	19.5
Fiji	..	..	..	26.9	26.3	28.2	30.0	31.6	30.1	34.0
Indonesia	12.1	15.3	12.5	12.2	13.8	13.5	13.1	12.6	12.9	12.4
Japan[1]	7.9	7.9	7.1	7.2	7.1	6.9	6.7	6.0	5.8	5.7
Kazakhstan	..	10.4	12.1	35.1	39.9	38.8	36.6	36.3	29.5	24.9
Korea[1]	21.6	19.7	14.5	15.1	12.2	12.0	11.8	10.8	10.9	10.5
Malaysia	27.5	20.5	17.1	17.3	14.9	14.2	14.1	14.1	11.0	9.0
New Zealand[1]	8.2	7.5	5.9	6.4	6.4	6.1	5.9	6.1	6.1	5.9
Papua New Guinea[2]	..	..	14.4	16.3	15.8	16.6	16.3	15.6	16.4	18.4
Philippines[3]	39.1	32.0	27.0	27.6	25.6	24.5	25.4	26.2	25.5	25.1
Samoa	..	..	37.8	40.2	36.1	34.3	36.1	35.3	36.5	38.7
Singapore	..	13.0	10.1	10.3	9.8	8.9	8.9	9.5	10.0	9.2
Solomon Islands	..	..	..	35.3	38.5	37.8	36.2	38.4	38.4	40.5
Thailand	..	37.0	31.5	32.1	29.9	28.2	29.1	27.1	28.3	29.0
Tokelau	..	..	52.2	48.9	46.3	44.4	42.3	51.9	48.9	45.4
Africa (21) average[4]	..	33.1	23.8	23.0	23.0	22.4	21.9	22.4	23.2	23.7
LAC average[5]	25.3	23.3	17.7	17.4	16.9	16.6	16.1	15.9	16.3	16.0
OECD average[1,6]	11.5	11.1	9.8	10.3	10.1	10.1	9.9	9.7	9.8	9.8

.. Not available

1. Australia, Japan, Korea and New Zealand are part of the OECD (36) group. Data for Australia, Japan, Korea, New Zealand and the OECD average are taken from OECD (2018), *Revenue Statistics*, https://doi.org/10.1787/2522770x.
2. Total revenues are not calculated for 2000 and 2001 as the data are incomplete and do not include customs revenues for these two years.
3. The data include revenues from VAT on imports, usually classified under heading 5110 (taxes on general consumption). This revenue could not be distinguished from revenue from other import duties.
4. Represents an unweighted average for the 21 African countries included in the publication *Revenue Statistics in Africa 2018*.
5. Represents an unweighted average for the 25 Latin American and Caribbean (LAC) countries included in the publication *Revenue Statistics in Latin America and the Caribbean 2018*.
6. Represents an unweighted average for the 36 OECD member countries included in the publication *Revenue Statistics 2018*.

StatLink https://doi.org/10.1787/888933854098

Table 3.16. Gross domestic product for tax reporting years at market prices, national currency

	1997	2000	2007	2010	2011	2012	2013	2014	2015	2016
Australia[1,2]	588	705	1 176	1 414	1 497	1 534	1 596	1 621	1 660	1 755
Cook Islands[2]	..	..	321 100	358 250	367 650	370 300	374 300	395 150	411 550	419 800
Fiji	3 018	3 572	5 440	6 024	6 769	7 110	7 716	8 462	9 150	9 785
Indonesia	754 614	1 520 683	4 323 057	6 864 133	7 831 726	8 615 705	9 546 134	10 569 705	11 526 333	12 406 774
Japan[1]	533 338	528 513	530 997	499 281	494 017	494 478	507 246	518 469	533 895	539 373
Kazakhstan	1 672	2 600	12 850	21 816	29 380	31 015	35 999	39 676	40 884	46 971
Korea	530 347	635 185	1 043 258	1 265 308	1 332 681	1 377 457	1 429 445	1 486 079	1 564 124	1 641 786
Malaysia	282	356	665	821	912	971	1 019	1 107	1 157	1 230
New Zealand[1,2]	105	122	189	206	215	219	237	245	258	274
Papua New Guinea	10 638	14 630	28 304	38 752	42 642	44 372	47 721	56 621	63 567	70 707
Philippines	2 689	3 581	6 893	9 004	9 708	10 561	11 538	12 634	13 322	14 481
Samoa[2,3]	733	867	1 598	1 693	1 804	1 841	1 853	1 908	2 002	2 094
Singapore[4]	150	168	276	331	351	366	385	401	419	434
Solomon Islands	1 840	1 938	3 949	5 493	7 127	7 825	8 250	8 646	9 139	9 798
Thailand	4 695	4 989	8 847	10 621	11 372	11 776	12 871	13 129	13 592	14 325
Tokelau[2]	..	..	8 399	9 597	10 250	10 595	11 501	12 355	14 223	14 838

.. Not available

Note: All units are in billions except for the Cook Islands, Fiji, Papua New Guinea, Samoa, the Solomon Islands and Tokelau. Due to the size of their economies, the GDP figures for the Cook Islands and Tokelau are expressed in thousands while they are in millions for Fiji, Papua New Guinea, Samoa, the Solomon Islands

1. The year Y is calculated (at annual rate) as the average of: Q2(Y) to Q1(Y+1) for Japan; and Q3(Y) to Q2(Y+1) for Australia and New Zealand.
2. Data are reported on a fiscal year basis beginning 1st July. For example, the data for 2016 represent the period from July 2016 to June 2017.
3. The year Y is calculated using the formula GDP(Y)/2+GDP(Y-1)/2. This is done in order to make the value of the GDP correspond more closely to a July(Y-1)-to-June(Y) fiscal year.
4. The year Y is calculated using the formula GDP(Y)*3/4+GDP(Y+1))/4 in order to make it correspond more closely to an April(Y)-to-March(Y+1) fiscal year.

Source: OECD National Accounts data for Australia, Indonesia, Japan, Korea and New Zealand; National statistical offices for the Cook Islands and Tokelau; CEIC for Kazakhstan, Malaysia, the Philippines, Thailand and Singapore; IMF's *World Economic Outlook* (April 2018) for Fiji, Papua New Guinea, Samoa and the Solomon Islands.

StatLink https://doi.org/10.1787/888933854117

Table 3.17. Gross domestic product for tax reporting years at market prices, in millions of US Dollars at market exchange rates

	1997	2000	2007	2010	2011	2012	2013	2014	2015	2016
Australia[1,2]	436 263	408 201	983 730	1 297 239	1 544 385	1 587 927	1 539 722	1 461 456	1 246 998	1 304 301
Cook Islands[2]	..	..	236	258	291	300	307	328	288	293
Fiji	2 090	1 678	3 378	3 141	3 775	3 972	4 190	4 484	4 344	4 666
Indonesia	261 966	181 212	473 016	755 392	892 401	918 104	912 590	890 555	860 854	932 230
Japan[1]	4 407 878	4 901 138	4 509 336	5 689 122	6 197 933	6 195 413	5 197 296	4 898 260	4 412 271	4 957 351
Kazakhstan	22 166	18 292	104 850	148 047	200 379	207 999	236 635	221 416	184 388	137 278
Korea	557 962	561 792	1 122 446	1 095 096	1 203 539	1 223 389	1 305 518	1 411 196	1 382 579	1 414 615
Malaysia	100 007	93 790	193 657	255 192	298 180	314 760	323 445	338 234	296 400	297 053
New Zealand[1,2]	69 287	55 432	138 908	148 339	169 860	177 147	194 086	203 477	180 026	190 924
Papua New Guinea	7 398	5 258	9 545	14 251	17 985	21 295	21 261	23 004	22 962	22 568
Philippines	91 234	81 023	149 360	199 591	224 143	250 092	271 836	284 585	292 774	304 906
Samoa[2,3]	286	279	590	667	756	800	811	821	826	801
Singapore[4]	96 808	96 787	187 241	248 764	280 283	294 865	305 629	310 872	302 391	313 434
Solomon Islands	495	381	516	681	933	1 064	1 130	1 174	1 158	1 235
Thailand	171 542	127 743	263 424	326 485	376 363	378 285	422 840	407 463	406 200	404 851
Tokelau[2]	..	..	6	7	8	9	9	10	10	10

.. Not available

Note: This table is produced based on GDP data in national currency from Table 3.16 and exchange rate data from Table 3.19.

1. The year Y is calculated (at annual rate) as the average of: Q2(Y) to Q1(Y+1) for Japan; and Q3(Y) to Q2(Y+1) for Australia and New Zealand.
2. Data are reported on a fiscal year basis beginning 1st July. For example, the data for 2016 represent the period from July 2016 to June 2017.
3. The year Y is calculated using the formula GDP(Y)/2+GDP(Y-1)/2. This is done in order to make the value of the GDP correspond more closely to a July(Y-1)-to-June(Y) fiscal year.
4. The year Y is calculated using the formula GDP(Y)*3/4+GDP(Y+1))/4 in order to make it correspond more closely to an April(Y)-to-March(Y+1) fiscal year.

StatLink https://doi.org/10.1787/888933854136

Table 3.18. **Total tax revenue in millions of US dollars at market exchange rates**

	1997	2000	2007	2010	2011	2012	2013	2014	2015	2016
Australia	125 058	124 385	290 788	328 349	400 524	427 972	418 120	399 343	348 153	362 049
Cook Islands	..	..	58	66	70	80	76	75	82	88
Fiji	..	..	..	679	855	936	984	1 078	1 089	1 127
Indonesia	19 906	14 264	57 550	85 782	108 580	114 616	114 026	108 322	103 683	108 360
Japan	1 153 894	1 263 376	1 241 967	1 509 609	1 702 132	1 749 052	1 500 082	1 482 193	1 351 487	1 516 166
Kazakhstan	..	3 621	27 329	35 169	49 189	49 614	53 445	46 682	28 652	20 451
Korea	108 274	120 547	278 198	256 154	290 720	303 158	317 220	347 014	347 879	371 150
Malaysia	19 694	13 180	28 690	35 283	45 554	50 652	51 098	51 818	43 794	42 338
New Zealand	23 510	18 037	47 059	44 906	51 051	56 057	59 151	63 532	56 832	60 282
Papua New Guinea	..	..	1 981	2 417	3 596	4 033	3 909	4 176	3 302	2 747
Philippines	15 201	12 770	24 304	29 501	33 928	39 530	44 023	47 563	49 779	51 782
Samoa	..	..	122	134	150	175	187	189	204	197
Singapore	..	14 743	24 821	31 436	36 746	40 336	40 635	41 979	40 141	42 414
Solomon Islands	..	..	..	171	237	279	300	308	303	298
Thailand	..	18 951	46 248	57 499	69 640	69 854	81 622	74 808	76 699	73 365
Tokelau	..	..	1	1	1	1	2	2	2	2

.. Not available

Note: This table is produced based on total tax revenues from Chapter 4 and exchange rate data from Table 3.19.

StatLink https://doi.org/10.1787/888933854155

Table 3.19. **Exchange rates used, national currency per US dollar**

	1997	2000	2007	2010	2011	2012	2013	2014	2015	2016
Australia	1.30	1.70	1.20	1.10	1.00	1.00	1.00	1.10	1.30	1.30
Cook Islands	1.50	2.20	1.40	1.40	1.30	1.20	1.20	1.20	1.40	1.40
Fiji	1.40	2.10	1.60	1.90	1.80	1.80	1.80	1.90	2.10	2.10
Indonesia	2 880.60	8 391.70	9 139.40	9 086.90	8 776.00	9 384.20	10 460.50	11 868.70	13 389.40	13 308.70
Japan	121.00	107.80	117.80	87.80	79.70	79.80	97.60	105.80	121.00	108.80
Kazakhstan	75.40	142.10	122.60	147.40	146.60	149.10	152.10	179.20	221.70	342.20
Korea	950.50	1 130.60	929.50	1 155.40	1 107.30	1 125.90	1 094.90	1 053.10	1 131.30	1 160.60
Malaysia	2.80	3.80	3.40	3.20	3.10	3.10	3.10	3.30	3.90	4.10
New Zealand	1.50	2.20	1.40	1.40	1.30	1.20	1.20	1.20	1.40	1.40
Papua New Guinea	1.40	2.80	3.00	2.70	2.40	2.10	2.20	2.50	2.80	3.10
Philippines	29.50	44.20	46.10	45.10	43.30	42.20	42.40	44.40	45.50	47.50
Samoa	2.60	3.10	2.70	2.50	2.40	2.30	2.30	2.30	2.40	2.60
Singapore	1.50	1.70	1.50	1.30	1.30	1.20	1.30	1.30	1.40	1.40
Solomon Islands	3.70	5.10	7.70	8.10	7.60	7.40	7.30	7.40	7.90	7.90
Thailand	27.40	39.10	33.60	32.50	30.20	31.10	30.40	32.20	33.50	35.40
Tokelau	1.50	2.20	1.40	1.40	1.30	1.20	1.20	1.20	1.40	1.40

Source: OECD National Accounts data for Australia, Indonesia, Japan, Korea and New Zealand; National statistical offices for the Cook Islands and Tokelau; CEIC for Kazakhstan, Malaysia, the Philippines, Thailand and Singapore; IMF's *World Economic Outlook* (April 2018) for Fiji, Papua New Guinea, Samoa and the Solomon Islands.

StatLink https://doi.org/10.1787/888933854174

Chapter 4

Country tables, tax revenues, 1997-2016

Table 4.1. **Australia**

Details of tax revenue

Billion AUD

	1997	2000	2007	2010	2011	2012	2013	2014	2015	2016
Total tax revenue	**168 582**	**214 752**	**347 545**	**357 958**	**388 183**	**413 406**	**433 342**	**443 049**	**463 350**	**487 078**
1000 Taxes on income, profits and capital gains	**95 367**	**124 427**	**206 134**	**202 184**	**227 861**	**238 829**	**246 073**	**255 966**	**262 357**	**278 764**
1100 Of individuals	70 782	80 991	127 587	138 163	152 884	162 410	169 972	183 023	191 747	198 534
1110 On income and profits	69 212	80 991	127 587	138 163	152 884	162 410	169 972	183 023	191 747	198 534
1120 On capital gains	1 570	0	0	0	0	0	0	0	0	0
1200 Corporate	24 585	43 436	78 547	64 021	74 977	76 419	76 101	72 943	70 610	80 230
1210 On profits	22 253	43 436	78 547	64 021	74 977	76 419	76 101	72 943	70 610	80 230
Income tax on companies	21 242	42 221	76 655	62 549	73 430	74 955	74 535	71 224	68 779	78 254
Dividend and interest taxes	693	846	1 892	1 472	1 547	1 464	1 566	1 719	1 831	1 976
Other withholding taxes	318	369	0	0	0	0	0	0	0	0
1220 On capital gains	2 332	0	0	0	0	0	0	0	0	0
1300 Unallocable between 1100 and 1200	0	0	0	0	0	0	0	0	0	0
2000 Social security contributions	**0**	**0**	**0**	**0**	**0**	**0**	**0**	**0**	**0**	**0**
2100 Employees	0	0	0	0	0	0	0	0	0	0
2110 On a payroll basis	..	..	..	..	..	..	..	..	..	..
2120 On an income tax basis	..	..	..	..	..	..	..	..	..	..
2200 Employers	0	0	0	0	0	0	0	0	0	0
2210 On a payroll basis	..	..	..	..	..	..	..	..	..	..
2220 On an income tax basis	..	..	..	..	..	..	..	..	..	..
2300 Self-employed or non-employed	0	0	0	0	0	0	0	0	0	0
2310 On a payroll basis	..	..	..	..	..	..	..	..	..	..
2320 On an income tax basis	..	..	..	..	..	..	..	..	..	..
2400 Unallocable between 2100, 2200 and 2300	0	0	0	0	0	0	0	0	0	0
2410 On a payroll basis	..	..	..	..	..	..	..	..	..	..
2420 On an income tax basis	..	..	..	..	..	..	..	..	..	..
3000 Taxes on payroll and workforce	**11 277**	**9 624**	**16 407**	**18 492**	**20 307**	**21 432**	**22 210**	**22 776**	**23 354**	**23 799**
4000 Taxes on property	**15 505**	**18 825**	**31 156**	**33 526**	**33 612**	**36 039**	**40 963**	**45 293**	**49 641**	**52 585**
4100 Recurrent taxes on immovable property	7 739	9 067	15 615	19 907	20 759	21 806	23 603	25 062	27 093	29 232
4110 Households	..	..	..	..	..	..	..	..	..	..
4120 Others	..	..	..	..	..	..	..	..	..	..
4200 Recurrent taxes on net wealth	0	0	0	0	0	0	0	0	0	0
4210 Individual	..	..	..	..	..	..	..	..	..	..
4220 Corporate	..	..	..	..	..	..	..	..	..	..
4300 Estate, inheritance and gift taxes	0	0	0	0	0	0	0	0	0	0
4310 Estate and inheritance taxes	..	..	..	..	..	..	..	..	..	..
Estate duty central government	..	..	..	..	..	..	..	..	..	..
St. and loc. estate probate and succession	..	..	..	..	..	..	..	..	..	..
4320 Gift taxes	..	..	..	..	..	..	..	..	..	..
4400 Taxes on financial and capital transactions	7 766	9 758	15 541	13 619	12 853	14 233	17 360	20 231	22 548	23 353
4500 Non-recurrent taxes	0	0	0	0	0	0	0	0	0	0
4510 On net wealth	..	..	..	..	..	..	..	..	..	..
4520 Other non-recurrent taxes	..	..	..	..	..	..	..	..	..	..
4600 Other recurrent taxes on property	0	0	0	0	0	0	0	0	0	0
5000 Taxes on goods and services	**46 433**	**61 876**	**93 848**	**103 756**	**106 403**	**117 106**	**124 096**	**119 014**	**127 998**	**131 930**
5100 Taxes on production, sale, transfer, etc.	37 359	56 178	84 851	92 007	94 236	97 184	103 419	104 528	110 185	113 155
5110 General taxes	14 085	25 830	45 486	49 329	50 004	51 462	56 819	57 830	61 815	64 251
5111 Value added taxes	0	23 854	44 381	48 093	48 849	50 313	55 517	56 462	60 312	62 727
5112 Sales tax	14 085	1 976	1 105	1 236	1 155	1 149	1 302	1 368	1 503	1 524
5113 Other	0	0	0	0	0	0	0	0	0	0
5120 Taxes on specific goods and services	23 274	30 348	39 365	42 678	44 232	45 722	46 600	46 698	48 370	48 904
5121 Excise duties	14 449	19 768	24 357	26 689	26 325	26 425	26 472	24 506	22 541	22 773
Excises central government	13 573	19 019	23 526	25 803	25 480	25 710	25 648	23 799	21 625	21 895
Statutory corporate payments	258	295	231	452	436	248	343	209	405	335
Primary production charges	618	454	600	434	409	467	481	498	511	543
5122 Profits of fiscal monopolies	0	0	0	0	0	0	0	0	0	0
5123 Customs and import duties	3 637	4 606	6 070	5 828	7 105	8 172	9 280	10 884	14 046	14 196
Customs duties central government	3 637	4 606	6 070	5 828	7 105	8 172	9 280	10 884	14 046	14 196
5124 Taxes on exports	6	0	10	11	12	9	10	12	11	11
Customs duties on coal exports	0	..	0	0	0	0	0	0	0	0
Other	6	..	10	11	12	9	10	12	11	11
5125 Taxes on investment goods	0	0	0	0	0	0	0	0	0	0

Table 4.1. **Australia** *(cont.)*

Details of tax revenue

Billion AUD

	1997	2000	2007	2010	2011	2012	2013	2014	2015	2016
5126 Taxes on specific services	5 182	5 974	8 928	10 150	10 790	11 116	10 838	11 296	11 772	11 924
Taxes race meetings	601	300	358	366	359	325	318	290	257	225
Poker machines	1 760	2 074	3 009	3 125	3 178	3 212	3 238	3 480	3 684	3 717
Lotteries	330	890	1 118	1 147	1 256	1 354	1 257	1 270	1 369	1 293
Levies on fire insurance companies	521	574	937	1 232	1 395	1 279	740	739	786	803
Other	1 970	2 136	3 506	4 280	4 602	4 946	5 285	5 517	5 676	5 886
5127 Other taxes on internat. trade and transactions	0	0	0	0	0	0	0	0	0	0
5128 Other taxes	0	0	0	0	0	0	0	0	0	0
5130 Unallocable between 5110 and 5120	0	0	0	0	0	0	0	0	0	0
5200 Taxes on use of goods and perform activities	9 074	5 698	8 997	11 749	12 167	19 922	20 677	14 486	17 813	18 775
5210 Recurrent taxes	8 956	5 698	8 997	11 749	12 167	19 922	20 677	14 486	17 813	18 775
5211 Paid by households: motor vehicles	2 188	3 908	6 196	7 229	7 631	8 246	8 591	9 155	9 586	9 930
5212 Paid by others: motor vehicles	1 350	125	189	232	254	285	301	308	318	344
Fees on motor vehicle registry	1 287	0	0	0	0	0	0	0	0	0
Drivers licences	0	0	0	0	0	0	0	0	0	0
Stamp duty on vehicle registry	63	125	189	232	254	285	301	308	318	344
5213 Paid in respect of other goods	5 418	1 665	2 611	4 288	4 283	11 390	11 786	5 022	7 910	8 501
Broadcasting tv licences	329	210	288	150	231	167	157	185	128	0
Business franchise lic. tobac. fuel	3 992	227	0	0	1	1	2	0	1	0
Other taxes	565	1 129	2 321	4 136	4 027	11 197	11 603	4 815	7 760	8 478
Liquor taxes	532	97	2	1	24	24	24	23	22	23
Dog licenses	0	0	0	0	0	0	0	0	0	0
5220 Non-recurrent taxes	118	0	0	0	0	0	0	0	0	0
5300 Unallocable between 5100 and 5200	0	0	0	0	0	0	0	0	0	0
6000 Other taxes	**0**	**0**	**0**	**0**	**0**	**0**	**0**	**0**	**0**	**0**
6100 Paid solely by business	..	..	..	..	..	..	..	..	..	..
6200 Other	..	..	..	..	..	..	..	..	..	..

Note: Data are on a fiscal year basis beginning 1st July.

From 1998 taxes are recorded on an accrual basis; prior to that they were on a cash basis.

Direct taxes paid by public trading enterprises are excluded from receipts.

The figures for total tax revenue do not match the published totals in Taxation Revenue Australia. The latter is based on an accrual IMF GFS methodology and there are some differences between that and the OECD equivalent.

Heading 5213 includes radio and television licenses fees, though these are usually not regarded as a tax revenue in the OECD list.

Headings for non-wastable tax credits 1110 and 1210 include the private health insurance tax offset, family benefit, baby bonus tax offsets (paid during the 2003-04 budget year), film tax offset, and research and development tax offsets. The estimation of non-wastable credits into the expenditure and transfer components is in accordance with the OECD guidelines on the treatment and the data for this memorandum item has been provided by the Australian Taxation Office.

Source: Australian Bureau of Statistics.

StatLink https://doi.org/10.1787/888933854193

Table 4.2. **Cook Islands**

Details of tax revenue

Thousand NZD

	1997	2000	2007	2010	2011	2012	2013	2014	2015	2016
Total tax revenue	..	..	**78 312**	**91 099**	**88 130**	**99 181**	**92 463**	**90 566**	**117 397**	**125 995**
1000 Taxes on income, profits and capital gains	..	..	**30 685**	**35 916**	**34 872**	**40 014**	**29 860**	**23 213**	**41 090**	**42 210**
1100 Of individuals	..	..	22 163	26 277	27 249	24 295	20 848	14 189	27 696	26 055
1110 On income and profits	..	..	22 163	26 277	27 249	24 295	20 848	14 189	27 696	26 055
Net Income Tax	..	..	22 163	26 361	23 886	22 173	20 032	11 963	24 768	24 298
Withholding Tax	..	..	0	-84	3 363	2 122	816	2 226	2 928	1 757
1120 On capital gains	..	..	0	0	0	0	0	0	0	0
1200 Corporate	..	..	8 523	9 638	7 623	15 718	9 012	9 024	13 394	16 155
1210 On profits	..	..	8 523	9 638	7 623	15 718	9 012	9 024	13 394	16 155
1220 On capital gains of corporates	..	..	0	0	0	0	0	0	0	0
1300 Unallocable between 1100 and 1200	..	..	0	0	0	0	0	0	0	0
2000 Social security contributions	..	..	**0**	**0**	**0**	**0**	**0**	**0**	**0**	**0**
2100 Employees	..	..	..	..	..	..	..	..	..	..
2110 On a payroll basis	..	..	..	..	..	..	..	..	..	..
2120 On an income tax basis	..	..	..	..	..	..	..	..	..	..
2200 Employers	..	..	..	..	..	..	..	..	..	..
2210 On a payroll basis	..	..	..	..	..	..	..	..	..	..
2220 On an income tax basis	..	..	..	..	..	..	..	..	..	..
2300 Self-employed or non-employed	..	..	..	..	..	..	..	..	..	..
2310 On a payroll basis	..	..	..	..	..	..	..	..	..	..
2320 On an income tax basis	..	..	..	..	..	..	..	..	..	..
2400 Unallocable between 2100, 2200 and 2300	..	..	..	..	..	..	..	..	..	..
2410 On a payroll basis	..	..	..	..	..	..	..	..	..	..
2420 On an income tax basis	..	..	..	..	..	..	..	..	..	..
3000 Taxes on payroll and workforce	..	..	**0**	**0**	**0**	**0**	**0**	**0**	**0**	**0**
4000 Taxes on property	..	..	**0**	**0**	**0**	**0**	**0**	**0**	**0**	**0**
4100 Recurrent taxes on immovable property	..	..	..	..	..	..	..	..	..	..
4110 Households	..	..	..	..	..	..	..	..	..	..
4120 Others	..	..	..	..	..	..	..	..	..	..
4200 Recurrent taxes on net wealth	..	..	..	..	..	..	..	..	..	..
4210 Individual	..	..	..	..	..	..	..	..	..	..
4220 Corporate	..	..	..	..	..	..	..	..	..	..
4300 Estate, inheritance and gift taxes	..	..	..	..	..	..	..	..	..	..
4310 Estate and inheritance taxes	..	..	..	..	..	..	..	..	..	..
4320 Gift taxes	..	..	..	..	..	..	..	..	..	..
4400 Taxes on financial and capital transactions	..	..	..	..	..	..	..	..	..	..
4500 Other non-reccurrent taxes on property	..	..	..	..	..	..	..	..	..	..
4510 On net wealth	..	..	..	..	..	..	..	..	..	..
4520 Other non-recurrent taxes	..	..	..	..	..	..	..	..	..	..
4600 Other recurrent taxes on property	..	..	..	..	..	..	..	..	..	..
5000 Taxes on goods and services	..	..	**47 627**	**55 183**	**53 251**	**59 167**	**62 603**	**67 353**	**76 307**	**83 784**
5100 Taxes on production, sale, transfer, etc	..	..	46 753	54 336	52 459	58 219	61 587	66 136	75 447	82 688
5110 General taxes on goods and services	..	..	33 955	37 381	34 830	36 754	41 681	47 453	54 660	58 124
5111 Value added taxes	..	..	33 955	37 381	34 830	36 754	41 681	47 453	54 659	58 124
Value Added Tax	..	..	41 689	45 454	45 839	46 417	52 902	62 549	67 855	70 574
VAT refunds	..	..	-5 043	-4 365	-5 960	-6 678	-7 521	-7 507	-7 433	-7 796
VAT on Crown Appropriations	..	..	-2 692	-3 707	-5 048	-2 985	-3 700	-7 589	-5 763	-4 653
5112 Sales tax	..	..	0	0	0	0	0	0	0	0
5113 Other	..	..	0	0	0	0	0	0	1	0
5120 Taxes on specific goods and services	..	..	12 799	16 955	17 629	21 466	19 907	18 682	20 787	24 564
5121 Excises	..	..	0	0	0	0	0	0	0	0
5122 Profits of fiscal monopolies	..	..	0	0	0	0	0	0	0	0
5123 Customs and import duties	..	..	9 810	11 052	11 391	15 459	11 899	10 536	12 320	14 330
5124 Taxes on exports	..	..	0	0	0	0	0	0	0	0
5125 Taxes on investment goods	..	..	0	0	0	0	0	0	0	0
5126 Taxes on specific services	..	..	2 989	5 903	6 238	6 007	8 008	8 146	8 468	10 234
5127 Other taxes on internat. trade and transactions	..	..	0	0	0	0	0	0	0	0
5128 Other taxes	..	..	0	0	0	0	0	0	0	0
5130 Unallocable between 5110 and 5120	..	..	0	0	0	0	0	0	0	0
5200 Taxes on use of goods and to perform activities	..	..	873	847	792	948	1 015	1 217	860	1 097
5210 Recurrent taxes	..	..	218	207	183	210	189	186	229	209
5211 Paid by households: motor vehicles	..	..	0	0	0	0	0	0	0	0
5212 Paid by others: motor vehicles	..	..	0	0	0	0	0	0	0	0
5213 Paid in respect of other goods	..	..	218	207	183	210	189	186	229	209

Table 4.2. **Cook Islands** *(cont.)*

Details of tax revenue

Thousand NZD

	1997	2000	2007	2010	2011	2012	2013	2014	2015	2016
5220 Non-recurrent taxes	..	..	655	640	609	738	827	1 032	631	888
5300 Unallocable between 5100 and 5200	..	..	0	0	0	0	0	0	0	0
6000 Other taxes	**..**	**..**	**0**	**0**	**7**	**0**	**0**	**0**	**0**	**0**
6100 Paid solely by business	..	..	..	..	..	..	..	..	..	..
6200 Other	..	..	..	..	..	..	..	..	..	..

Note: Data are reported on a fiscal year basis beginning 1st July. For example, the data for 2016 represent the period from July 2016 to June 2017.
The data are on a cash basis.
Figures exclude tax revenues collected by sub-national governments as the data are not available.
Source: Ministry of Finance and Economic Management of the Cook Islands.

StatLink https://doi.org/10.1787/888933854212

Table 4.3. **Fiji**

Details of tax revenue

Million FJD

	1997	2000	2007	2010	2011	2012	2013	2014	2015	2016
Total tax revenue	..	..	..	**1 302**	**1 533**	**1 676**	**1 811**	**2 035**	**2 293**	**2 363**
1000 Taxes on income, profits and capital gains	..	..	..	**426**	**461**	**455**	**422**	**471**	**574**	**706**
1100 Of individuals	..	..	..	184	202	138	145	166	187	198
1110 On income and profits	..	..	..	184	202	138	145	166	187	198
PAYE	..	..	..	184	202	115	118	140	159	167
Social responsibility tax	..	..	..	0	0	13	9	8	8	11
Fringe benefit tax	..	..	..	0	0	9	18	19	20	21
1120 On capital gains	..	..	..	..	..	..	..	..	..	..
1200 Corporate	..	..	..	242	259	317	277	305	386	508
1210 On profits	..	..	..	242	259	317	277	305	386	508
Company Tax	..	..	..	161	177	246	203	208	291	348
Dividend and Withholding	..	..	..	73	72	66	72	85	85	105
Provisional tax	..	..	..	11	11	11	11	11	10	49
Other income taxes	..	..	..	30	34	36	30	30	45	44
Income tax refunds	..	..	..	-34	-35	-42	-40	-28	-45	-38
1220 On capital gains of corporates	..	..	..	..	..	..	..	..	..	..
1300 Unallocable between 1100 and 1200	..	..	..	0	0	0	0	0	0	0
2000 Social security contributions	..	..	..	**0**	**0**	**0**	**0**	**0**	**0**	**0**
2100 Employees	..	..	..	..	..	..	..	..	..	..
2110 On a payroll basis	..	..	..	..	..	..	..	..	..	..
2120 On an income tax basis	..	..	..	..	..	..	..	..	..	..
2200 Employers	..	..	..	..	..	..	..	..	..	..
2210 On a payroll basis	..	..	..	..	..	..	..	..	..	..
2220 On an income tax basis	..	..	..	..	..	..	..	..	..	..
2300 Self-employed or non-employed	..	..	..	..	..	..	..	..	..	..
2310 On a payroll basis	..	..	..	..	..	..	..	..	..	..
2320 On an income tax basis	..	..	..	..	..	..	..	..	..	..
2400 Unallocable between 2100, 2200 and 2300	..	..	..	..	..	..	..	..	..	..
2410 On a payroll basis	..	..	..	..	..	..	..	..	..	..
2420 On an income tax basis	..	..	..	..	..	..	..	..	..	..
3000 Taxes on payroll and workforce	..	..	..	**0**	**0**	**0**	**0**	**0**	**0**	**0**
4000 Taxes on property	..	..	..	**0**	**13**	**21**	**44**	**68**	**71**	**78**
4100 Recurrent taxes on immovable property	..	..	..	..	0	0	0	0	0	0
4110 Households	..	..	..	..	..	..	..	..	..	..
4120 Others	..	..	..	..	..	..	..	..	..	..
4200 Recurrent taxes on net wealth	..	..	..	..	0	0	0	0	0	0
4210 Individual	..	..	..	..	..	..	..	..	..	..
4220 Corporate	..	..	..	..	..	..	..	..	..	..
4300 Estate, inheritance and gift taxes	..	..	..	..	0	0	0	0	0	0
4310 Estate and inheritance taxes	..	..	..	..	..	..	..	..	..	..
4320 Gift taxes	..	..	..	..	..	..	..	..	..	..
4400 Taxes on financial and capital transactions	..	..	..	..	13	21	44	68	71	78
4500 Other non-reccurrent taxes on property	..	..	..	..	0	0	0	0	0	0
4510 On net wealth	..	..	..	..	..	..	..	..	..	..
4520 Other non-recurrent taxes	..	..	..	..	..	..	..	..	..	..
4600 Other recurrent taxes on property	..	..	..	..	0	0	0	0	0	0
5000 Taxes on goods and services	..	..	..	**877**	**1 059**	**1 200**	**1 346**	**1 496**	**1 648**	**1 579**
5100 Taxes on production, sale, transfer, etc	..	..	..	877	1 057	1 198	1 345	1 496	1 648	1 578
5110 General taxes on goods and services	..	..	..	526	655	725	803	852	958	774
5111 Value added taxes	..	..	..	496	618	676	751	794	893	653
Gross value added taxes	..	..	..	646	809	880	1 020	1 102	1 204	943
VAT refunds	..	..	..	-150	-190	-204	-269	-308	-311	-290
5112 Sales tax	..	..	..	0	0	0	0	0	0	0
5113 Other	..	..	..	31	36	49	52	58	65	121
5120 Taxes on specific goods and services	..	..	..	350	403	473	543	644	690	804
5121 Excises	..	..	..	88	90	102	127	139	145	246
Environmental levy	..	..	..	0	0	0	0	0	0	67
Import excises	..	..	..	20	23	27	38	43	43	47
Domestic excises	..	..	..	81	76	83	92	98	106	134
Other excises	..	..	..	5	6	8	2	2	2	2
Rebates	..	..	..	-17	-15	-16	-5	-6	-6	-5
5122 Profits of fiscal monopolies	..	..	..	0	0	0	0	0	0	0
5123 Customs and import duties	..	..	..	252	247	259	311	365	392	398
5124 Taxes on exports	..	..	..	9	8	7	4	10	10	10

Table 4.3. **Fiji** *(cont.)*

Details of tax revenue

Million FJD

	1997	2000	2007	2010	2011	2012	2013	2014	2015	2016
5125 Taxes on investment goods	..	..	..	0	0	0	0	0	0	0
5126 Taxes on specific services	..	..	..	0	59	105	101	130	143	150
5127 Other taxes on internat. trade and transactions	..	..	..	0	0	0	0	0	0	0
5128 Other taxes	..	..	..	0	0	0	0	0	0	0
5130 Unallocable between 5110 and 5120	..	..	..	0	0	0	0	0	0	0
5200 Taxes on use of goods and to perform activities	..	..	..	0	1	2	1	1	0	1
5210 Recurrent taxes	..	..	..	0	1	1	0	0	0	0
5211 Paid by households: motor vehicles	..	..	..	..	0	0	0	0	0	0
5212 Paid by others: motor vehicles	..	..	..	..	0	0	0	0	0	0
5213 Paid in respect of other goods	..	..	..	..	1	1	0	0	0	0
5220 Non-recurrent taxes	..	..	..	0	0	0	0	0	0	0
5300 Unallocable between 5100 and 5200	..	..	..	0	0	0	0	0	0	0
6000 Other taxes	**..**	**..**	**..**	**0**	**0**	**0**	**0**	**0**	**0**	**0**
6100 Paid solely by business	..	..	..	..	..	..	..	..	..	..
6200 Other	..	..	..	..	..	..	..	..	..	..

Note: Year ending 31st December.
The data are on a cash basis.
Figures exclude tax revenues collected by sub-national governments as the data are not available.
The resource tax and the tourist VAT refund registration fee (about 0.5% of GDP in 2016) are not included in tax revenues. These revenues are considered as non-tax revenues in accordance with the OECD classification, as set out in the Interpretative Guide in Annex A.

Source: Revenue and Customs Service of Fiji.

StatLink https://doi.org/10.1787/888933854231

Table 4.4. **Indonesia**

Details of tax revenue

Billion IDR

	1997	2000	2007	2010	2011	2012	2013	2014	2015	2016
Total tax revenue	**57 340**	**119 697**	**525 969**	**779 484**	**952 896**	**1 075 587**	**1 192 769**	**1 285 634**	**1 388 247**	**1 442 137**
1000 Taxes on income, profits and capital gains	**27 062**	**57 073**	**238 431**	**357 046**	**431 122**	**465 070**	**506 443**	**546 181**	**602 308**	**666 212**
1100 Of individuals	..	..	77 250	122 031	150 537	171 210	197 987	238 058	292 819	380 045
1110 On income and profits	..	..	..	..	..	..	..	..	..	..
1120 On capital gains	..	..	..	..	..	..	..	..	..	..
1200 Corporate	..	..	161 181	235 015	280 585	293 859	308 456	308 123	309 489	286 167
1210 On profits	..	..	..	..	..	..	..	..	..	..
1220 On capital gains	..	..	..	..	..	..	..	..	..	..
1300 Unallocable between 1100 and 1200	27 062	57 073	0	0	0	0	0	0	0	0
2000 Social security contributions	..	..	..	..	..	..	..	..	..	..
2100 Employees	..	..	..	..	..	..	..	..	..	..
2110 On a payroll basis	..	..	..	..	..	..	..	..	..	..
2120 On an income tax basis	..	..	..	..	..	..	..	..	..	..
2200 Employers	..	..	..	..	..	..	..	..	..	..
2210 On a payroll basis	..	..	..	..	..	..	..	..	..	..
2220 On an income tax basis	..	..	..	..	..	..	..	..	..	..
2300 Self-employed or non-employed	..	..	..	..	..	..	..	..	..	..
2310 On a payroll basis	..	..	..	..	..	..	..	..	..	..
2320 On an income tax basis	..	..	..	..	..	..	..	..	..	..
2400 Unallocable between 2100, 2200 and 2300	..	..	..	..	..	..	..	..	..	..
2410 On a payroll basis	..	..	..	..	..	..	..	..	..	..
2420 On an income tax basis	..	..	..	..	..	..	..	..	..	..
3000 Taxes on payroll and workforce	**0**	**0**	**0**	**0**	**0**	**0**	**0**	**0**	**0**	**0**
4000 Taxes on property	**2 413**	**4 456**	**29 677**	**36 607**	**29 892**	**28 969**	**25 305**	**23 476**	**29 250**	**19 443**
4100 Recurrent taxes on immovable property	2 413	3 525	23 724	28 581	29 893	28 969	25 305	23 476	29 250	19 443
4110 Households	..	..	..	..	..	..	..	..	..	..
4120 Others	..	..	..	..	..	..	..	..	..	..
4200 Recurrent taxes on net wealth	0	0	0	0	0	0	0	0	0	0
4210 Individual	..	..	..	..	..	..	..	..	..	..
4220 Corporate	..	..	..	..	..	..	..	..	..	..
4300 Estate, inheritance and gift taxes	0	0	0	0	0	0	0	0	0	0
4310 Estate and inheritance taxes	..	..	..	..	..	..	..	..	..	..
4320 Gift taxes	..	..	..	..	..	..	..	..	..	..
4400 Taxes on financial and capital transactions	0	931	5 953	8 026	-1	0	0	0	0	0
Tax on acquisition of land and buildings	..	931	5 953	8 026	-1	..	..	..	..	..
4500 Non-recurrent taxes	0	0	0	0	0	0	0	0	0	0
4510 On net wealth	..	..	..	..	..	..	..	..	..	..
4520 Other non-recurrent taxes	..	..	..	..	..	..	..	..	..	..
4600 Other recurrent taxes on property	0	0	0	0	0	0	0	0	0	0
5000 Taxes on goods and services	**27 274**	**53 547**	**220 143**	**325 685**	**408 932**	**482 269**	**540 622**	**570 915**	**603 292**	**591 209**
5100 Taxes on production, sale, transfer, etc	27 274	53 547	220 143	325 685	408 932	482 269	540 622	570 915	603 292	591 209
5110 General taxes	20 351	35 232	154 527	230 605	277 800	337 585	384 714	409 182	423 711	412 213
5111 Value added taxes	20 351	35 232	154 527	230 605	277 800	337 585	384 714	409 182	423 711	412 213
5112 Sales tax	0	0	0	0	0	0	0	0	0	0
5113 Other	0	0	0	0	0	0	0	0	0	0
5120 Taxes on specific goods and services	6 923	18 315	65 616	95 080	131 131	144 684	155 909	161 734	179 581	178 996
5121 Excises	4 263	11 287	44 679	66 166	77 010	95 028	108 452	118 086	144 641	143 525
5122 Profits of fiscal monopolies	0	0	0	0	0	0	0	0	0	0
5123 Customs and import duties	2 579	6 697	16 699	20 017	25 266	28 418	31 621	32 319	31 213	32 472
5124 Taxes on exports	81	331	4 237	8 898	28 856	21 238	15 835	11 329	3 727	2 999
5125 Taxes on investment goods	0	0	0	0	0	0	0	0	0	0
5126 Taxes on specific services	0	0	0	0	0	0	0	0	0	0
5127 Other taxes on internat. trade and transactions	0	0	0	0	0	0	0	0	0	0
5128 Other taxes	0	0	0	0	0	0	0	0	0	0
5130 Unallocable between 5110 and 5120	0	0	0	0	0	0	0	0	0	0
5200 Taxes on use of goods and to perform activities	0	0	0	0	0	0	0	0	0	0
5210 Recurrent taxes	..	..	..	..	..	..	..	..	..	..
5211 Paid by households: motor vehicles	..	..	..	..	..	..	..	..	..	..
5212 Paid by others: motor vehicles	..	..	..	..	..	..	..	..	..	..
5213 Paid in respect of other goods	..	..	..	..	..	..	..	..	..	..
5220 Non-recurrent taxes	..	..	..	..	..	..	..	..	..	..
5300 Unallocable between 5100 and 5200	0	0	0	0	0	0	0	0	0	0
6000 Other taxes	**591**	**4 621**	**37 718**	**60 146**	**82 951**	**99 279**	**120 400**	**145 062**	**153 397**	**165 272**
6100 Paid solely by business	0	0	0	0	0	0	0	0	0	0

Table 4.4. **Indonesia** *(cont.)*

Details of tax revenue

Billion IDR

	1997	2000	2007	2010	2011	2012	2013	2014	2015	2016
6200 Other	591	4 621	37 718	60 146	82 951	99 279	120 400	145 062	153 397	165 272
Other local level	0	3 784	34 981	56 177	79 023	95 069	115 463	138 769	147 829	157 167
Other non local level	591	837	2 738	3 969	3 928	4 211	4 937	6 293	5 568	8 105

Note: Year ending 31st December.

The data are on a cash basis.

The figures for social security contributions (heading 2000) are not available but they are thought to be negligible as they relate only to the "Asuransi Kesehatan" - a health insurance programme for employees in for-profit state-owned enterprises.

Source: Ministry of Finance of Indonesia.

StatLink https://doi.org/10.1787/888933854250

Table 4.5. **Japan**

Details of tax revenue

Billion JPY

	1997	2000	2007	2010	2011	2012	2013	2014	2015	2016
Total tax revenue	**139 617**	**136 236**	**146 248**	**132 484**	**135 671**	**139 598**	**146 405**	**156 886**	**163 533**	**164 963**
1000 Taxes on income, profits and capital gains	**51 673**	**47 398**	**53 174**	**40 034**	**40 910**	**43 352**	**47 534**	**49 939**	**50 969**	**50 448**
1100 Of individuals	29 809	28 677	28 600	24 663	24 951	25 946	28 150	29 655	30 847	30 670
1110 On income and profits	29 809	28 677	28 600	24 663	24 951	25 946	28 150	29 655	30 847	30 670
Income tax	19 183	18 789	16 080	12 984	13 476	14 044	15 865	17 139	18 178	17 978
Prefectural inhabitants tax	3 183	3 621	5 008	4 699	4 608	4 783	5 090	5 215	5 252	5 128
Municipal inhabitants tax	7 172	6 044	7 294	6 795	6 688	6 942	7 015	7 114	7 224	7 365
Enterprise tax	271	223	218	184	179	178	181	186	194	198
1120 On capital gains	0	0	0	0	0	0	0	0	0	0
1200 Corporate	21 864	18 721	24 573	15 372	15 959	17 406	19 384	20 284	20 122	19 778
1210 On profits	21 864	18 721	24 573	15 372	15 959	17 406	19 384	20 284	20 122	19 778
Corporation tax	13 477	11 747	14 744	8 968	9 351	10 408	11 698	11 464	10 832	10 332
Prefectural inhabitants tax	1 026	879	1 206	777	800	846	854	963	859	763
Municipal inhabitants tax	2 532	2 176	3 015	1 954	2 011	2 129	2 157	2 445	2 324	2 209
Enterprise tax	4 830	3 918	5 608	2 253	2 240	2 354	2 674	3 017	3 510	4 063
Local special corporate tax	0	0	0	1 420	1 556	1 670	2 001	2 395	2 081	1 782
Local corporate tax	0	0	0	0	0	0	0	1	516	629
1220 On capital gains	0	0	0	0	0	0	0	0	0	0
1300 Unallocable between 1100 and 1200	0	0	0	0	0	0	0	0	0	0
2000 Social security contributions	**47 861**	**47 968**	**53 325**	**54 461**	**56 325**	**58 088**	**59 803**	**62 252**	**64 465**	**66 614**
2100 Employees	19 682	19 830	21 975	23 593	24 432	25 192	25 984	27 168	28 224	29 311
2110 On a payroll basis	19 682	19 830	21 975	23 593	24 432	25 192	25 984	27 168	28 224	29 311
2120 On an income tax basis	0	0	0	0	0	0	0	0	0	0
2200 Employers	22 826	22 456	24 243	24 674	25 736	26 343	27 143	28 374	29 479	30 560
2210 On a payroll basis	22 826	22 456	24 243	24 674	25 736	26 343	27 143	28 374	29 479	30 560
2220 On an income tax basis	0	0	0	0	0	0	0	0	0	0
2300 Self-employed or non-employed	5 352	5 683	7 108	6 194	6 156	6 553	6 676	6 710	6 763	6 742
2310 On a payroll basis	5 352	5 683	7 108	6 194	6 156	6 553	6 676	6 710	6 763	6 742
2320 On an income tax basis	0	0	0	0	0	0	0	0	0	0
2400 Unallocable between 2100, 2200 and 2300	0	0	0	0	0	0	0	0	0	0
2410 On a payroll basis	..	..	..	..	..	..	..	..	0	0
2420 On an income tax basis	..	..	..	..	..	..	..	..	0	0
3000 Taxes on payroll and workforce	**0**	**0**	**0**	**0**	**0**	**0**	**0**	**0**	**0**	**0**
4000 Taxes on property	**15 679**	**14 294**	**13 138**	**12 878**	**13 100**	**12 716**	**12 940**	**13 306**	**13 400**	**13 772**
4100 Recurrent taxes on immovable property	10 410	10 414	9 949	10 225	10 237	9 799	9 882	10 016	10 005	10 165
Prefectural property tax	8	11	14	5	3	2	2	2	2	3
Municipal property tax	8 822	9 041	8 729	8 961	8 966	8 580	8 653	8 769	8 755	8 894
City planning tax	1 326	1 318	1 202	1 256	1 268	1 216	1 227	1 244	1 244	1 262
Special landholding tax	94	43	4	3	1	1	1	2	3	7
Water and land utilization tax	0	0	0	0	0	0	0	0	0	0
Land value tax	160	1	0	0	0	0	0	0	0	0
4110 Households	..	..	..	..	..	..	..	..	..	..
4120 Others	..	..	..	..	..	..	..	..	..	..
4200 Recurrent taxes on net wealth	0	0	0	0	0	0	0	0	0	0
4210 Individual	..	..	..	..	..	..	..	..	..	..
4220 Corporate	..	..	..	..	..	..	..	..	..	..
4300 Estate, inheritance and gift taxes	2 413	1 782	1 503	1 250	1 474	1 504	1 574	1 883	1 968	2 131
4310 Estate and inheritance taxes	..	..	..	..	..	..	..	..	..	..
Inheritance tax	..	..	..	..	..	..	..	..	..	..
4320 Gift taxes	..	..	..	..	..	..	..	..	..	..
Tax on gifts	..	..	..	..	..	..	..	..	..	..
4400 Taxes on financial and capital transactions	2 856	2 099	1 686	1 403	1 388	1 413	1 483	1 407	1 426	1 476
Bourse tax	40	0	0	0	0	0	0	0	0	0
Securities transaction	404	0	0	0	0	0	0	0	0	0
Bank of Japan note issue tax	0	0	0	0	0	0	0	0	0	0
Stamp revenues	1 681	1 532	1 202	1 024	1 047	1 078	1 126	1 035	1 050	1 079
Real property acquisition tax	731	567	485	379	342	336	357	372	377	397
4500 Non-recurrent taxes	0	0	0	0	0	0	0	0	0	0
4510 On net wealth	..	..	..	..	..	..	..	..	..	..
4520 Other non-recurrent taxes	..	..	..	..	..	..	..	..	..	..
4600 Other recurrent taxes on property	0	0	0	0	0	0	0	0	0	0
5000 Taxes on goods and services	**24 058**	**26 227**	**26 256**	**24 730**	**24 966**	**25 056**	**25 744**	**30 991**	**34 286**	**33 711**
5100 Taxes on production, sale, transfer, etc.	21 132	23 180	23 241	22 160	22 410	22 592	23 313	28 587	31 871	31 254
5110 General taxes	10 112	12 350	12 841	12 675	12 745	12 902	13 479	19 135	22 400	21 931

Table 4.5. **Japan** *(cont.)*

Details of tax revenue

Billion JPY

	1997	2000	2007	2010	2011	2012	2013	2014	2015	2016
5111 Value added taxes	10 112	12 350	12 841	12 675	12 745	12 902	13 479	19 135	22 400	21 931
5112 Sales tax	0	0	0	0	0	0	0	0	0	0
5113 Other	0	0	0	0	0	0	0	0	0	0
5120 Taxes on specific goods and services	11 021	10 830	10 400	9 485	9 665	9 690	9 834	9 452	9 470	9 323
5121 Excise duties	9 764	9 837	9 374	8 622	8 719	8 721	8 728	8 308	8 351	8 316
Liquor tax	1 962	1 816	1 524	1 389	1 369	1 350	1 371	1 328	1 338	1 320
Sugar excises	0	0	0	0	0	0	0	0	0	0
Local gasoline tax	276	296	302	294	283	281	275	266	264	261
Gasoline tax	2 583	2 769	2 820	2 750	2 648	2 622	2 574	2 486	2 465	2 434
Liquefied petroleum gas tax	29	28	27	24	23	21	21	19	18	17
Aviation fuel tax	104	104	104	89	60	64	67	67	66	66
Commodity tax	0	0	0	0	0	0	0	0	0	0
Playing-card tax	0	0	0	0	0	0	0	0	0	0
Prefectural tobacco tax	248	282	278	256	293	289	173	155	153	149
Municipal tobacco tax	799	865	853	788	900	887	983	950	936	911
Timber delivery tax	0	0	0	0	0	0	0	0	0	0
Mineral product tax	2	2	2	2	2	2	2	2	2	2
Electricity and gas tax	0	0	0	0	0	0	0	0	0	0
Diesel oil tax	1 331	1 208	1 034	918	932	925	943	936	925	933
Vehicle acquisition tax	562	464	425	192	168	210	193	86	137	146
Promotion of power resources development tax	354	375	352	349	331	328	328	321	316	320
Petroleum and coal tax	497	489	513	502	519	567	600	631	630	702
Tobacco tax	1 018	876	925	908	1 032	1 018	1 038	919	954	914
Special tobacco tax	0	264	214	163	160	158	161	142	148	141
5122 Profits of fiscal monopolies	0	0	0	0	0	0	0	0	0	0
Monopoly profits	..	..	..	..	..	..	..	..	..	..
5123 Customs and import duties	1 012	877	941	786	874	897	1 034	1 073	1 049	939
Customs duty	1 012	877	941	786	874	897	1 034	1 073	1 049	939
5124 Taxes on exports	0	0	0	0	0	0	0	0	0	0
5125 Taxes on investment goods	0	0	0	0	0	0	0	0	0	0
5126 Taxes on specific services	245	116	85	77	72	73	71	70	70	68
Travel tax	0	0	0	0	0	0	0	0	0	0
Admission tax	0	0	0	0	0	0	0	0	0	0
Local entertainment tax	0	0	0	0	0	0	0	0	0	0
Golf course utilization tax	98	81	60	55	51	51	49	48	48	46
Meal and lodging tax	0	0	0	0	0	0	0	0	0	0
Special local consumption tax	125	12	0	0	0	0	0	0	0	0
Bathing tax	22	23	25	22	21	22	22	22	23	22
5127 Other taxes on internat. trade and transactions	0	0	0	0	0	0	0	0	0	0
5128 Other taxes	0	0	0	0	0	0	0	0	0	0
5130 Unallocable between 5110 and 5120	0	0	0	0	0	0	0	0	0	0
5200 Taxes on use of goods and perform activities	2 926	3 047	3 015	2 570	2 557	2 464	2 431	2 404	2 416	2 457
5210 Recurrent taxes	2 905	3 027	2 993	2 548	2 535	2 442	2 409	2 382	2 393	2 435
Automobile tax	1 705	1 765	1 717	1 616	1 597	1 586	1 574	1 556	1 543	1 535
Light vehicle tax	113	125	164	178	180	184	189	195	200	238
Motor vehicle tonnage tax	1 084	1 134	1 110	753	755	669	643	629	649	660
Hunter licence tax	2	2	0	0	0	0	0	0	0	0
Hunting tax	1	1	2	2	2	2	2	2	1	1
Mine lot tax	1	1	0	0	0	0	0	0	0	0
5211 Paid by households: motor vehicles	..	..	..	..	..	..	..	..	..	..
5212 Paid by others: motor vehicles	..	..	..	..	..	..	..	..	..	..
5213 Paid in respect of other goods	..	..	..	..	..	..	..	..	..	..
5220 Non-recurrent taxes	21	20	22	21	22	22	22	23	22	22
5300 Unallocable between 5100 and 5200	0	0	0	0	0	0	0	0	0	0
6000 Other taxes	**346**	**348**	**356**	**381**	**371**	**386**	**384**	**399**	**413**	**418**
6100 Paid solely by business	325	324	313	330	339	350	348	356	361	366
Business office tax	325	324	313	330	339	350	348	356	361	366
6200 Other	22	24	43	52	32	36	36	43	52	52
Taxes not in local tax law	21	24	43	52	32	36	36	43	52	52
Other	0	0	0	0	0	0	0	0	0	0

Table 4.5. **Japan** *(cont.)*

Details of tax revenue

Note: Data are on a fiscal year basis beginning 1st April.

From 1990, data are on accrual basis.

The figures for different groups of taxes are reported on different reporting bases, namely: Social security contributions (heading 2000) : in principle accrual basis, Central government taxes : accrual basis (revenues accrued during the fiscal year plus cash receipts collected before the end of May (the end of April until 1977), Local government taxes : accrual basis (due to be paid during the fiscal year and cash receipts collected before the end of May).

The Japanese authorities take the view that the Enterprise tax (classified in 1100 and 1200) and the Mineral product tax (classified in 5121) should be classified in heading 6000 since under articles 72 and 519 of the Local Tax Law these taxes are regarded as levies on the business or mining activity itself.

Heading 2000 includes some unidentifiable voluntary contributions.

Heading 2300: Includes contibutions to the National pension, National Health Insurance and the Farmer's pension fund. Contributions to the Farmer's pension fund are not available for the years before 1999.

Heading 4100: Municipal property tax, includes Prefectural property tax from 1990 to 1994 because data is not available to provide a breakdown.

Heading 5121: Municipal tobacco tax, includes Prefectural tobacco tax from 1990 to 1994 because data is not available to provide a breakdown.

Heading 5121: In sub-item Petroleum and coal tax, the data before 2003 refer to petroleum tax.

Source: Tax Bureau, Ministry of Finance.

StatLink https://doi.org/10.1787/888933854269

Table 4.6. **Kazakhstan**

Details of tax revenue

Million KZT

	1997	2000	2007	2010	2011	2012	2013	2014	2015	2016
Total tax revenue	..	**514 722**	**3 349 275**	**5 182 314**	**7 212 132**	**7 398 056**	**8 130 544**	**8 364 983**	**6 352 921**	**6 997 524**
1000 Taxes on income, profits and capital gains	..	**214 545**	**1 797 785**	**2 072 357**	**2 774 181**	**2 826 237**	**2 928 127**	**3 113 992**	**2 467 977**	**2 610 413**
1100 Of individuals	..	51 016	221 025	312 332	376 245	438 498	492 991	552 280	598 807	691 778
1110 On income and profits	..	51 016	221 025	312 332	376 245	438 498	492 991	552 280	598 807	691 778
From non-foreign citizens	..	51 016	221 025	276 089	336 185	395 988	442 561	492 913	566 974	688 023
From foreign citizens	..	0	0	36 243	40 060	42 509	50 430	59 367	31 832	3 755
1120 On capital gains	..	..	..	..	..	..	..	..	..	..
1200 Corporate	..	163 529	1 576 760	1 760 025	2 397 936	2 387 739	2 435 136	2 561 712	1 869 170	1 918 635
1210 On profits	..	163 529	1 576 760	1 760 025	2 397 936	2 387 739	2 435 136	2 561 712	1 869 170	1 918 635
From non-oil companies	..	163 529	766 979	847 057	1 094 909	1 052 499	1 039 044	1 172 635	1 236 561	1 445 066
From oil companies	..	0	0	0	0	0	0	0	0	0
From oil companies to National Fund	..	0	809 782	912 968	1 303 027	1 335 241	1 396 092	1 389 077	632 609	473 569
1220 On capital gains	..	..	..	..	..	..	..	..	..	..
1300 Unallocable between 1100 and 1200	..	0	0	0	0	0	0	0	0	0
2000 Social security contributions	..	**0**	**49 904**	**131 041**	**157 105**	**183 225**	**203 361**	**225 948**	**240 590**	**256 181**
2100 Employees	..	..	..	..	..	..	..	..	..	..
2110 On a payroll basis	..	..	..	..	..	..	..	..	..	..
2120 On an income tax basis	..	..	..	..	..	..	..	..	..	..
2200 Employers	..	..	..	..	..	..	..	..	..	..
2210 On a payroll basis	..	..	..	..	..	..	..	..	..	..
2220 On an income tax basis	..	..	..	..	..	..	..	..	..	..
2300 Self-employed or non-employed	..	..	..	..	..	..	..	..	..	..
2310 On a payroll basis	..	..	..	..	..	..	..	..	..	..
2320 On an income tax basis	..	..	..	..	..	..	..	..	..	..
2400 Unallocable between 2100, 2200 and 2300	..	..	49 904	131 041	157 105	183 225	203 361	225 948	240 590	256 181
2410 On a payroll basis	..	..	..	..	..	..	..	..	..	..
2420 On an income tax basis	..	..	..	..	..	..	..	..	..	..
3000 Taxes on payroll and workforce	..	**99 082**	**295 733**	**253 830**	**296 843**	**340 997**	**380 477**	**427 985**	**464 674**	**530 440**
The social tax	..	99 082	295 733	253 830	296 843	340 997	380 477	427 985	464 674	530 440
4000 Taxes on property	..	**21 013**	**73 822**	**124 632**	**134 109**	**144 757**	**160 845**	**192 063**	**226 853**	**227 862**
4100 Recurrent taxes on immovable property	..	20 504	71 592	122 146	131 194	141 344	157 424	188 331	224 752	226 815
4110 Households	..	3 230	2 936	4 402	4 919	5 577	6 153	9 385	10 164	11 906
4120 Others	..	17 274	68 655	117 744	126 275	135 767	151 271	178 946	214 588	214 909
Uniform land tax	..	235	428	762	818	820	830	876	833	944
Property tax	..	13 699	59 140	104 745	113 842	123 461	138 015	165 795	200 710	200 685
Land tax	..	3 340	9 086	12 238	11 615	11 486	12 426	12 275	13 045	13 281
4200 Recurrent taxes on net wealth	..	0	0	0	0	0	0	0	0	0
4210 Individual	..	..	..	..	..	..	..	..	..	..
4220 Corporate	..	..	..	..	..	..	..	..	..	..
4300 Estate, inheritance and gift taxes	..	0	0	0	0	0	0	0	0	0
4310 Estate and inheritance taxes	..	..	..	..	..	..	..	..	..	..
4320 Gift taxes	..	..	..	..	..	..	..	..	..	..
4400 Taxes on financial and capital transactions	..	509	2 231	2 486	2 915	3 413	3 421	3 732	2 101	1 047
4500 Non-recurrent taxes	..	0	0	0	0	0	0	0	0	0
4510 On net wealth	..	..	..	..	..	..	..	..	..	..
4520 Other non-recurrent taxes	..	..	..	..	..	..	..	..	..	..
4600 Other recurrent taxes on property	..	0	0	0	0	0	0	0	0	0
5000 Taxes on goods and services	..	**179 452**	**1 131 122**	**2 600 449**	**3 849 891**	**3 902 837**	**4 457 631**	**4 404 920**	**2 952 686**	**3 372 218**
5100 Taxes on production, sale, transfer, etc	..	168 678	1 032 930	2 497 709	3 740 606	3 782 126	4 300 462	4 237 236	2 816 629	3 238 137
5110 General taxes	..	115 159	629 279	677 229	865 087	914 194	1 327 433	1 197 258	943 051	1 495 682
5111 Value added taxes	..	115 159	629 279	677 229	865 087	914 194	1 327 433	1 197 258	943 051	1 495 682
Domestic VAT	..	75 625	137 290	197 358	208 652	134 144	445 876	333 943	203 247	525 318
VAT on imported goods	..	39 534	464 361	435 869	607 850	723 304	819 129	789 302	667 404	860 801
Other VAT	..	0	27 628	44 002	48 585	56 746	62 428	74 013	72 399	109 563
5112 Sales tax	..	0	0	0	0	0	0	0	0	0
5113 Other	..	0	0	0	0	0	0	0	0	0
5120 Taxes on specific goods and services	..	53 519	403 651	1 820 480	2 875 519	2 867 932	2 973 029	3 039 978	1 873 579	1 742 455
5121 Excises	..	19 285	58 753	61 423	76 400	93 143	103 651	147 057	161 068	205 231
Alcohol	..	12 939	18 189	15 691	24 098	29 493	29 659	38 788	36 345	40 712
Tobacco	..	5 182	10 953	22 903	29 400	37 700	45 644	78 695	98 346	121 403
Petroleum product	..	1 164	20 970	20 966	20 790	22 599	24 139	25 221	26 216	42 042
Automobiles	..	0	8 641	1 864	2 111	3 351	4 208	4 352	931	0
Others	..	0	0	0	1	0	2	0	-770	1 075
5122 Profits of fiscal monopolies	..	0	0	0	0	0	0	0	0	0

Table 4.6. **Kazakhstan** *(cont.)*

Details of tax revenue

Million KZT

	1997	2000	2007	2010	2011	2012	2013	2014	2015	2016
5123 Customs and import duties	..	18 471	150 355	354 487	322 316	314 994	297 959	279 313	189 522	266 484
5124 Taxes on exports	..	0	611	492 870	1 323 625	1 264 458	1 466 254	1 513 573	920 175	807 011
Taxes on exports	..	..	0	22 060	499 207	457 410	585 857	778 853	692 855	688 122
Taxes on exports to National Fund	..	..	611	470 810	824 418	807 048	880 397	734 720	227 320	118 889
5125 Taxes on investment goods	..	0	0	0	0	0	0	0	0	0
5126 Taxes on specific services	..	0	6 184	14 566	16 451	16 770	18 862	21 036	24 798	25 856
Telecommunication	..	..	3 624	5 535	5 881	5 309	5 476	6 167	8 151	8 124
Placement of outdoor advertisements	..	..	2 560	3 723	4 664	5 016	5 652	5 981	6 076	5 855
Gambling business	..	..	0	3 693	4 393	5 064	6 385	7 598	9 231	10 518
Others	..	..	0	1 614	1 513	1 381	1 350	1 291	1 340	1 359
5127 Other taxes on internat. trade and transactions	..	0	0	0	0	0	0	0	0	0
5128 Other taxes	..	15 763	187 748	897 133	1 136 727	1 178 567	1 086 303	1 078 999	578 015	437 873
Production of useful minerals of non-oil sector companies	..	15 763	16 510	122 128	148 494	159 313	168 186	122 909	118 073	159 276
Production of useful minerals of oil sector companies	..	0	0	0	0	0	0	0	0	0
Production of useful minerals of oil sector co. to National Fund	..	0	171 238	775 005	988 233	1 019 253	918 117	956 090	459 942	278 597
5130 Unallocable between 5110 and 5120	..	0	0	0	0	0	0	0	0	0
5200 Taxes on use of goods and perform activities	..	10 774	98 192	102 740	109 285	120 711	157 169	167 683	136 057	134 081
5210 Recurrent taxes	..	5 901	11 340	26 262	29 975	30 961	36 029	38 844	42 278	46 879
5211 Paid by households: motor vehicles	..	3 930	8 099	21 565	24 631	25 172	29 629	31 656	34 466	38 572
5212 Paid by others: motor vehicles	..	1 971	3 241	4 697	5 344	5 789	6 401	7 188	7 812	8 307
5213 Paid in respect of other goods	..	0	0	0	0	0	0	0	0	0
5220 Non-recurrent taxes	..	4 873	86 852	76 478	79 310	89 750	121 140	128 840	93 779	87 202
Emissions into the environment	..	0	70 958	57 982	58 466	67 183	93 179	97 712	63 379	67 216
Others	..	4 873	15 894	18 497	20 843	22 567	27 960	31 128	30 399	19 985
5300 Unallocable between 5100 and 5200	..	0	0	0	0	0	0	0	0	0
6000 Other taxes	..	**629**	**909**	**6**	**4**	**3**	**103**	**75**	**141**	**410**
6100 Paid solely by business	..	0	0	0	0	0	0	0	0	0
6200 Other	..	629	909	6	4	3	103	75	141	410

Note: Year ending 31st December.

Data are on a cash basis.

The share of Kazakhstan under production sharing contracts of oil companies, the bonuses of oil and non-oil sector companies, the levy for the use of the radio-frequency spectrum, the payment to compensate for historic costs as well as certain other items are classified as non-tax revenues according to the OECD Interpretative Guide, but are considered as tax revenues in Kazakhstan.

Headings 1210, 5124 and 5128: These categories include revenues that are paid to the National Fund of Kazakhstan. This fund was created in 2000 as a stabilisation fund and includes revenues levied from oil and gas companies.

Heading 2000: Social security contribution revenues are not considered as tax revenues in Kazakhstan, but are considered as tax revenues under the OECD Interpretative Guide, subject to certain criteria. The figures in 2016 are estimated.

Heading 4120: The uniform land tax is a presumptive tax for farmers and peasants' households. Such payers are not obliged to pay personal income tax, land tax, environmental fees, transport tax, property tax and other mandatory payments to the budget. The uniform land tax is levied on the value of land in use.

Source: Ministry of Finance of Kazakhstan.

StatLink https://doi.org/10.1787/888933854288

Table 4.7. **Korea**

Details of tax revenue

Billion KRW

	1997	2000	2007	2010	2011	2012	2013	2014	2015	2016
Total tax revenue	**102 916**	**136 295**	**258 571**	**295 968**	**321 915**	**341 336**	**347 332**	**365 428**	**393 559**	**430 752**
1000 Taxes on income, profits and capital gains	**26 916**	**39 254**	**82 239**	**82 905**	**96 845**	**101 944**	**101 792**	**106 353**	**119 151**	**134 503**
1100 Of individuals	16 543	19 950	43 276	42 098	47 299	51 185	53 311	59 457	67 600	75 711
1110 On income and profits	14 586	18 569	31 984	33 935	39 910	43 730	46 654	51 410	55 744	62 028
Income tax	0	0	0	0	0	0	0	0	0	0
Dividends and interest income tax	0	0	4 682	4 425	4 896	5 152	4 889	4 628	4 561	4 125
Wages and salaries income tax	0	0	14 124	15 517	18 337	19 627	21 931	25 359	27 055	30 994
Other income tax	0	0	2 607	2 986	3 365	3 595	3 432	3 805	4 467	5 346
Global income tax	12 911	16 128	6 151	6 369	8 300	9 938	10 901	11 486	12 784	14 348
Defence tax on income tax	0	0	0	0	0	0	0	0	0	0
Education tax on income tax	0	0	0	0	0	0	0	0	0	0
Rural dev. tax on interest, bus. Inc. & cap. gains relief	149	156	160	179	156	125	124	115	105	109
Inhabitant tax on income tax (local)	1 526	2 285	4 260	4 459	4 856	5 293	5 377	6 017	6 772	7 106
1120 On capital gains	1 957	1 381	11 292	8 163	7 389	7 455	6 657	8 047	11 856	13 683
Capital gains tax	1 957	1 381	11 292	8 163	7 389	7 455	6 657	8 047	11 856	13 683
1200 Corporate	10 158	19 271	38 963	40 807	49 546	50 759	48 481	46 896	51 551	58 792
1210 On profits	10 158	19 271	38 963	40 807	49 546	50 759	48 481	46 896	51 551	58 792
Corporation tax - withholding	5 501	8 577	8 360	9 095	10 534	11 516	12 176	12 172	12 317	11 986
Corporation tax - final returns	3 924	9 302	27 057	28 173	34 339	34 416	31 679	30 478	32 713	40 130
Defence tax on corporation tax	0	0	0	0	0	0	0	0	0	0
Inhabitant tax on corporation tax (local)	733	1 142	3 152	3 094	3 953	4 258	4 118	3 882	6 217	6 270
Rural development tax corporate income	0	251	394	445	720	569	508	364	304	406
Excess profit tax	0	0	0	0	0	0	0	0	0	0
1220 On capital gains	0	0	0	0	0	0	0	0	0	0
Capital gains tax	..	..	..	..	..	..	..	..	..	..
1300 Unallocable between 1100 and 1200	215	33	0	0	0	0	0	0	0	0
Business income tax	0	0	..	..	..	..	..	..	..	..
Real estate income tax	0	0	..	..	..	..	..	..	..	..
Defence tax on real estate & business income	0	0	..	..	..	..	..	..	..	..
Rural dev. tax on bus. inc. & cap. gains relief	211	30	..	..	..	..	..	..	..	..
Inhabitant tax before 1990 (local)	1	0	..	..	..	..	..	..	..	..
Farm land tax (local)	3	3	..	..	..	..	..	..	..	..
Inhabitant tax on farm land tax (local)	0	0	..	..	..	..	..	..	..	..
2000 Social security contributions	**14 583**	**22 759**	**53 588**	**69 090**	**77 234**	**84 380**	**91 596**	**98 184**	**104 693**	**112 658**
2100 Employees	6 376	8 578	21 773	28 213	31 875	35 670	38 396	41 355	44 281	48 077
Veterans' relief fund	0	0	0	0	0	0	0	0	0	0
Soldiers' annuity fund	0	0	0	0	0	0	0	0	0	0
Unemployment assurance	264	598	1 164	1 358	1 698	2 138	2 418	2 866	3 076	3 251
National welfare pension fund	3 597	4 325	9 338	11 004	11 832	12 867	13 890	14 823	15 821	16 862
Social benefit fund	0	0	0	0	0	0	0	0	0	0
Health Insurance	1 149	2 066	8 180	11 783	13 954	15 718	17 128	18 492	19 868	21 470
Teachers' pensions	219	279	581	868	940	1 229	1 077	1 081	1 125	1 410
Government employees pensions	1 013	1 144	2 202	2 878	3 106	3 345	3 435	3 593	3 876	4 533
Military personal pensions	134	166	308	322	345	373	448	500	515	551
2110 On a payroll basis	..	8 578	21 773	28 213	31 875	35 670	38 396	41 355	44 281	48 077
2120 On an income tax basis	..	0	0	0	0	0	0	0	0	0
2200 Employers	5 901	9 409	23 557	30 856	34 366	36 911	41 518	44 806	47 846	51 190
Ind. works' insurance fund	1 819	1 876	4 431	4 632	4 632	5 508	5 436	5 797	6 062	6 283
Soldiers' annuity fund	0	0	0	0	0	0	0	0	0	0
Pneumoconiosis fund	0	0	0	0	0	0	0	0	0	0
Unemployment insurance	653	1 449	2 474	2 860	3 347	4 166	4 545	5 150	5 499	5 790
Veterans' relief fund	0	0	0	0	0	0	0	0	0	0
National welfare pension fund	1 814	4 340	9 383	11 052	11 833	12 930	13 958	14 909	15 895	16 928
Social benefit fund	0	0	0	0	0	0	0	0	0	0
Health Insurance	1 459	1 547	6 844	11 718	13 889	13 576	16 826	18 133	19 493	21 074
Teachers' pensions	156	197	425	594	665	731	753	0	0	0
Government employees pensions	0	0	0	0	0	0	0	817	897	1 115
2210 On a payroll basis	..	9 409	23 557	30 856	34 366	36 911	41 518	44 806	47 846	51 190
2220 On an income tax basis	..	0	0	0	0	0	0	0	0	0
2300 Self-employed or non-employed	2 306	4 772	8 258	10 021	10 993	11 799	11 682	12 023	12 566	13 391
2310 On a payroll basis	0	0	0	0	0	0	0	0	0	0
2320 On an income tax basis	2 306	4 772	8 258	10 021	10 993	11 799	11 682	12 023	12 566	13 391
2400 Unallocable between 2100, 2200 and 2300	0	0	0	0	0	0	0	0	0	0
2410 On a payroll basis	..	..	..	..	..	..	..	..	..	..

Table 4.7. **Korea** *(cont.)*

Details of tax revenue

Billion KRW

	1997	2000	2007	2010	2011	2012	2013	2014	2015	2016
2420 On an income tax basis	..	..	..	..	..	..	..	..	..	..
3000 Taxes on payroll and workforce	**309**	**258**	**619**	**714**	**803**	**868**	**981**	**1 042**	**1 122**	**1 293**
Workshop tax on workforce (local)	309	258	619	714	803	868	981	1 042	1 122	1 293
Vocational training promotion fund	0	0	0	0	0	0	0	0	0	0
4000 Taxes on property	**13 088**	**16 846**	**33 109**	**33 516**	**36 555**	**36 213**	**35 847**	**40 305**	**48 625**	**49 820**
4100 Recurrent taxes on immovable property	2 986	3 385	9 196	9 270	9 779	10 315	10 809	11 654	12 486	13 095
Property tax (local)	577	728	3 755	4 817	7 617	8 049	8 267	8 780	9 294	9 930
City planning tax on urban real estate (local)	731	815	1 883	2 465	5	3	0	0	0	0
Community facilities tax (local)	268	341	543	650	705	766	912	1 138	1 351	1 450
Tax on excessive land holdings (local)	0	0	0	0	0	0	0	0	0	0
Tax on aggregate land holdings (local)	1 279	1 282	5	0	0	0	0	0	0	0
Rural dev. tax on local agg. land holdings tax	63	81	1	0	0	0	0	0	0	0
Tax on excessively increased land value	-1	0	0	0	0	0	0	0	0	0
Comprehensive real estate tax	0	0	2 414	1 029	1 102	1 131	1 224	1 307	1 399	1 294
Rural dev. tax on comprehensive real estate tax	0	0	483	208	223	228	250	265	267	240
4110 Households	0	0	0	0	0	0	0	0	0	0
4120 Others	68	138	112	101	127	138	156	164	175	181
Workshop tax on property (local)	68	138	112	101	127	138	156	164	175	181
4200 Recurrent taxes on net wealth	0	0	0	0	0	0	0	0	0	0
4210 Individual	..	..	..	..	..	..	..	..	..	..
4220 Corporate	..	..	..	..	..	..	..	..	..	..
4300 Estate, inheritance and gift taxes	1 161	989	2 842	3 076	3 333	4 021	4 290	4 625	5 044	5 350
4310 Estate and inheritance taxes	605	449	1 059	1 203	1 259	1 719	1 587	1 696	1 944	1 995
Inheritance tax	605	449	1 059	1 203	1 259	1 719	1 587	1 696	1 944	1 995
Defence tax on inheritance tax	0	0	0	0	0	0	0	0	0	0
4320 Gift taxes	556	540	1 783	1 873	2 074	2 302	2 703	2 929	3 100	3 355
Gift tax	556	540	1 783	1 873	2 074	2 302	2 703	2 929	3 100	3 355
Defence tax on gift tax	0	0	0	0	0	0	0	0	0	0
4400 Taxes on financial and capital transactions	8 774	11 935	21 071	21 170	23 443	21 877	20 748	24 026	31 095	31 375
Registration tax (local)	4 257	4 528	7 254	7 370	7 680	7 645	1 312	1 485	1 831	1 708
Registration tax	0	0	0	0	0	0	0	0	0	0
Defence tax on registration tax	0	0	0	0	0	0	0	0	0	0
Rural dev. tax on local acquisition tax	164	246	627	632	982	853	874	843	969	954
Rural dev. tax on local registration tax	211	66	143	144	2	2	1	1	1	0
Securities transactions tax	262	2 736	3 469	3 667	4 279	3 681	3 077	3 121	4 670	4 468
Rural dev. tax on securities transaction tax	170	823	1 729	2 010	2 515	1 769	1 529	1 459	1 861	1 637
Acquisition tax (local)	3 319	3 148	7 261	6 825	7 361	7 326	13 318	16 391	20 810	21 702
Stamp tax	390	388	588	522	624	601	637	726	953	906
4500 Non-recurrent taxes	167	537	0	0	0	0	0	0	0	0
Asset revaluation tax	167	537	..	..	..	..	..	..	..	..
4510 On net wealth	..	..	..	..	..	..	..	..	..	..
4520 Other non-recurrent taxes	..	..	..	..	..	..	..	..	..	..
4600 Other recurrent taxes on property	0	0	0	0	0	0	0	0	0	0
5000 Taxes on goods and services	**43 978**	**52 271**	**80 861**	**99 769**	**100 551**	**106 402**	**106 717**	**109 451**	**110 326**	**121 197**
5100 Taxes on production, sale, transfer, etc.	41 699	50 023	78 414	96 573	93 983	99 731	99 970	102 531	103 254	113 644
5110 General taxes	19 488	23 212	40 942	51 800	54 868	58 702	59 105	62 975	60 162	68 229
5111 Value added taxes	19 488	23 212	40 942	51 800	54 868	58 702	59 105	62 975	60 162	68 229
Value added tax	19 488	23 212	40 942	51 800	54 868	58 702	59 105	62 975	60 162	68 229
5112 Sales tax	0	0	0	0	0	0	0	0	0	0
Business tax	..	..	..	..	..	..	..	..	..	..
5113 Other	0	0	0	0	0	0	0	0	0	0
5120 Taxes on specific goods and services	22 211	26 811	37 472	44 773	39 115	41 029	40 865	39 556	43 092	45 415

Table 4.7. **Korea** *(cont.)*

Details of tax revenue

Billion KRW

	1997	2000	2007	2010	2011	2012	2013	2014	2015	2016
5121 Excise duties	14 616	18 155	27 880	31 340	25 401	28 410	27 661	28 226	31 857	34 762
Commodity tax	0	0	0	0	0	0	0	0	0	0
Defence tax on commodity tax	0	0	0	0	0	0	0	0	0	0
Liquor tax	1 790	1 963	2 268	2 878	2 529	2 999	2 947	2 852	3 228	3 209
Defence tax on liquor tax	0	0	0	0	0	0	0	0	0	0
Education tax on liquor tax	418	516	580	724	644	774	764	728	808	813
Textile tax	0	0	0	0	0	0	0	0	0	0
Petroleum tax	0	0	0	0	0	0	0	0	0	0
Transport tax on petrol products	5 547	8 404	11 464	13 970	11 546	13 809	13 248	13 440	14 055	15 303
Education tax on transport tax	758	1 247	1 715	2 133	1 726	2 030	1 895	2 074	2 154	2 289
Electricity and gas tax	0	0	0	0	0	0	0	0	0	0
Special excise tax	3 036	2 985	5 161	5 066	5 537	5 336	5 484	5 624	8 001	8 881
Defence tax on special excise tax	0	0	0	0	0	0	0	0	0	0
Education tax on special excise tax	804	498	607	501	589	525	485	495	515	463
Rural development on special excise tax	26	37	54	24	45	56	56	60	61	60
Tobacco sales tax (local)	0	0	0	0	0	0	0	0	0	0
Tobacco consumption tax (local)	2 236	2 251	2 761	2 875	2 785	2 881	2 782	2 953	3 035	3 744
Motor fuel tax (local)	0	254	3 270	3 169	0	0	0	0	0	0
5122 Profits of fiscal monopolies	0	0	0	0	0	0	0	0	0	0
Monopoly profit	..	..	..	..	..	..	..	..	..	..
5123 Customs and import duties	5 941	5 936	7 690	11 046	11 350	10 220	11 012	9 132	8 907	8 434
Customs duties	5 798	5 800	7 411	10 666	10 990	9 816	10 562	8 721	8 495	8 045
Defence tax on customs duties	0	0	0	0	0	0	0	0	0	0
Special customs duties	0	0	0	0	0	0	0	0	0	0
Tonnage tax	0	0	0	0	0	0	0	0	0	0
Education tax on imports	116	99	234	336	322	375	429	390	390	366
Rural dev. tax on customs exemptions	27	37	45	44	38	29	21	21	22	23
Previous year receipts	0	0	0	0	0	0	0	0	0	0
5124 Taxes on exports	0	0	0	0	0	0	0	0	0	0
5125 Taxes on investment goods	0	0	0	0	0	0	0	0	0	0
5126 Taxes on specific services	1 654	2 720	1 902	2 387	2 364	2 399	2 192	2 198	2 328	2 219
Telephone tax	789	1 457	0	0	0	0	0	0	0	0
Defence tax on telephone tax	0	0	0	0	0	0	0	0	0	0
Entertainment tax	0	0	0	0	0	0	0	0	0	0
Defence tax on entertainment tax	0	0	0	0	0	0	0	0	0	0
Entertainment tax (local)	0	0	0	0	0	0	0	0	0	0
Travel tax	0	0	0	0	0	0	0	0	0	0
Admission tax	0	0	0	0	0	0	0	0	0	0
Defence tax on admission tax	0	0	0	0	0	0	0	0	0	0
Education tax on banking & insurance	369	473	721	951	966	932	938	920	1 004	951
Horse race tax (local)	361	566	864	1 068	1 072	1 129	1 042	1 073	1 089	1 060
Rural dev. tax on horse race tax	18	84	165	215	214	221	212	205	235	208
Butchery tax (local)	47	51	52	58	5	0	0	0	0	0
Regional development tax (local)	71	89	100	95	107	117	0	0	0	0
5127 Other taxes on internat. trade and transactions	0	0	0	0	0	0	0	0	0	0
5128 Other taxes	0	0	0	0	0	0	0	0	0	0
5130 Unallocable between 5110 and 5120	0	0	0	0	0	0	0	0	0	0
5200 Taxes on use of goods and perform activities	2 279	2 248	2 447	3 196	6 568	6 671	6 747	6 920	7 072	7 553
5210 Recurrent taxes	2 279	2 248	2 447	3 196	6 568	6 671	6 747	6 920	7 072	7 553
License tax (local)	225	241	77	76	78	78	0	0	0	0
Automobile tax (local)	2 054	2 007	2 370	3 120	6 490	6 593	6 747	6 920	7 072	7 553
5211 Paid by households: motor vehicles	..	..	..	..	..	..	..	..	..	..
5212 Paid by others: motor vehicles	..	..	..	..	..	..	..	..	..	..
5213 Paid in respect of other goods	..	..	..	..	..	..	..	..	..	..
5220 Non-recurrent taxes	0	0	0	0	0	0	0	0	0	0
5300 Unallocable between 5100 and 5200	0	0	0	0	0	0	0	0	0	0
6000 Other taxes	**4 041**	**4 907**	**8 155**	**9 974**	**9 927**	**11 529**	**10 399**	**10 093**	**9 642**	**11 281**
6100 Paid solely by business	0	0	0	0	0	0	0	0	0	0
6200 Other	4 041	4 907	8 155	9 974	9 927	11 529	10 399	10 093	9 642	11 281
Unallocable tax revenue	0	0	0	0	0	0	0	0	0	0
Previous year tax	779	1 474	2 965	4 449	4 232	5 768	4 774	4 049	3 435	4 147
Previous year tax (local)	340	474	672	654	728	680	601	589	392	868
Unallocable defence tax	-8	-3	0	0	0	0	0	0	0	0
Education tax on local taxes	2 931	2 962	4 518	4 871	4 967	5 081	5 024	5 455	5 815	6 266

Table 4.7. **Korea** *(cont.)*

Details of tax revenue

Note: Year ending 31st December.

Data are on cash basis.

Heading 2000: From 1997 the contributions to the three funds (civil servant pension fund, private school teachers pension fund and medical insurance fund) are classified as security social contributions. The reasons for the change are that the contributions either became mandatory or the fund started to be managed by public authorities in that year, thereby meeting the OECD definition of social security contributions.

Heading 2200: From 2007, this includes long-term care insurance.

Source: Ministry of Finance and Economy, Ministry of Home Affairs.

StatLink https://doi.org/10.1787/888933854307

Table 4.8. **Malaysia**

Details of tax revenue

Million MYR

	1997	2000	2007	2010	2011	2012	2013	2014	2015	2016
Total tax revenue	**55 493**	**50 083**	**98 569**	**113 573**	**139 288**	**156 298**	**160 920**	**169 513**	**170 971**	**175 325**
1000 Taxes on income, profits and capital gains	**27 648**	**27 339**	**65 671**	**75 058**	**98 018**	**111 676**	**114 113**	**120 284**	**105 751**	**103 967**
1100 Of individuals	6 429	7 015	11 661	17 805	20 203	22 977	23 055	24 423	26 321	27 566
1110 On income and profits	6 429	7 015	11 661	17 805	20 203	22 977	23 055	24 423	26 321	27 566
1120 On capital gains	..	..	..	..	..	..	..	..	..	..
1200 Corporate	20 552	19 923	52 615	55 156	74 653	85 239	87 949	92 223	75 275	72 127
1210 On profits	20 552	19 923	52 615	55 156	74 653	85 239	87 949	92 223	75 275	72 127
Company income tax	16 688	13 905	32 149	36 266	46 888	51 288	58 175	65 240	63 679	63 625
Petroleum income tax	3 861	6 010	20 453	18 713	27 748	33 934	29 753	26 956	11 559	8 422
Offshore business activity tax	3	8	13	15	17	18	20	27	37	81
Levy on electricity	0	0	0	162	0	0	1	0	0	0
1220 On capital gains	..	..	..	..	..	..	..	..	..	..
1300 Unallocable between 1100 and 1200	666	402	1 395	2 097	3 162	3 459	3 109	3 639	4 155	4 274
Cooperatives income tax	143	87	189	378	357	345	286	169	80	90
Withholding income tax	0	0	1 190	1 268	1 519	2 097	2 008	2 184	2 316	2 562
Other income tax	0	0	17	21	17	21	23	24	30	43
Real property gains tax	523	247	0	303	509	608	785	1 210	1 729	1 492
Exit levy	0	41	0	0	0	0	0	0	0	0
Windfall levy on crude palm oil	0	0	0	0	0	0	0	0	0	0
Windfall levy on crude palm kernel oil	0	26	0	0	0	0	0	0	0	0
Levy on fresh fruit bunch	0	0	0	127	761	388	7	51	1	87
2000 Social security contributions	**0**	**990**	**1 690**	**2 008**	**2 172**	**2 326**	**2 518**	**2 689**	**2 847**	**3 216**
2100 Employees	..	218	371	439	475	508	552	588	..	..
2110 On a payroll basis	..	218	371	439	475	508	552	588	..	..
2120 On an income tax basis	..	0	0	0	0	0	0	0	..	..
2200 Employers	..	772	1 319	1 569	1 697	1 818	1 966	2 101	..	..
2210 On a payroll basis	..	772	1 319	1 569	1 697	1 818	1 966	2 101	..	..
2220 On an income tax basis	..	0	0	0	0	0	0	0	..	..
2300 Self-employed or non-employed	..	0	0	0	0	0	0	0	..	..
2310 On a payroll basis	..	..	..	..	..	..	..	..	..	..
2320 On an income tax basis	..	..	..	..	..	..	..	..	..	..
2400 Unallocable between 2100, 2200 and 2300	..	0	0	0	0	0	0	0	2 847	3 216
2410 On a payroll basis	..	..	..	..	..	..	..	..	..	..
2420 On an income tax basis	..	..	..	..	..	..	..	..	..	..
3000 Taxes on payroll and workforce	**0**	**0**	**0**	**0**	**0**	**0**	**0**	**0**	**0**	**0**
4000 Taxes on property	**19**	**2**	..	..	..	**2**	**1**	**2**	**1**	**3**
4100 Recurrent taxes on immovable property	0	0	..	..	..	0	0	0	0	0
4110 Households	..	..	..	..	..	..	..	..	..	..
4120 Others	..	..	..	..	..	..	..	..	..	..
4200 Recurrent taxes on net wealth	0	0	..	..	..	0	0	0	0	0
4210 Individual	..	..	..	..	..	..	..	..	..	..
4220 Corporate	..	..	..	..	..	..	..	..	..	..
4300 Estate, inheritance and gift taxes	19	2	..	..	..	2	1	2	1	3
4310 Estate and inheritance taxes	19	2	..	..	..	2	1	2	1	3
Estate duty	19	2	..	..	..	2	1	2	1	3
4320 Gift taxes	0	0	..	..	..	0	0	0	0	0
4400 Taxes on financial and capital transactions	0	0	..	..	..	0	0	0	0	0
4500 Non-recurrent taxes	0	0	..	..	..	0	0	0	0	0
4510 On net wealth	..	..	..	..	..	..	..	..	..	..
4520 Other non-recurrent taxes	..	..	..	..	..	..	..	..	..	..
4600 Other recurrent taxes on property	0	0	..	..	..	0	0	0	0	0
5000 Taxes on goods and services	**25 061**	**19 910**	**27 483**	**32 268**	**34 114**	**36 647**	**37 871**	**40 030**	**56 353**	**62 415**
5100 Taxes on production, sale, transfer, etc	23 195	17 990	25 772	30 218	31 883	34 317	35 421	37 411	53 669	59 649
5110 General taxes	6 167	5 968	6 642	8 171	8 577	9 496	10 068	10 939	32 235	41 309
5111 Value added taxes	0	0	0	0	0	0	0	0	27 012	41 206
5112 Sales tax	6 167	5 968	6 642	8 171	8 577	9 496	10 068	10 939	5 223	103
On local goods	4 160	3 894	4 178	4 886	4 995	5 358	5 626	6 130	3 207	..
On imported goods	2 008	2 074	2 464	3 285	3 583	4 138	4 442	4 809	2 016	..
5113 Other	0	0	0	0	0	0	0	0	0	0
5120 Taxes on specific goods and services	15 266	10 245	16 897	19 624	20 765	22 184	22 756	23 930	18 862	15 854
5121 Excise duties	6 053	3 803	8 990	11 770	11 517	12 187	12 193	12 925	11 890	11 705
On local goods	6 053	3 803	7 910	9 350	8 415	8 420	8 395	8 456	7 999	7 721
On imported goods	0	0	1 081	2 420	3 102	3 767	3 798	4 468	3 891	3 984
5122 Profits of fiscal monopolies	0	0	0	0	0	0	0	0	0	0

Table 4.8. **Malaysia** *(cont.)*

Details of tax revenue

Million MYR

	1997	2000	2007	2010	2011	2012	2013	2014	2015	2016
5123 Customs and import duties	6 524	3 599	2 424	1 966	2 026	2 282	2 524	2 670	2 732	2 905
5124 Taxes on exports	1 053	1 032	2 322	1 810	2 081	1 968	1 930	1 893	1 039	980
5125 Taxes on investment goods	0	0	0	0	0	0	0	0	0	0
5126 Taxes on specific services	1 475	1 701	3 013	3 926	4 982	5 583	5 944	6 278	3 038	103
Pool betting duties and sweepstakes	0	0	0	0	0	0	0	0	0	0
Service tax	1 475	1 701	3 013	3 926	4 982	5 583	5 944	6 278	3 038	103
5127 Other taxes on internat. trade and transactions	160	110	147	151	159	164	165	165	163	160
5128 Other taxes	0	0	0	0	0	0	0	0	0	0
5130 Unallocable between 5110 and 5120	1 761	1 777	2 233	2 423	2 541	2 638	2 597	2 542	2 572	2 486
5200 Taxes on use of goods and to perform activities	1 866	1 920	1 711	2 050	2 231	2 329	2 450	2 619	2 684	2 766
5210 Recurrent taxes	1 863	1 918	1 709	2 047	2 227	2 326	2 447	2 617	2 681	2 763
5211 Paid by households: motor vehicles	1 852	1 909	1 688	1 992	2 183	2 283	2 407	2 532	2 630	2 714
Motor vehicle licences	1 852	1 909	1 688	1 992	2 183	2 283	2 407	2 532	2 630	2 714
5212 Paid by others: motor vehicles	11	9	20	18	5	3	3	3	3	3
Commercial vehicle licences	11	9	19	17	5	3	3	3	3	3
Tour vehicle licences	0	0	1	1	1	0	0	0	0	0
5213 Paid in respect of other goods	0	0	0	38	39	39	37	81	48	46
Petroleum permits	0	0	0	1	1	1	0	4	2	2
Bank licences fees	0	0	0	37	38	39	37	78	46	44
5220 Non-recurrent taxes	3	2	3	2	4	3	2	2	3	3
Environment pollution licences	2	2	3	2	4	3	2	2	3	3
Film rental tax	1	0	0	0	0	0	0	0	0	0
5300 Unallocable between 5100 and 5200	0	0	0	0	0	0	0	0	0	0
6000 Other taxes	**2 764**	**1 841**	**3 725**	**4 240**	**4 984**	**5 648**	**6 417**	**6 508**	**6 018**	**5 724**
6100 Paid solely by business	0	0	0	0	0	0	0	0	0	0
6200 Other	2 764	1 841	3 725	4 240	4 984	5 648	6 417	6 508	6 018	5 724
Share transfer tax	0	0	0	0	0	0	0	0	0	0
Stamp duties	2 714	1 799	3 404	4 192	4 929	5 595	6 364	6 458	5 974	5 688
Other direct taxes	50	42	321	48	55	53	53	51	45	37

Note: Year ending 31st December.

The data are on a cash basis.

Heading 2000: Starting from 2015, the breakdown for social security contributions is not available and the data are given as a lump sum.

Heading 4000: Taxes on property do not include local tax items (Quit Rent and Assessment Tax) as the data are unavailable.

Heading 5111: Starting from 2015, VAT is sourced from the IMF's Government Finance Statistics dataset.

Source: Ministry of Finance of Malaysia, Social Security Organisation, State Government Financial Report.

StatLink https://doi.org/10.1787/888933854326

Table 4.9. **New Zealand**

Details of tax revenue

Billion NZD

	1997	2000	2007	2010	2011	2012	2013	2014	2015	2016
Total tax revenue	**35 560**	**39 765**	**64 046**	**62 310**	**64 653**	**69 225**	**72 187**	**76 609**	**81 511**	**86 597**
1000 Taxes on income, profits and capital gains	**21 260**	**23 861**	**40 308**	**33 494**	**34 288**	**37 980**	**39 415**	**41 818**	**44 724**	**48 134**
1100 Of individuals	15 669	17 126	26 965	23 519	23 339	25 530	26 555	28 726	30 298	31 869
1110 On income and profits	15 669	17 126	26 965	23 519	23 339	25 530	26 555	28 726	30 298	31 869
1120 On capital gains	0	0	0	0	0	0	0	0	0	0
1200 Corporate	3 926	4 914	9 069	7 609	8 484	9 889	10 344	10 250	11 407	13 461
1210 On profits	3 926	4 914	9 069	7 609	8 484	9 889	10 344	10 250	11 407	13 461
1220 On capital gains	0	0	0	0	0	0	0	0	0	0
1300 Unallocable between 1100 and 1200	1 665	1 821	4 274	2 366	2 465	2 561	2 516	2 842	3 019	2 804
NRWT	662	760	1 506	467	497	417	427	470	733	594
Property speculation	0	0	0	0	0	0	0	0	0	0
Absentee income tax	0	0	0	0	0	0	0	0	0	0
Interest	961	990	2 699	1 704	1 676	1 628	1 643	1 829	1 660	1 468
Dividends	42	71	69	195	292	516	446	543	626	742
Other	0	0	0	0	0	0	0	0	0	0
2000 Social security contributions	**0**	**0**	**0**	**0**	**0**	**0**	**0**	**0**	**0**	**0**
2100 Employees	0	0	0	0	0	0	0	0	0	0
2110 On a payroll basis	..	..	..	..	..	..	..	..	..	..
2120 On an income tax basis	..	..	..	..	..	..	..	..	..	..
2200 Employers	0	0	0	0	0	0	0	0	0	0
2210 On a payroll basis	..	..	..	..	..	..	..	..	..	..
2220 On an income tax basis	..	..	..	..	..	..	..	..	..	..
2300 Self-employed or non-employed	0	0	0	0	0	0	0	0	0	0
2310 On a payroll basis	..	..	..	..	..	..	..	..	..	..
2320 On an income tax basis	..	..	..	..	..	..	..	..	..	..
2400 Unallocable between 2100, 2200 and 2300	0	0	0	0	0	0	0	0	0	0
2410 On a payroll basis	..	..	..	..	..	..	..	..	..	..
2420 On an income tax basis	..	..	..	..	..	..	..	..	..	..
3000 Taxes on payroll and workforce	**0**	**0**	**0**	**0**	**0**	**0**	**0**	**0**	**0**	**0**
4000 Taxes on property	**1 918**	**2 112**	**3 417**	**4 119**	**4 297**	**4 386**	**4 585**	**4 793**	**5 058**	**5 280**
4100 Recurrent taxes on immovable property	1 732	2 049	3 322	4 031	4 208	4 302	4 492	4 693	4 974	5 201
Local govt rates and services	1 732	2 049	3 322	4 031	4 208	4 302	4 492	4 693	4 974	5 201
Land tax	0	0	0	0	0	0	0	0	0	0
4110 Households	..	..	..	..	..	..	..	..	..	..
4120 Others	..	..	..	..	..	..	..	..	..	..
4200 Recurrent taxes on net wealth	0	0	0	0	0	0	0	0	0	0
4210 Individual	..	..	..	..	..	..	..	..	..	..
4220 Corporate	..	..	..	..	..	..	..	..	..	..
4300 Estate, inheritance and gift taxes	0	2	3	2	0	0	0	0	0	0
4310 Estate and inheritance taxes	..	0	0	0	..	..	..	..	..	..
4320 Gift taxes	..	2	3	2	..	..	..	..	..	..
4400 Taxes on financial and capital transactions	186	61	92	86	89	84	93	100	84	79
Instrument duty	173	51	85	82	85	81	91	100	84	79
Cheque duty	13	10	7	4	4	3	2	0	0	0
4500 Non-recurrent taxes	0	0	0	0	0	0	0	0	0	0
4510 On net wealth	..	..	..	..	..	..	..	..	..	..
4520 Other non-recurrent taxes	..	..	..	..	..	..	..	..	..	..
4600 Other recurrent taxes on property	0	0	0	0	0	0	0	0	0	0
5000 Taxes on goods and services	**12 382**	**13 792**	**20 290**	**24 692**	**26 063**	**26 856**	**28 184**	**29 996**	**31 727**	**33 176**
5100 Taxes on production, sale, transfer, etc.	11 603	12 887	18 832	23 107	24 437	25 193	26 344	28 011	29 584	30 925
5110 General taxes	8 696	9 885	15 046	19 143	20 314	21 004	22 063	23 306	24 587	25 847
5111 Value added taxes	8 696	9 885	15 046	19 143	20 314	21 004	22 063	23 306	24 587	25 847
5112 Sales tax	0	0	0	0	0	0	0	0	0	0
Motor vehicles	..	..	..	..	..	..	..	..	..	..
Other sales tax	..	..	..	..	..	..	..	..	..	..
5113 Other	0	0	0	0	0	0	0	0	0	0
5120 Taxes on specific goods and services	2 907	3 002	3 786	3 964	4 123	4 189	4 281	4 705	4 997	5 078

Table 4.9. **New Zealand** *(cont.)*

Details of tax revenue

Billion NZD

	1997	2000	2007	2010	2011	2012	2013	2014	2015	2016
5121 Excise duties	2 018	2 148	1 627	1 782	1 814	1 866	1 854	2 050	2 280	2 231
On alcoholic beverages	439	436	573	622	656	664	650	651	672	684
Beer	218	201	290	207	252	251	250	253	262	265
Wine	106	100	163	181	213	220	204	216	216	218
Spirits	115	135	120	234	191	193	196	182	194	201
Tobacco	681	764	159	220	244	281	273	310	362	352
Motor vehicles	0	0	0	0	0	0	0	0	0	0
Refined sugar	0	0	0	0	0	0	0	0	0	0
CA petroleum fuels	786	810	819	872	847	855	865	1 018	1 185	1 137
NRF fuel excise	0	0	0	0	0	0	0	0	0	0
Local petroleum fuels	25	27	30	32	31	32	31	35	33	34
CA mileage tax	0	0	0	0	0	0	0	0	0	0
NRF mileage tax	0	0	0	0	0	0	0	0	0	0
Road user charges	0	0	0	0	0	0	0	0	0	0
Energy resources levy	87	111	46	36	36	34	35	36	28	24
5122 Profits of fiscal monopolies	0	0	0	0	0	0	0	0	0	0
5123 Customs and import duties	750	648	1 857	1 916	2 038	2 056	2 160	2 391	2 442	2 550
5124 Taxes on exports	0	0	0	0	0	0	0	0	0	0
5125 Taxes on investment goods	0	0	0	0	0	0	0	0	0	0
5126 Taxes on specific services	139	206	302	266	271	267	267	264	275	297
Lottery (national)	103	167	290	253	258	253	254	249	260	281
Lottery (overseas)	0	0	0	0	0	0	0	0	0	0
Racing	36	39	12	13	13	14	13	15	15	16
Film hire tax	0	0	0	0	0	0	0	0	0	0
Domestic air travel tax	0	0	0	0	0	0	0	0	0	0
5127 Other taxes on internat. trade and transactions	0	0	0	0	0	0	0	0	0	0
Foreign fishing vessels tax	..	..	..	..	..	..	..	..	..	..
Foreign travel tax	..	..	..	..	..	..	..	..	..	..
International departure tax	..	..	..	..	..	..	..	..	..	..
5128 Other taxes	0	0	0	0	0	0	0	0	0	0
5130 Unallocable between 5110 and 5120	0	0	0	0	0	0	0	0	0	0
5200 Taxes on use of goods and perform activities	779	905	1 458	1 585	1 626	1 663	1 840	1 985	2 143	2 251
5210 Recurrent taxes	779	905	1 458	1 585	1 626	1 663	1 840	1 985	2 143	2 251
Motor vehicle registration	158	181	226	172	175	174	187	181	214	223
Heavy traffic fees	466	532	851	1 016	1 045	1 066	1 205	1 283	1 381	1 469
Accident compensation levies	0	0	0	0	0	0	0	0	0	0
5211 Paid by households: motor vehicles	0	0	0	0	0	0	0	0	0	0
5212 Paid by others: motor vehicles	0	0	0	0	0	0	0	0	0	0
5213 Paid in respect of other goods	155	192	381	397	406	423	448	521	548	559
Local authority fees and charges	155	192	381	397	406	423	448	521	548	559
5220 Non-recurrent taxes	0	0	0	0	0	0	0	0	0	0
5300 Unallocable between 5100 and 5200	0	0	0	0	0	0	0	0	0	0
6000 Other taxes	**0**	**0**	**31**	**5**	**5**	**3**	**3**	**2**	**2**	**7**
6100 Paid solely by business	..	..	0	0	0	0	0	0	0	0
6200 Other	..	..	31	5	5	3	3	2	2	7

Note: For the years before 1989 data are on a fiscal year basis ending 31st March. The figures provided for 1989 and onwards relate to the financial year ending 30th June of the following year.

From 1993, data are on accrual basis.

Heading 1000: Tax credits to exporters under the export incentives schemes are non-wastable, but that part of the excess of tax liability paid out to taxpayers is not identifiable.

Heading 1100: The figures up to 1969 include revenues collected by a social security income tax. The base of this tax was the same as the ordinary income tax base and the two have now been incorporated into a single income tax.

Heading 5121: From October 1986 incorporates that portion of the selective impost on wine, spirits, tobacco and motor vehicles which was formerly collected and reported as sales tax. The revenue collected on those imported goods which are subject to the equivalent of the domestic excise has been classified as excise duty. In this respect, there is a discontinuity between the excises recorded before and after October 1986.

Heading 5210: The other local authority licence fees include some small items which could be regarded as non-tax revenues.

Heading for non-wastable tax credits 1110 comprises four Family assistance tax credits. The total in item 1100 is net of the tax expenditure component but not net of the transfer component.

Source: Local Authorities Statistics, Department of Statistics, Wellington.

StatLink https://doi.org/10.1787/888933854345

Table 4.10. **Papua New Guinea**

Details of tax revenue

Million PGK

	1997	2000	2007	2010	2011	2012	2013	2014	2015	2016
Total tax revenue	..	..	**5 875**	**6 573**	**8 526**	**8 403**	**8 773**	**10 279**	**9 142**	**8 606**
1000 Taxes on income, profits and capital gains	..	**936**	**4 287**	**4 562**	**5 951**	**5 632**	**5 878**	**6 889**	**5 956**	**5 286**
1100 Of individuals	..	552	1 001	1 553	2 159	2 645	2 827	3 200	3 037	2 844
1110 On income and profits	..	552	1 001	1 553	2 159	2 645	2 827	3 200	3 037	2 844
1120 On capital gains	..	..	..	..	..	..	..	..	..	..
1200 Corporate	..	384	3 285	3 009	3 793	2 987	3 051	3 689	2 919	2 441
1210 On profits	..	384	3 285	3 009	3 793	2 987	3 051	3 689	2 919	2 441
Corporate Income Tax	..	262	724	1 201	1 373	1 677	2 067	2 629	2 375	2 094
Mining and Petroleum Tax	..	0	2 334	1 476	2 073	1 033	667	794	169	92
Royalty Tax and Management fee	..	4	5	10	16	18	28	37	18	44
Dividend witholding tax	..	54	204	279	291	186	245	186	195	133
Interest witholding tax	..	64	19	42	40	72	45	43	162	79
1220 On capital gains of corporates	..	..	..	..	..	..	..	..	..	..
1300 Unallocable between 1100 and 1200	..	0	0	0	0	0	0	0	0	0
2000 Social security contributions	..	**0**	**0**	**0**	**0**	**0**	**0**	**0**	**0**	**0**
2100 Employees	..	..	..	..	..	..	..	..	..	..
2110 On a payroll basis	..	..	..	..	..	..	..	..	..	..
2120 On an income tax basis	..	..	..	..	..	..	..	..	..	..
2200 Employers	..	..	..	..	..	..	..	..	..	..
2210 On a payroll basis	..	..	..	..	..	..	..	..	..	..
2220 On an income tax basis	..	..	..	..	..	..	..	..	..	..
2300 Self-employed or non-employed	..	..	..	..	..	..	..	..	..	..
2310 On a payroll basis	..	..	..	..	..	..	..	..	..	..
2320 On an income tax basis	..	..	..	..	..	..	..	..	..	..
2400 Unallocable between 2100, 2200 and 2300	..	..	..	..	..	..	..	..	..	..
2410 On a payroll basis	..	..	..	..	..	..	..	..	..	..
2420 On an income tax basis	..	..	..	..	..	..	..	..	..	..
3000 Taxes on payroll and workforce	..	**1**	**2**	**2**	**4**	**4**	**6**	**16**	**0**	**14**
4000 Taxes on property	..	**44**	**85**	**65**	**64**	**70**	**67**	**137**	**51**	**79**
4100 Recurrent taxes on immovable property	..	0	0	0	0	0	0	0	0	0
4110 Households	..	..	..	..	..	..	..	..	..	..
4120 Others	..	..	..	..	..	..	..	..	..	..
4200 Recurrent taxes on net wealth	..	0	0	0	0	0	0	0	0	0
4210 Individual	..	..	..	..	..	..	..	..	..	..
4220 Corporate	..	..	..	..	..	..	..	..	..	..
4300 Estate, inheritance and gift taxes	..	0	0	0	0	0	0	0	0	0
4310 Estate and inheritance taxes	..	..	..	..	..	..	..	..	..	..
4320 Gift taxes	..	..	..	..	..	..	..	..	..	..
4400 Taxes on financial and capital transactions	..	44	85	65	64	70	67	137	51	79
4500 Other non-reccurrent taxes on property	..	0	0	0	0	0	0	0	0	0
4510 On net wealth	..	..	..	..	..	..	..	..	..	..
4520 Other non-recurrent taxes	..	..	..	..	..	..	..	..	..	..
4600 Other recurrent taxes on property	..	0	0	0	0	0	0	0	0	0
5000 Taxes on goods and services	..	**325**	**1 501**	**1 944**	**2 507**	**2 697**	**2 822**	**3 237**	**3 134**	**3 227**
5100 Taxes on production, sale, transfer, etc	..	325	1 501	1 944	2 507	2 697	2 822	3 237	3 134	3 227
5110 General taxes on goods and services	..	325	654	874	1 162	1 300	1 388	1 636	1 637	1 646
5111 Value added taxes	..	321	648	865	1 154	1 291	1 379	1 623	1 571	1 638
Goods and services tax (inland Collection)	..	177	468	629	876	1 019	1 036	1 180	1 068	1 103
GST transfers to provinces	..	144	180	236	278	272	343	443	503	535
5112 Sales tax	..	0	0	0	0	0	0	0	0	0
5113 Other	..	4	6	9	8	9	9	13	66	8
5120 Taxes on specific goods and services	..	..	846	1 070	1 345	1 397	1 434	1 601	1 497	1 581
5121 Excises	..	..	455	611	737	855	814	889	802	876
5122 Profits of fiscal monopolies	..	0	0	0	0	0	0	0	0	0
5123 Customs and import duties	..	..	136	189	281	223	257	273	243	243
5124 Taxes on exports	..	..	155	174	211	180	212	275	316	294
5125 Taxes on investment goods	..	0	0	0	0	0	0	0	0	0
5126 Taxes on specific services	..	61	100	97	116	139	151	164	136	168
Gaming taxes	..	58	97	93	111	133	145	158	126	164
Departure tax	..	3	3	4	5	6	6	6	9	4
5127 Other taxes on internat. trade and transactions	..	0	0	0	0	0	0	0	0	0
5128 Other taxes	..	0	0	0	0	0	0	0	0	0
5130 Unallocable between 5110 and 5120	..	0	0	0	0	0	0	0	0	0
5200 Taxes on use of goods and to perform activities	..	0	0	0	0	0	0	0	0	0

Table 4.10. **Papua New Guinea** *(cont.)*

Details of tax revenue

Million PGK

	1997	2000	2007	2010	2011	2012	2013	2014	2015	2016
5210 Recurrent taxes	..	..	..	..	..	..	..	..	..	..
5211 Paid by households: motor vehicles	..	..	..	..	..	..	..	..	..	..
5212 Paid by others: motor vehicles	..	..	..	..	..	..	..	..	..	..
5213 Paid in respect of other goods	..	..	..	..	..	..	..	..	..	..
5220 Non-recurrent taxes	..	..	..	..	..	..	..	..	..	..
5300 Unallocable between 5100 and 5200	..	0	0	0	0	0	0	0	0	0
6000 Other taxes	**..**	**0**	**0**	**0**	**0**	**0**	**0**	**0**	**0**	**0**
6100 Paid solely by business	..	..	..	..	..	..	..	..	..	..
6200 Other	..	..	..	..	..	..	..	..	..	..

Note: Year ending 31st December.

The data are on a cash basis.

Figures exclude tax revenues collected by sub-national governments as the data are not available.

Totals are not calculated for 2000 and 2001 as the data are incomplete and do not include customs revenues for these two years.

Source: Ministry of Treasury and Finance of Papua New Guinea.

StatLink https://doi.org/10.1787/888933854364

Table 4.11. **Philippines**

Details of tax revenue

Million PHP

	1997	2000	2007	2010	2011	2012	2013	2014	2015	2016
Total tax revenue	**447 976**	**564 343**	**1 121 594**	**1 330 768**	**1 469 547**	**1 669 306**	**1 868 601**	**2 111 568**	**2 265 085**	**2 459 258**
1000 Taxes on income, profits and capital gains	**164 170**	**217 798**	**453 338**	**521 707**	**612 432**	**691 232**	**767 819**	**840 680**	**912 198**	**992 949**
1100 Of individuals	59 749	83 006	141 673	167 605	194 025	223 165	246 894	283 873	309 439	344 081
1110 On income and profits	53 370	78 229	135 504	158 325	184 076	210 645	232 725	267 703	292 548	325 446
1120 On capital gains	6 379	4 777	6 170	9 280	9 949	12 520	14 169	16 170	16 891	18 635
1200 Corporate	95 449	116 980	282 504	326 967	392 400	432 850	486 898	523 183	569 454	617 473
1210 On profits	94 427	114 871	280 090	323 116	387 499	421 937	476 311	513 978	561 434	607 708
1220 On capital gains	1 022	2 110	2 414	3 851	4 902	10 913	10 587	9 205	8 020	9 766
1300 Unallocable between 1100 and 1200	8 973	17 812	29 160	27 135	26 007	35 217	34 027	33 624	33 305	31 395
2000 Social security contributions	**36 500**	**74 200**	**131 830**	**168 430**	**186 203**	**215 356**	**236 575**	**284 360**	**319 077**	**343 560**
2100 Employees	..	..	..	..	..	..	..	..	..	..
2110 On a payroll basis	..	..	..	..	..	..	..	..	..	..
2120 On an income tax basis	..	..	..	..	..	..	..	..	..	..
2200 Employers	2 800	19 900	26 520	34 300	38 008	54 215	54 662	80 130	97 598	101 002
2210 On a payroll basis	..	..	..	..	..	..	..	..	..	..
2220 On an income tax basis	..	..	..	..	..	..	..	..	..	..
2300 Self-employed or non-employed	..	..	..	..	..	..	..	..	..	..
2310 On a payroll basis	..	..	..	..	..	..	..	..	..	..
2320 On an income tax basis	..	..	..	..	..	..	..	..	..	..
2400 Unallocable between 2100, 2200 and 2300	33 700	54 300	105 310	134 130	148 195	161 141	181 913	204 230	221 479	242 558
2410 On a payroll basis	..	..	..	..	..	..	..	..	..	..
2420 On an income tax basis	..	..	..	..	..	..	..	..	..	..
3000 Taxes on payroll and workforce	**0**	**0**	**0**	**0**	**0**	**0**	**0**	**0**	**0**	**0**
4000 Taxes on property	**4 178**	**17 401**	**32 354**	**39 070**	**44 590**	**50 943**	**56 269**	**60 026**	**63 990**	**66 275**
4100 Recurrent taxes on immovable property	0	14 947	27 387	31 876	36 043	39 315	41 191	45 458	48 999	50 838
Real property tax (local government)	..	14 947	27 387	31 876	36 043	39 315	41 191	45 458	48 999	50 838
4110 Households	..	..	..	..	..	..	..	..	..	..
4120 Others	..	..	..	..	..	..	..	..	..	..
4200 Recurrent taxes on net wealth	0	0	0	0	0	0	0	0	0	0
4210 Individual	..	..	..	..	..	..	..	..	..	..
4220 Corporate	..	..	..	..	..	..	..	..	..	..
4300 Estate, inheritance and gift taxes	881	480	962	1 981	2 400	3 626	3 275	5 450	5 636	6 638
4310 Estate and inheritance taxes	677	302	650	1 451	1 635	2 315	1 650	3 489	3 341	4 723
4320 Gift taxes	204	178	312	531	765	1 312	1 625	1 960	2 294	1 915
4400 Taxes on financial and capital transactions	3 297	1 974	4 005	5 213	6 147	8 002	11 803	9 118	9 356	8 798
Stock transactions (RA 7717)	3 297	1 974	4 005	5 213	6 147	8 002	11 803	9 118	9 356	8 798
4500 Non-recurrent taxes	0	0	0	0	0	0	0	0	0	0
4510 On net wealth	..	..	..	..	..	..	..	..	..	..
4520 Other non-recurrent taxes	..	..	..	..	..	..	..	..	..	..
4600 Other recurrent taxes on property	0	0	0	0	0	0	0	0	0	0
5000 Taxes on goods and services	**225 025**	**237 243**	**456 497**	**549 890**	**568 870**	**648 504**	**735 896**	**844 442**	**884 132**	**962 763**
5100 Taxes on production, sale, transfer, etc	222 627	234 202	448 164	540 595	558 770	638 148	724 888	832 656	872 832	949 396
5110 General taxes	47 273	53 879	145 013	173 284	183 082	229 594	250 149	278 794	295 502	331 414
5111 Value added taxes	47 273	53 879	145 013	173 284	183 082	229 594	250 149	278 794	295 502	331 414
5112 Sales tax	0	0	0	0	0	0	0	0	0	0
5113 Other	0	0	0	0	0	0	0	0	0	0
5120 Taxes on specific goods and services	175 354	180 323	303 151	367 312	375 687	408 554	474 739	553 862	577 330	617 982
5121 Excises	63 048	61 677	54 998	67 203	67 993	72 346	118 856	135 315	158 319	163 505
Alcohol products	13 412	12 997	18 786	21 781	22 873	23 896	33 535	37 525	42 214	50 272
Tobacco products	16 027	17 427	23 206	31 730	25 997	32 942	71 608	82 725	99 505	95 055
Petroleum products	29 272	28 297	10 036	9 832	9 963	10 159	8 503	9 419	11 888	13 111
Automobiles	0	0	0	0	2 026	2 935	2 542	2 636	2 452	3 128
Mineral products	77	243	942	1 306	6 986	2 206	2 494	2 814	2 079	1 758
Others	4 259	2 712	2 028	2 555	148	208	174	196	182	181
5122 Profits of fiscal monopolies	0	0	0	0	0	0	0	0	0	0
5123 Customs and import duties	94 800	95 006	209 439	259 241	265 108	289 866	304 925	369 277	367 534	396 365
5124 Taxes on exports	0	0	0	0	0	0	0	0	0	0
5125 Taxes on investment goods	0	0	0	0	0	0	0	0	0	0
5126 Taxes on specific services	17 506	23 639	38 714	40 868	42 587	46 342	50 958	49 270	51 477	58 111
Banks and financial institutions	9 696	9 538	19 434	22 857	23 514	25 338	30 199	26 677	26 915	29 602
Travel tax (CHED/NCAA)	386	1 043	1 581	1 512	1 660	1 709	1 885	1 827	1 770	1 694
Immigration tax (BID)	18	47	42	59	61	64	69	72	72	87
Others	7 406	13 011	17 657	16 440	17 351	19 231	18 805	20 694	22 720	26 728
5127 Other taxes on internat. trade and transactions	0	0	0	0	0	0	0	0	0	0

Table 4.11. **Philippines** *(cont.)*

Details of tax revenue

Million PHP

	1997	2000	2007	2010	2011	2012	2013	2014	2015	2016
5128 Other taxes	0	0	0	0	0	0	0	0	0	0
5130 Unallocable between 5110 and 5120	0	0	0	0	0	0	0	0	0	0
5200 Taxes on use of goods and perform activities	2 398	3 041	8 333	9 295	10 100	10 356	11 008	11 786	11 300	13 367
5210 Recurrent taxes	2 398	3 041	8 333	9 295	10 100	10 356	11 008	11 786	11 300	13 367
LTO-Motor vehicle users' tax	2 398	3 041	8 333	9 295	10 100	10 356	11 008	11 786	11 300	13 367
5211 Paid by households: motor vehicles	..	..	..	..	..	..	..	..	..	..
5212 Paid by others: motor vehicles	..	..	..	..	..	..	..	..	..	..
5213 Paid in respect of other goods	0	0	0	0	0	0	0	0	0	0
5220 Non-recurrent taxes	0	0	0	0	0	0	0	0	0	0
5300 Unallocable between 5100 and 5200	0	0	0	0	0	0	0	0	0	0
6000 Other taxes	**18 103**	**17 702**	**47 575**	**51 671**	**57 452**	**63 271**	**72 042**	**82 060**	**85 687**	**93 711**
6100 Paid solely by business	0	0	0	0	0	0	0	0	0	0
6200 Other	18 103	17 702	47 575	51 671	57 452	63 271	72 042	82 060	85 687	93 711
Documentary stamp tax	16 477	16 170	35 147	42 629	47 879	52 455	60 356	69 036	72 073	80 151
DENR-Forest charges	116	175	164	239	150	204	132	133	128	136
Miscellaneous taxes	1 510	1 356	8 944	4 391	4 724	5 788	5 874	6 051	6 219	5 888
Other taxes (local government)	0	0	3 319	4 412	4 700	4 823	5 679	6 840	7 267	7 535

Note:

Year ending 31st December.

The data are on a cash basis.

Heading 5123: This category includes VAT and excises levied on imports.

Source: Department of Finance of the Philippines.

StatLink https://doi.org/10.1787/888933854383

Table 4.12. **Samoa**

Details of tax revenue

Million WST

	1997	2000	2007	2010	2011	2012	2013	2014	2015	2016
Total tax revenue	..	..	**330**	**341**	**359**	**403**	**427**	**440**	**495**	**514**
1000 Taxes on income, profits and capital gains	..	..	**78**	**84**	**91**	**101**	**103**	**107**	**114**	**117**
1100 Of individuals	..	..	42	46	53	55	58	59	64	69
1110 On income and profits	..	..	42	46	53	55	58	59	64	69
1120 On capital gains	..	..	0	0	0	0	0	0	0	0
1200 Corporate	..	..	36	38	39	46	45	48	51	48
1210 On profits	..	..	36	38	39	46	45	48	51	48
1220 On capital gains of corporates	..	..	0	0	0	0	0	0	0	0
1300 Unallocable between 1100 and 1200	..	..	0	0	0	0	0	0	0	0
2000 Social security contributions	..	..	**0**	**0**	**0**	**0**	**0**	**0**	**0**	**0**
2100 Employees	..	..	..	..	..	..	..	..	..	..
2110 On a payroll basis	..	..	..	..	..	..	..	..	..	..
2120 On an income tax basis	..	..	..	..	..	..	..	..	..	..
2200 Employers	..	..	..	..	..	..	..	..	..	..
2210 On a payroll basis	..	..	..	..	..	..	..	..	..	..
2220 On an income tax basis	..	..	..	..	..	..	..	..	..	..
2300 Self-employed or non-employed	..	..	..	..	..	..	..	..	..	..
2310 On a payroll basis	..	..	..	..	..	..	..	..	..	..
2320 On an income tax basis	..	..	..	..	..	..	..	..	..	..
2400 Unallocable between 2100, 2200 and 2300	..	..	..	..	..	..	..	..	..	..
2410 On a payroll basis	..	..	..	..	..	..	..	..	..	..
2420 On an income tax basis	..	..	..	..	..	..	..	..	..	..
3000 Taxes on payroll and workforce	..	..	**0**	**0**	**0**	**0**	**0**	**0**	**0**	**0**
4000 Taxes on property	..	..	**2**	**0**	**0**	**0**	**0**	**0**	**0**	**0**
4100 Recurrent taxes on immovable property	..	..	0	0	0	0	0	0	0	0
4110 Households	..	..	..	..	..	..	..	..	..	..
4120 Others	..	..	..	..	..	..	..	..	..	..
4200 Recurrent taxes on net wealth	..	..	0	0	0	0	0	0	0	0
4210 Individual	..	..	..	..	..	..	..	..	..	..
4220 Corporate	..	..	..	..	..	..	..	..	..	..
4300 Estate, inheritance and gift taxes	..	..	0	0	0	0	0	0	0	0
4310 Estate and inheritance taxes	..	..	..	..	..	..	..	..	..	..
4320 Gift taxes	..	..	..	..	..	..	..	..	..	..
4400 Taxes on financial and capital transactions	..	..	2	0	0	0	0	0	0	0
4500 Other non-reccurrent taxes on property	..	..	0	0	0	0	0	0	0	0
4510 On net wealth	..	..	..	..	..	..	..	..	..	..
4520 Other non-recurrent taxes	..	..	..	..	..	..	..	..	..	..
4600 Other recurrent taxes on property	..	..	0	0	0	0	0	0	0	0
5000 Taxes on goods and services	..	..	**251**	**257**	**267**	**302**	**324**	**332**	**380**	**397**
5100 Taxes on production, sale, transfer, etc	..	..	251	257	267	302	324	332	380	397
5110 General taxes on goods and services	..	..	126	119	138	164	170	177	200	198
5111 Value added taxes	..	..	126	119	138	164	170	177	200	198
VAGST on Imports	..	..	100	0	0	0	0	0	0	0
VAGST on sales of goods and services	..	..	26	0	0	0	0	0	0	0
5112 Sales tax	..	..	0	0	0	0	0	0	0	0
5113 Other	..	..	0	0	0	0	0	0	0	0
5120 Taxes on specific goods and services	..	..	125	137	130	139	154	155	181	199
5121 Excises	..	..	78	95	89	87	96	99	120	134
Petroleum Levy	..	..	3	..	..	..	..	..	..	..
Import Excise	..	..	29	..	..	..	..	..	..	..
Domestic Excise	..	..	47	..	..	..	..	..	..	..
5122 Profits of fiscal monopolies	..	..	0	0	0	0	0	0	0	0
5123 Customs and import duties	..	..	43	38	35	45	53	50	54	55
5124 Taxes on exports	..	..	0	0	0	0	0	0	0	0
5125 Taxes on investment goods	..	..	0	0	0	0	0	0	0	0
5126 Taxes on specific services	..	..	4	4	5	6	5	6	6	10
5127 Other taxes on internat. trade and transactions	..	..	0	0	0	0	0	0	0	0
5128 Other taxes	..	..	0	0	0	0	0	0	0	0
5130 Unallocable between 5110 and 5120	..	..	0	0	0	0	0	0	0	0
5200 Taxes on use of goods and to perform activities	..	..	0	0	0	0	0	0	0	0
5210 Recurrent taxes	..	..	..	..	..	..	..	..	..	..
5211 Paid by households: motor vehicles	..	..	..	..	..	..	..	..	..	..
5212 Paid by others: motor vehicles	..	..	..	..	..	..	..	..	..	..
5213 Paid in respect of other goods	..	..	..	..	..	..	..	..	..	..

Table 4.12. **Samoa** *(cont.)*

Details of tax revenue

Million WST

	1997	2000	2007	2010	2011	2012	2013	2014	2015	2016
5220 Non-recurrent taxes	..	..	..	..	..	..	..	..	..	..
5300 Unallocable between 5100 and 5200	..	..	0	0	0	0	0	0	0	0
6000 Other taxes	**..**	**..**	**0**	**0**	**0**	**0**	**0**	**0**	**0**	**0**
6100 Paid solely by business	..	..	..	..	..	..	..	..	..	..
6200 Other	..	..	..	..	..	..	..	..	..	..

Note: Data are reported on a fiscal year basis beginning 1st July. For example, the data for 2016 represent the period from July 2016 to June 2017.

The data are on a cash basis.

Figures exclude tax revenues collected by sub-national governments as the data are not available.

The data from 2009 were provided on the basis of the IMF's GFSM 2014 classification. Prior to this year, data were provided on a different basis. The differences between the two sets of data are indicated below for the relevant tax revenue categories.

Heading 1000: Income tax revenues from 2009 onwards are net of income tax refunds. Prior to 2009, the income tax revenue figures are gross of refunds.

Heading 5111: VAGST revenues from 2009 onwards do not include aid, loan payments by Treasury and VAGST paid by government departments.

Heading 5123: Import duty from 2009 onwards does not include aid and loan payments by Treasury.

Heading 5126: Data from 2009 include revenues from fisheries' licences. Fisheries' licences revenues are usually classified as non-tax revenues according to the OECD classification set out in Annex A of the Interpretative Guide, but could not be distinguished from other revenues from taxes on specific services.

Source: Bureau of Statistics of Samoa.

StatLink https://doi.org/10.1787/888933854402

Table 4.13. **Singapore**

Details of tax revenue

Million SGD

	1997	2000	2007	2010	2011	2012	2013	2014	2015	2016
Total tax revenue	..	**25 627**	**36 630**	**41 848**	**46 076**	**50 119**	**51 146**	**54 110**	**55 647**	**58 699**
1000 Taxes on income, profits and capital gains	..	**13 538**	**16 621**	**18 687**	**20 579**	**22 411**	**22 050**	**23 940**	**24 890**	**26 378**
1100 Of individuals	..	3 543	4 537	6 470	6 871	7 714	7 688	8 927	9 235	10 526
1110 On income and profits	..	3 543	4 537	6 470	6 871	7 714	7 688	8 927	9 235	10 526
1120 On capital gains	..	..	..	..	..	..	..	..	..	..
1200 Corporate	..	9 509	10 934	11 260	12 450	13 360	13 209	13 887	14 253	14 378
1210 On profits	..	9 509	10 934	11 260	12 450	13 360	13 209	13 887	14 253	14 378
From corporate profits	..	8 316	9 250	10 687	12 096	12 821	12 680	13 372	13 815	13 602
Statutory board contributions	..	1 192	1 683	573	353	539	530	516	438	776
1220 On capital gains	..	..	..	..	..	..	..	..	..	..
1300 Unallocable between 1100 and 1200	..	486	1 150	957	1 258	1 337	1 152	1 126	1 402	1 474
Withholding taxes	..	486	1 150	957	1 258	1 337	1 152	1 126	1 402	1 474
2000 Social security contributions	..	**0**	**0**	**0**	**0**	**0**	**0**	**0**	**0**	**0**
2100 Employees	..	..	..	..	..	..	..	..	..	..
2110 On a payroll basis	..	..	..	..	..	..	..	..	..	..
2120 On an income tax basis	..	..	..	..	..	..	..	..	..	..
2200 Employers	..	..	..	..	..	..	..	..	..	..
2210 On a payroll basis	..	..	..	..	..	..	..	..	..	..
2220 On an income tax basis	..	..	..	..	..	..	..	..	..	..
2300 Self-employed or non-employed	..	..	..	..	..	..	..	..	..	..
2310 On a payroll basis	..	..	..	..	..	..	..	..	..	..
2320 On an income tax basis	..	..	..	..	..	..	..	..	..	..
2400 Unallocable between 2100, 2200 and 2300	..	..	..	..	..	..	..	..	..	..
2410 On a payroll basis	..	..	..	..	..	..	..	..	..	..
2420 On an income tax basis	..	..	..	..	..	..	..	..	..	..
3000 Taxes on payroll and workforce	..	**0**	**0**	**0**	**0**	**0**	**0**	**0**	**0**	**0**
4000 Taxes on property	..	**2 863**	**6 259**	**6 080**	**7 077**	**8 078**	**8 112**	**7 124**	**7 224**	**7 638**
4100 Recurrent taxes on immovable property	..	1 535	2 428	2 798	3 899	3 760	4 179	4 340	4 456	4 359
4110 Households	..	..	..	..	..	..	..	..	..	..
4120 Others	..	..	..	..	..	..	..	..	..	..
4200 Recurrent taxes on net wealth	..	0	0	0	0	0	0	0	0	0
4210 Individual	..	..	..	..	..	..	..	..	..	..
4220 Corporate	..	..	..	..	..	..	..	..	..	..
4300 Estate, inheritance and gift taxes	..	71	154	5	3	8	3	1	-1	0
4310 Estate and inheritance taxes	..	71	154	5	3	8	3	1	-1	0
4320 Gift taxes	..	0	0	0	0	0	0	0	0	0
4400 Taxes on financial and capital transactions	..	1 257	3 677	3 277	3 175	4 310	3 930	2 784	2 769	3 278
4500 Non-recurrent taxes	..	0	0	0	0	0	0	0	0	0
4510 On net wealth	..	..	..	..	..	..	..	..	..	..
4520 Other non-recurrent taxes	..	..	..	..	..	..	..	..	..	..
4600 Other recurrent taxes on property	..	0	0	0	0	0	0	0	0	0
5000 Taxes on goods and services	..	**7 967**	**12 053**	**14 376**	**15 113**	**15 288**	**15 736**	**16 949**	**17 657**	**18 638**
5100 Taxes on production, sale, transfer, etc	..	5 462	9 864	12 525	13 193	13 485	14 081	15 346	15 897	16 490
5110 General taxes	..	2 121	6 165	8 198	8 687	9 038	9 513	10 215	10 345	11 078
5111 Value added taxes	..	2 121	6 165	8 198	8 687	9 038	9 513	10 215	10 345	11 078
5112 Sales tax	..	0	0	0	0	0	0	0	0	0
5113 Other	..	0	0	0	0	0	0	0	0	0
5120 Taxes on specific goods and services	..	3 341	3 699	4 327	4 506	4 447	4 568	5 131	5 552	5 412
5121 Excises	..	1 847	1 985	2 048	2 133	2 142	2 189	2 540	2 833	2 730
Liquors	..	..	414	470	496	517	518	634	638	640
Tobacco	..	..	700	889	967	969	1 043	1 228	1 205	986
Petroleum Products	..	..	386	419	416	415	414	419	584	596
Motor Vehicles	..	..	483	267	248	233	206	251	399	502
Compressed Natural Gas Unit Duty	..	..	0	0	1	3	3	3	2	1
Others	..	..	3	5	5	5	5	6	5	5
5122 Profits of fiscal monopolies	..	0	0	0	0	0	0	0	0	0
5123 Customs and import duties	..	..	..	..	..	..	..	..	..	..
5124 Taxes on exports	..	0	0	0	0	0	0	0	0	0
5125 Taxes on investment goods	..	0	0	0	0	0	0	0	0	0
5126 Taxes on specific services	..	1 494	1 714	2 279	2 373	2 305	2 379	2 591	2 719	2 682
Betting duty	..	1 494	1 714	2 279	2 373	2 305	2 379	2 591	2 719	2 682
5127 Other taxes on internat. trade and transactions	..	0	0	0	0	0	0	0	0	0
5128 Other taxes	..	0	0	0	0	0	0	0	0	0
5130 Unallocable between 5110 and 5120	..	0	0	0	0	0	0	0	0	0

Table 4.13. **Singapore** *(cont.)*

Details of tax revenue

Million SGD

	1997	2000	2007	2010	2011	2012	2013	2014	2015	2016
5200 Taxes on use of goods and perform activities	..	2 506	2 189	1 851	1 920	1 803	1 655	1 603	1 760	2 148
5210 Recurrent taxes	..	..	..	..	..	..	..	..	..	..
5211 Paid by households: motor vehicles	..	..	..	..	..	..	..	..	..	..
5212 Paid by others: motor vehicles	..	..	..	..	..	..	..	..	..	..
5213 Paid in respect of other goods	..	..	..	..	..	..	..	..	..	..
5220 Non-recurrent taxes	..	..	..	..	..	..	..	..	..	..
5300 Unallocable between 5100 and 5200	..	0	0	0	0	0	0	0	0	0
6000 Other taxes	**..**	**1 259**	**1 698**	**2 706**	**3 307**	**4 342**	**5 248**	**6 097**	**5 876**	**6 045**
6100 Paid solely by business	..	0	0	0	0	0	0	0	0	0
6200 Other	..	1 259	1 698	2 706	3 307	4 342	5 248	6 097	5 876	6 045

Note: Data are on a fiscal year basis ending 31st March. For example, the data for 2016 represent the period from 01 April 2016 to 31 March 2017.
The data are on a cash basis.
Heading 2000: There are no social security contributions in Singapore.
Heading 4100: Recurrent taxes on immovable property include tax levied on all private properties, as well as properties owned by statutory boards.
Heading 5121: Comprises excises, customs and import duties.
Source: Ministry of Finance of Singapore.

StatLink https://doi.org/10.1787/888933854421

Table 4.14. **Solomon Islands**

Details of tax revenue

Million SBD

	1997	2000	2007	2010	2011	2012	2013	2014	2015	2016
Total tax revenue	..	..	**482**	**1 376**	**1 812**	**2 053**	**2 189**	**2 269**	**2 392**	**2 361**
1000 Taxes on income, profits and capital gains	..	..	**189**	**418**	**468**	**564**	**642**	**622**	**719**	**690**
1100 Of individuals	..	..	141	280	325	377	403	404	437	411
1110 On income and profits	..	..	141	280	325	377	403	404	437	411
1120 On capital gains	..	..	..	..	..	..	..	..	..	..
1200 Corporate	..	..	48	137	143	186	239	218	283	278
1210 On profits	..	..	48	137	143	186	239	218	283	278
Dividend Withholding Tax (WHT)	..	..	14	41	45	54	87	74	118	106
Non-resident WHT	..	..	16	43	52	56	75	63	71	68
Resident WHT	..	..	19	53	46	76	78	81	94	105
1220 On capital gains of corporates	..	..	..	..	..	..	..	..	..	..
1300 Unallocable between 1100 and 1200	..	..	0	0	0	0	0	0	0	0
2000 Social security contributions	..	..	**0**	**0**	**0**	**0**	**0**	**0**	**0**	**0**
2100 Employees	..	..	..	..	..	..	..	..	..	..
2110 On a payroll basis	..	..	..	..	..	..	..	..	..	..
2120 On an income tax basis	..	..	..	..	..	..	..	..	..	..
2200 Employers	..	..	..	..	..	..	..	..	..	..
2210 On a payroll basis	..	..	..	..	..	..	..	..	..	..
2220 On an income tax basis	..	..	..	..	..	..	..	..	..	..
2300 Self-employed or non-employed	..	..	..	..	..	..	..	..	..	..
2310 On a payroll basis	..	..	..	..	..	..	..	..	..	..
2320 On an income tax basis	..	..	..	..	..	..	..	..	..	..
2400 Unallocable between 2100, 2200 and 2300	..	..	..	..	..	..	..	..	..	..
2410 On a payroll basis	..	..	..	..	..	..	..	..	..	..
2420 On an income tax basis	..	..	..	..	..	..	..	..	..	..
3000 Taxes on payroll and workforce	..	..	**0**	**0**	**0**	**0**	**0**	**0**	**0**	**0**
4000 Taxes on property	..	..	**9**	**8**	**18**	**9**	**11**	**14**	**19**	**17**
4100 Recurrent taxes on immovable property	..	..	0	0	0	0	0	0	0	0
4110 Households	..	..	..	..	..	..	..	..	..	..
4120 Others	..	..	..	..	..	..	..	..	..	..
4200 Recurrent taxes on net wealth	..	..	0	0	0	0	0	0	0	0
4210 Individual	..	..	..	..	..	..	..	..	..	..
4220 Corporate	..	..	..	..	..	..	..	..	..	..
4300 Estate, inheritance and gift taxes	..	..	0	0	0	0	0	0	0	0
4310 Estate and inheritance taxes	..	..	..	..	..	..	..	..	..	..
4320 Gift taxes	..	..	..	..	..	..	..	..	..	..
4400 Taxes on financial and capital transactions	..	..	9	8	18	9	11	14	19	17
4500 Other non-reccurrent taxes on property	..	..	0	0	0	0	0	0	0	0
4510 On net wealth	..	..	..	..	..	..	..	..	..	..
4520 Other non-recurrent taxes	..	..	..	..	..	..	..	..	..	..
4600 Other recurrent taxes on property	..	..	0	0	0	0	0	0	0	0
5000 Taxes on goods and services	..	..	**283**	**951**	**1 326**	**1 480**	**1 536**	**1 633**	**1 654**	**1 655**
5100 Taxes on production, sale, transfer, etc	..	..	283	944	1 318	1 472	1 527	1 619	1 638	1 638
5110 General taxes on goods and services	..	..	283	458	620	696	734	747	721	682
5111 Value added taxes	..	..	0	0	0	0	0	0	0	0
5112 Sales tax	..	..	283	458	620	696	734	747	721	682
5113 Other	..	..	0	0	0	0	0	0	0	0
5120 Taxes on specific goods and services	..	..	0	486	698	775	793	872	917	956
5121 Excises	..	..	0	106	132	150	138	158	144	158
Tobacco	..	..	0	59	77	93	79	96	89	95
Beer	..	..	0	34	47	54	55	59	49	56
Spirits	..	..	0	12	8	3	3	4	6	7
Other	..	..	0	0	0	0	0	0	0	0
5122 Profits of fiscal monopolies	..	..	0	0	0	0	0	0	0	0
5123 Customs and import duties	..	..	0	136	186	202	229	217	214	215
5124 Taxes on exports	..	..	0	245	380	423	426	496	560	582
Export duty on minerals	..	..	0	2	6	13	11	6	1	2
Export duty on shells	..	..	0	1	1	3	1	1	1	0
Export duty on fish	..	..	0	2	2	2	1	1	1	1
Export duty on timber/log	..	..	0	240	369	404	409	487	469	579
Export duty on other products	..	..	0	0	2	0	4	2	88	1
5125 Taxes on investment goods	..	..	0	0	0	0	0	0	0	0
5126 Taxes on specific services	..	..	0	0	0	0	0	0	0	0
5127 Other taxes on internat. trade and transactions	..	..	0	0	0	0	0	0	0	0

Table 4.14. **Solomon Islands** *(cont.)*

Details of tax revenue

Million SBD

	1997	2000	2007	2010	2011	2012	2013	2014	2015	2016
5128 Other taxes	..	..	0	0	0	0	0	0	0	0
5130 Unallocable between 5110 and 5120	..	..	0	0	0	0	0	0	0	0
5200 Taxes on use of goods and to perform activities	..	..	0	7	8	8	9	14	16	17
5210 Recurrent taxes	..	..	..	7	8	8	9	14	16	17
5211 Paid by households: motor vehicles	..	..	..	0	0	0	0	0	0	0
5212 Paid by others: motor vehicles	..	..	..	0	0	0	0	0	0	0
5213 Paid in respect of other goods	..	..	..	7	8	8	9	14	16	17
5220 Non-recurrent taxes	..	..	..	0	0	0	0	0	0	0
5300 Unallocable between 5100 and 5200	..	..	0	0	0	0	0	0	0	0
6000 Other taxes	..	..	**0**	**0**	**0**	**0**	**0**	**0**	**0**	**0**
6100 Paid solely by business	..	..	..	..	..	..	..	..	..	..
6200 Other	..	..	..	..	..	..	..	..	..	..

Note: Year ending 31st December.

The data are on a cash basis.

Figures exclude tax revenues collected by sub-national governments as the data are not available.

Some revenues (e.g. customs fees, penalties) amounting to about 1 million in 2016 are considered as non-tax revenues according to the OECD classification, described in the Interpretative Guide in Annex A. The national classification of Solomon Islands classifies these revenues as tax revenues.

Heading 5123: the data for 2008 are estimated as they are not available.

Source: Ministry of Finance and Treasury of the Solomon Islands.

StatLink https://doi.org/10.1787/888933854440

Table 4.15. **Thailand**

Details of tax revenue

Million THB

	1997	2000	2007	2010	2011	2012	2013	2014	2015	2016
Total tax revenue	..	**740 147**	**1 553 133**	**1 870 452**	**2 104 237**	**2 174 559**	**2 484 530**	**2 410 488**	**2 566 481**	**2 595 796**
1000 Taxes on income, profits and capital gains	..	**235 421**	**614 883**	**682 860**	**852 749**	**863 268**	**943 208**	**881 591**	**895 205**	**894 058**
1100 Of individuals	..	87 420	177 205	187 687	214 273	240 984	267 979	237 147	268 290	283 003
1110 On income and profits	..	..	..	..	..	..	..	..	..	..
1120 On capital gains	..	..	..	..	..	..	..	..	..	..
1200 Corporate	..	148 001	437 678	495 173	638 477	622 285	675 229	644 444	626 915	611 055
1210 On profits	..	..	..	..	..	..	..	..	..	..
1220 On capital gains of corporates	..	..	..	..	..	..	..	..	..	..
1300 Unallocable between 1100 and 1200	..	0	0	0	0	0	0	0	0	0
2000 Social security contributions	..	**27 073**	**79 809**	**132 394**	**98 342**	**103 205**	**103 112**	**128 174**	**144 803**	**145 693**
2100 Employees	..	12 704	37 717	0	0	49 733	46 633	58 031	66 027	68 574
2110 On a payroll basis	..	..	..	..	..	..	..	..	..	..
2120 On an income tax basis	..	..	..	..	..	..	..	..	..	..
2200 Employers	..	14 369	40 567	127 844	94 552	49 733	51 761	63 615	70 103	72 714
2210 On a payroll basis	..	..	..	..	..	..	..	..	..	..
2220 On an income tax basis	..	..	..	..	..	..	..	..	..	..
2300 Self-employed or non-employed	..	0	1 525	4 549	3 790	3 739	4 718	6 528	8 674	4 405
2310 On a payroll basis	..	..	..	..	..	..	..	..	..	..
2320 On an income tax basis	..	..	..	..	..	..	..	..	..	..
2400 Unallocable between 2100, 2200 and 2300	..	0	0	0	0	0	0	0	0	0
2410 On a payroll basis	..	..	..	..	..	..	..	..	..	..
2420 On an income tax basis	..	..	..	..	..	..	..	..	..	..
3000 Taxes on payroll and workforce	..	**0**	**0**	**0**	**0**	**0**	**0**	**0**	**0**	**0**
4000 Taxes on property	..	**16 283**	**18 317**	**24 666**	**42 872**	**48 787**	**57 579**	**62 627**	**68 157**	**60 364**
4100 Recurrent taxes on immovable property	..	9 094	18 317	24 592	17 255	22 387	23 749	32 396	33 530	33 751
4110 Households	..	..	..	..	..	..	..	..	..	..
4120 Others	..	..	..	..	..	..	..	..	..	..
4200 Recurrent taxes on net wealth	..	0	0	74	0	0	0	0	0	0
4210 Individual	..	..	..	..	..	..	..	..	..	..
4220 Corporate	..	..	..	..	..	..	..	..	..	..
4300 Estate, inheritance and gift taxes	..	0	0	0	0	0	0	0	0	0
4310 Estate and inheritance taxes	..	..	..	..	..	..	..	..	..	..
4320 Gift taxes	..	..	..	..	..	..	..	..	..	..
4400 Taxes on financial and capital transactions	..	7 189	0	0	25 617	26 400	33 830	30 231	34 627	26 613
4500 Other non-reccurrent taxes on property	..	0	0	0	0	0	0	0	0	0
4510 On net wealth	..	..	..	..	..	..	..	..	..	..
4520 Other non-recurrent taxes	..	..	..	..	..	..	..	..	..	..
4600 Other recurrent taxes on property	..	0	0	0	0	0	0	0	0	0
5000 Taxes on goods and services	..	**457 826**	**829 490**	**1 016 829**	**1 097 212**	**1 145 801**	**1 364 636**	**1 322 691**	**1 440 639**	**1 477 287**
5100 Taxes on production, sale, transfer, etc	..	444 986	808 624	990 052	1 069 279	1 114 508	1 231 644	1 182 176	1 262 437	1 312 202
5110 General taxes on goods and services	..	171 113	319 655	388 856	440 648	501 104	509 847	527 902	535 121	558 192
5111 Value added taxes	..	169 425	319 655	388 856	437 086	497 022	509 847	527 902	535 121	558 192
5112 Sales tax	..	1 688	0	0	3 561	4 083	0	0	0	0
5113 Other	..	0	0	0	0	0	0	0	0	0
5120 Taxes on specific goods and services	..	273 873	488 969	601 197	628 631	613 403	721 797	654 274	727 316	754 010
5121 Excises	..	180 884	351 498	478 257	488 496	451 003	554 499	480 479	559 388	589 363
5122 Profits of fiscal monopolies	..	5 310	8 210	4 879	4 879	5 664	3 458	9 869	8 106	5 148
5123 Customs and import duties	..	84 902	87 440	92 675	99 111	115 328	109 788	105 270	100 156	97 400
5124 Taxes on exports	..	2 329	4 164	168	239	320	252	267	202	103
5125 Taxes on investment goods	..	0	0	0	0	0	0	0	0	0
5126 Taxes on specific services	..	448	37 657	25 218	35 906	41 089	53 801	58 388	59 463	61 996
5127 Other taxes on internat. trade and transactions	..	0	0	0	0	0	0	0	0	0
5128 Other taxes	..	0	0	0	0	0	0	0	0	0
5130 Unallocable between 5110 and 5120	..	0	0	0	0	0	0	0	0	0
5200 Taxes on use of goods and to perform activities	..	12 840	20 866	26 777	27 933	31 294	132 992	140 515	178 202	165 084
5210 Recurrent taxes	..	..	..	..	..	..	..	..	..	..
5211 Paid by households: motor vehicles	..	..	..	..	..	..	..	..	..	..
5212 Paid by others: motor vehicles	..	..	..	..	..	..	..	..	..	..
5213 Paid in respect of other goods	..	..	..	..	..	..	..	..	..	..
5220 Non-recurrent taxes	..	..	..	..	..	..	..	..	..	..
5300 Unallocable between 5100 and 5200	..	0	0	0	0	0	0	0	0	0
6000 Other taxes	..	**3 544**	**10 634**	**13 703**	**13 062**	**13 498**	**15 995**	**15 405**	**17 677**	**18 394**
6100 Paid solely by business	..	..	..	..	..	..	..	..	..	..
6200 Other	..	..	..	..	..	..	..	..	..	..

Note: Data are on a fiscal year basis ending 30th September. For example, the data for 2016 represent the period from 01 October 2015 to 30 September 2016.

The data are on a cash basis.

Tax revenues submitted by the Ministry of Finance for 2000-2012 are based on data gathered by the IMF.

Source: Ministry of Finance in Thailand.

StatLink https://doi.org/10.1787/888933854459

Table 4.16. **Tokelau**

Details of tax revenue

Thousand NZD

	1997	2000	2007	2010	2011	2012	2013	2014	2015	2016
Total tax revenue	..	..	**1 198**	**1 694**	**1 594**	**1 620**	**1 865**	**2 107**	**2 151**	**2 176**
1000 Taxes on income, profits and capital gains	..	..	**573**	**866**	**856**	**901**	**1 076**	**1 014**	**1 100**	**1 188**
1100 Of individuals	..	..	573	866	856	901	1 076	1 014	1 100	1 188
1110 On income and profits	..	..	..	..	..	..	..	..	..	..
1120 On capital gains	..	..	..	..	..	..	..	..	..	..
1200 Corporate	..	..	0	0	0	0	0	0	0	0
1210 On profits	..	..	..	..	..	..	..	..	..	..
1220 On capital gains of corporates	..	..	..	..	..	..	..	..	..	..
1300 Unallocable between 1100 and 1200	..	..	0	0	0	0	0	0	0	0
2000 Social security contributions	..	..	**0**	**0**	**0**	**0**	**0**	**0**	**0**	**0**
2100 Employees	..	..	..	..	..	..	..	..	..	..
2110 On a payroll basis	..	..	..	..	..	..	..	..	..	..
2120 On an income tax basis	..	..	..	..	..	..	..	..	..	..
2200 Employers	..	..	..	..	..	..	..	..	..	..
2210 On a payroll basis	..	..	..	..	..	..	..	..	..	..
2220 On an income tax basis	..	..	..	..	..	..	..	..	..	..
2300 Self-employed or non-employed	..	..	..	..	..	..	..	..	..	..
2310 On a payroll basis	..	..	..	..	..	..	..	..	..	..
2320 On an income tax basis	..	..	..	..	..	..	..	..	..	..
2400 Unallocable between 2100, 2200 and 2300	..	..	..	..	..	..	..	..	..	..
2410 On a payroll basis	..	..	..	..	..	..	..	..	..	..
2420 On an income tax basis	..	..	..	..	..	..	..	..	..	..
3000 Taxes on payroll and workforce	..	..	**0**	**0**	**0**	**0**	**0**	**0**	**0**	**0**
4000 Taxes on property	..	..	**0**	**0**	**0**	**0**	**0**	**0**	**0**	**0**
4100 Recurrent taxes on immovable property	..	..	..	..	..	..	..	..	..	..
4110 Households	..	..	..	..	..	..	..	..	..	..
4120 Others	..	..	..	..	..	..	..	..	..	..
4200 Recurrent taxes on net wealth	..	..	..	..	..	..	..	..	..	..
4210 Individual	..	..	..	..	..	..	..	..	..	..
4220 Corporate	..	..	..	..	..	..	..	..	..	..
4300 Estate, inheritance and gift taxes	..	..	..	..	..	..	..	..	..	..
4310 Estate and inheritance taxes	..	..	..	..	..	..	..	..	..	..
4320 Gift taxes	..	..	..	..	..	..	..	..	..	..
4400 Taxes on financial and capital transactions	..	..	..	..	..	..	..	..	..	..
4500 Other non-reccurrent taxes on property	..	..	..	..	..	..	..	..	..	..
4510 On net wealth	..	..	..	..	..	..	..	..	..	..
4520 Other non-recurrent taxes	..	..	..	..	..	..	..	..	..	..
4600 Other recurrent taxes on property	..	..	..	..	..	..	..	..	..	..
5000 Taxes on goods and services	..	..	**625**	**828**	**738**	**719**	**789**	**1 093**	**1 051**	**988**
5100 Taxes on production, sale, transfer, etc	..	..	625	828	738	719	789	1 093	1 051	988
5110 General taxes on goods and services	..	..	0	0	0	0	0	0	0	0
5111 Value added taxes	..	..	..	..	..	..	..	..	..	..
5112 Sales tax	..	..	..	..	..	..	..	..	..	..
5113 Other	..	..	..	..	..	..	..	..	..	..
5120 Taxes on specific goods and services	..	..	625	828	738	719	789	1 093	1 051	988
5121 Excises	..	..	624	827	736	718	767	1 091	1 050	984
Duty On Tobacco	..	..	258	379	342	416	395	600	558	539
Duty On Liqour	..	..	178	222	186	118	212	288	288	251
Duty On General Goods : resale	..	..	188	226	208	184	160	203	204	194
5122 Profits of fiscal monopolies	..	..	0	0	0	0	0	0	0	0
5123 Customs and import duties	..	..	0	0	0	0	0	0	0	0
5124 Taxes on exports	..	..	0	0	0	0	0	0	0	0
5125 Taxes on investment goods	..	..	0	0	0	0	0	0	0	0
5126 Taxes on specific services	..	..	1	1	2	1	22	2	1	4
5127 Other taxes on internat. trade and transactions	..	..	0	0	0	0	0	0	0	0
5128 Other taxes	..	..	0	0	0	0	0	0	0	0
5130 Unallocable between 5110 and 5120	..	..	0	0	0	0	0	0	0	0
5200 Taxes on use of goods and to perform activities	..	..	0	0	0	0	0	0	0	0
5210 Recurrent taxes	..	..	..	..	..	..	..	..	..	..
5211 Paid by households: motor vehicles	..	..	..	..	..	..	..	..	..	..
5212 Paid by others: motor vehicles	..	..	..	..	..	..	..	..	..	..
5213 Paid in respect of other goods	..	..	..	..	..	..	..	..	..	..
5220 Non-recurrent taxes	..	..	..	..	..	..	..	..	..	..
5300 Unallocable between 5100 and 5200	..	..	0	0	0	0	0	0	0	0

Table 4.16. **Tokelau** *(cont.)*

Details of tax revenue

Thousand NZD

	1997	2000	2007	2010	2011	2012	2013	2014	2015	2016
6000 Other taxes	..	..	**0**	**0**	**0**	**0**	**0**	**0**	**0**	**0**
6100 Paid solely by business	..	..	..	..	..	..	..	..	..	..
6200 Other	..	..	..	..	..	..	..	..	..	..

Note: Data are reported on a fiscal year basis beginning 1st July. For example, the data for 2016 represent the period from July 2016 to June 2017.
The data are on a cash basis.

Source: National Statistics Office of Tokelau.

StatLink https://doi.org/10.1787/888933854478

Chapter 5

Country tables, non-tax revenues 2007-16

Table 5.1. **Total non-tax revenue as percentage of GDP in selected Pacific economies, 2007-16**

	2007	2008	2009	2010	2011	2012	2013	2014	2015	2016
Cook Islands	5.5	5.1	9.0	12.8	8.0	8.2	14.1	16.8	9.0	11.5
Papua New Guinea	4.0	4.1	3.5	4.7	3.3	3.1	2.4	3.1	3.1	2.9
Samoa[1]	7.8	10.0	3.6	9.3	5.8	4.6	6.7	4.8	4.9	4.8
Tokelau[2]	149.3	157.6	165.2	154.6	196.4	192.6	246.6	173.4	252.5	236.5

Note: Figures exclude non-tax revenues collected by sub-national governments as the data are not available.
1. The data prior to 2009 are reported on a different basis (for more information see Table 5.7).
2. Tokelau receives significant revenues from foreign vessels for access to Tokelau fishing waters. In the 2008 SNA, these revenues are recorded as part of GNI, but they do not add to GDP.

StatLink https://doi.org/10.1787/888933854497

Table 5.2. **Non-tax revenue of main headings as percentage of GDP in selected Pacific economies, 2016**

	Grants	Property income	Sales of goods and services	Fines, penalties and forfeits	Miscellaneous and unidentified revenue
Cook Islands	4.6	5.1	0.6	0.1	1.2
Papua New Guinea	2.0	0.7	0.0	0.0	0.1
Samoa[1]	2.0	0.3	2.0	0.5	0.0
Tokelau[2]	80.9	150.6	5.0	0.0	0.0

Note: Figures exclude non-tax revenues collected by sub-national governments as the data are not available.
1. The data prior to 2009 are reported on a different basis (for more information see Table 5.7).
2. Tokelau receives significant revenues from foreign vessels for access to Tokelau fishing waters. In the 2008 SNA, these revenues are recorded as part of GNI, but they do not add to GDP.

StatLink https://doi.org/10.1787/888933853737

Table 5.3. **Non-tax revenue of main headings as percentage of total non-tax revenues in selected Pacific economies, 2016**

	Grants	Property income	Sales of goods and services	Fines, penalties and forfeits	Miscellaneous and unidentified revenue
Cook Islands	39.7	44.2	5.0	1.1	10.0
Papua New Guinea	69.3	25.6	0.0	0.0	5.1
Samoa	40.9	6.4	41.4	11.4	0.0
Tokelau	34.2	63.7	2.1	0.0	0.0

Note: Figures exclude non-tax revenues collected by sub-national governments as the data are not available.

StatLink https://doi.org/10.1787/888933853756

Table 5.4. **Total non-tax revenue in selected Pacific economies in millions of US dollars at market exchange rates**

	2007	2008	2009	2010	2011	2012	2013	2014	2015	2016
Cook Islands	12.9	12.3	19.8	33.1	23.2	24.6	43.2	55.0	26.0	33.7
Papua New Guinea	381.7	475.8	407.3	671.6	588.5	657.6	513.0	718.5	703.0	658.8
Samoa	46.0	65.8	20.6	61.8	44.1	36.8	54.7	39.8	40.4	38.2
Tokelau	9.2	10.5	9.9	10.7	15.9	16.5	23.3	17.8	25.1	24.5

Note: This table is derived by dividing the total non-tax revenue figures for each country (in millions of national currency) by the exchange rate figures shown in Table 3.19.

StatLink https://doi.org/10.1787/888933854516

Table 5.5. Cook Islands

Details of non-tax revenue

Thousand NZD

	2007	2008	2009	2010	2011	2012	2013	2014	2015	2016
Total non-tax revenue	**17 586**	**17 270**	**31 279**	**45 942**	**29 270**	**30 322**	**52 704**	**66 251**	**37 097**	**48 379**
Grants	5 034	6 003	12 807	22 411	16 808	17 908	32 018	44 449	12 000	19 214
Crown Aid Revenue	0	0	0	0	0	0	0	0	1 000	1 877
OIDGF Aid Fund	177	109	348	306	1	0	27 374	22 619	5 000	7 730
NZODA Revenue	4 097	4 907	10 412	20 123	15 617	15 508	0	8 645	0	0
AusAid Revenue	0	0	0	0	0	0	0	0	0	0
UNESCO Revenue	65	47	48	0	0	1	86	87	0	0
UNDP Revenue	223	607	220	619	301	424	507	1 122	0	0
EU Revenue	22	0	78	179	187	91	1 929	955	0	0
Other	450	334	1 702	1 183	701	1 884	2 121	11 021	6 000	9 607
Property income	9 768	7 219	7 421	9 327	8 542	8 994	10 839	15 613	11 307	21 366
Rents and royalties	595	1 091	2 844	3 528	3 872	4 877	5 503	10 887	7 714	18 057
Fishing Licences	595	1 091	2 844	3 528	3 872	4 196	1 855	8 064	7 714	14 197
Fisheries Catch Revenue	0	0	0	0	0	0	2 877	1 777	0	2 312
Fisheries - US Treaties	0	0	0	0	0	681	771	1 046	0	1 548
Interest and dividends	9 173	6 128	4 577	5 800	4 670	4 117	5 336	4 725	3 593	3 309
Dividend Income	2 350	2 948	2 328	2 672	2 099	2 060	0	0	0	0
Interest Income (Crown Accounts)	3 795	3 114	2 183	3 100	2 547	2 058	2 145	1 820	1 673	2 140
Interest Inc from SOE Advances	69	66	65	28	24	0	707	976	1 102	787
Other dividends	2 958	0	0	0	0	0	2 484	1 929	818	382
Other property income	0	0	0	0	0	0	0	0	0	0
Sales of goods and services	2 157	2 409	3 015	2 843	2 813	2 477	2 450	3 347	3 497	2 401
Immigration Fees	495	512	509	496	562	534	663	656	715	886
Financial Supervisory Comm	325	177	732	605	486	279	303	899	917	324
Numismatic Revenue	386	517	515	457	439	400	274	501	600	354
Drivers Licence Fees	403	677	717	718	715	557	452	125	292	87
Censorship Fees	0	29	19	12	10	8	6	5	2	2
Upper Air Space Fees	354	361	392	442	463	506	460	985	545	545
Other fees	193	136	131	112	138	193	294	175	426	203
Fines, penalties and forfeits	81	118	131	72	59	39	35	1 249	23	553
Miscellaneous and unidentified revenue	545	1 521	7 905	11 289	1 048	904	7 362	1 594	10 271	4 844
Total tax and non-tax revenue	95 898	97 295	121 912	137 041	117 400	129 502	145 167	156 817	154 494	174 373

Note: Data are reported on a fiscal year basis beginning 1st July. For example, the data for 2016 represent the period from July 2016 to June 2017.
The data are on a cash basis.
Figures exclude tax revenues collected by sub-national governments as the data are not available.
Source: Ministry of Finance and Economic Management of the Cook Islands.

StatLink https://doi.org/10.1787/888933854535

Table 5.6. Papua New Guinea

Details of non-tax revenue

Million PGK

	2007	2008	2009	2010	2011	2012	2013	2014	2015	2016
Total non-tax revenue	**1 132**	**1 285**	**1 122**	**1 826**	**1 395**	**1 370**	**1 151**	**1 768**	**1 946**	**2 064**
Grants	721	1 002	878	1 391	1 045	1 091	878	868	820	1 430
Property income	291	189	145	341	253	172	55	666	911	529
Rents and royalties	0	0	0	0	0	0	0	0	0	0
Interest and dividends	291	189	145	341	253	172	55	666	911	529
Dividends	65	26	0	40	49	50	55	152	455	228
Mining and Petroleum Dividends	226	163	138	299	191	122	0	514	456	301
SWF Receipts	0	0	0	0	0	0	0	0	0	0
Interests and fees from lending	1	1	7	1	13	0	0	0	0	0
Other property income	0	0	0	0	0	0	0	0	0	0
Sales of goods and services	0	0	0	0	0	0	0	0	0	0
Fines, penalties and forfeits	0	0	0	0	0	0	0	0	0	0
Miscellaneous and unidentified revenue	120	93	100	95	98	106	219	235	215	105
Total tax and non-tax revenue	7 007	7 141	6 213	8 399	9 921	9 773	9 925	12 047	11 088	10 670

Note: Year ending 31st December.
The data are on a cash basis.
Figures exclude non-tax revenues collected by sub-national governments as the data are not available.
Source: Ministry of Treasury and Finance of Papua New Guinea.

StatLink https://doi.org/10.1787/888933854554

Table 5.7. **Samoa**

Details of non-tax revenue

Million WST

	2007	2008	2009	2010	2011	2012	2013	2014	2015	2016
Total non-tax revenue	**125**	**167**	**59**	**157**	**105**	**85**	**125**	**92**	**98**	**100**
Grants	77	111	14	105	49	48	82	41	45	41
Property income	24	31	15	8	18	4	3	11	7	6
Rents and royalties	24	31	1	1	1	1	1	1	1	1
Interest and dividends	0	0	15	7	18	3	2	11	6	6
Other property income	0	0	0	0	0	0	0	0	0	0
Sales of goods and services	23	25	17	31	23	19	23	33	37	41
Administrative fees	..	..	..	28	19	13	15	23	26	28
Incidental sales by nonmarket establishments	..	..	..	2	5	6	8	10	11	13
Fines, penalties and forfeits	0	0	2	1	1	2	3	7	8	11
Miscellaneous and unidentified revenue	0	0	10	11	13	12	15	0	0	0
Total tax and non-tax revenue	455	492	411	498	464	488	552	532	593	614

.. Not available

Note: Data are reported on a fiscal year basis beginning 1st July. For example, the data for 2016 represent the period from July 2016 to June 2017.

The data are on a cash basis.

Figures exclude non-tax revenues collected by sub-national governments as the data are not available.

The data from 2009 were provided on the basis of the IMF's GFSM 2014 classification. Prior to this year, data were provided on a different basis. The differences between the two sets of data are indicated below for the relevant non-tax revenue categories.

Heading Grants: Data from 2009 include only cash grants whereas data prior to that year also include aid-funded projects.

Heading Sales of Goods and Services: Data from 2009 exclude fisheries' licences currently included in tax revenues under Heading "5126 taxes on specific services" (more information can be found in Table 4.12) . Fisheries' licences revenues are usually classified as non-tax revenues according to the OECD classification set out in Annex A of the Interpretative Guide.

Source: Bureau of Statistics of Samoa.

StatLink https://doi.org/10.1787/888933854573

Table 5.8. **Tokelau**

Details of non-tax revenue

Thousand NZD

	2007	2008	2009	2010	2011	2012	2013	2014	2015	2016
Total non-tax revenue	**12 537**	**14 704**	**15 582**	**14 836**	**20 129**	**20 402**	**28 361**	**21 424**	**35 911**	**35 088**
Grants	10 508	12 858	13 899	13 115	14 680	11 700	20 293	12 354	12 000	12 000
New Zealand Budgetary Grants	10 508	12 858	13 899	13 115	14 680	11 700	20 283	12 305	12 000	12 000
External donor funding	0	0	0	0	0	0	10	49	0	0
Property income	1 478	1 225	1 162	1 051	4 668	7 915	7 244	8 363	23 139	22 340
Rents and royalties	1 257	1 043	1 081	955	4 578	7 864	7 188	8 067	23 039	21 866
Tokelau EEZ Revenues (Others)	872	1 008	1 072	426	2 311	480	662	1 059	2 746	0
Fishing Licenses - Tokelau EEZ	309	35	0	232	223	3 402	2 428	1 587	14 790	114
FFA : US Tuna Treaty - Tokelau Shares	76	0	9	297	2 044	3 982	4 098	5 421	5 503	21 752
Interest and dividends	221	182	81	96	90	51	56	296	100	474
Other property income	0	0	0	0	0	0	0	0	0	0
Sales of goods and services	551	621	521	670	781	787	824	707	772	748
Handicrafts & Tourism (ENDRE)	0	0	0	0	0	0	0	0	154	4
Commemorative coins	0	0	0	0	64	60	30	71	0	0
Stamp sales	0	0	0	0	5	6	7	0	0	0
Transport - Boatfares	159	147	115	117	140	112	151	132	123	174
Transport - Freights Payments	291	374	318	409	329	350	316	397	386	430
Transport - Sale of Assets	0	0	0	1	3	0	8	0	6	10
Charter fees	25	12	0	10	0	0	0	0	0	0
Postage	2	1	2	3	3	2	2	1	1	0
Registry Certificates: Birth & Death	1	2	2	1	1	1	2	2	2	4
Service Fees	19	15	18	45	122	121	25	22	20	37
Miscellaneous Revenues	1	0	0	1	42	61	97	0	0	0
Revenue - Debt Recovery (MISC)	0	0	0	0	0	0	118	0	0	2
Gains - Sale of Assets (Vehicles)	0	0	0	0	0	0	0	0	66	19
House Rental Subsidies	22	39	52	46	46	43	56	66	1	55
Tokelau Savings Bank Passbook Fees	0	0	0	0	0	0	0	1	2	1
Trust Fund Revenue	31	31	14	37	26	31	12	15	11	12
Tokelau Higano: accommodation	..	..	..	..	..	..	..	..	..	..
Fines, penalties and forfeits	0	0	0	0	0	0	0	0	0	0
Miscellaneous and unidentified revenue	0	0	0	0	0	0	0	0	0	0
Total tax and non-tax revenue	13 735	16 207	17 043	16 530	21 723	22 022	30 226	23 531	38 062	37 264

.. Not available

Note: Data are reported on a fiscal year basis beginning 1st July. For example, the data for 2016 represent the period from July 2016 to June 2017.

The data are on a cash basis.

Source: National Statistics Office of Tokelau.

StatLink https://doi.org/10.1787/888933854592

ANNEX A

The OECD Classification of Taxes and Interpretative Guide[1]

Table of contents

A.1. The OECD classification of taxes

1. 1000 Taxes on income, profits and capital gains
    - 1100 Taxes on income, profits and capital gains of individuals
        - 1110 On income and profits
        - 1120 On capital gains
    - 1200 Corporate taxes on income, profits and capital gains
        - 1210 On income and profits
        - 1220 On capital gains
    - 1300 Unallocable as between 1100 and 1200
2. 2000 Social security contributions
    - 2100 Employees
        - 2110 On a payroll basis
        - 2120 On an income tax basis
    - 2200 Employers
        - 2210 On a payroll basis
        - 2220 On an income tax basis
    - 2300 Self-employed or non-employed
        - 2310 On a payroll basis
        - 2320 On an income tax basis
    - 2400 Unallocable as between 2100, 2200 and 2300
        - 2410 On a payroll basis
        - 2420 On an income tax basis
3. 3000 Taxes on payroll and workforce
4. 4000 Taxes on property
    - 4100 Recurrent taxes on immovable property
        - 4110 Households
        - 4120 Other
    - 4200 Recurrent taxes on net wealth
        - 4210 Individual
        - 4220 Corporate
    - 4300 Estate, inheritance and gift taxes
        - 4310 Estate and inheritance taxes
        - 4320 Gift taxes
    - 4400 Taxes on financial and capital transactions
    - 4500 Other non-recurrent taxes on property
        - 4510 On net wealth
        - 4520 Other non-recurrent taxes
    - 4600 Other recurrent taxes on property

5. 5000 Taxes on goods and services

5100 Taxes on production, sale, transfer, leasing and delivery of goods and rendering of services

5110 General taxes

5111 Value added taxes

5112 Sales taxes

5113 Other general taxes on goods and services

5120 Taxes on specific goods and services

5121 Excises

5122 Profits on fiscal monopolies

5123 Customs and import duties

5124 Taxes on exports

5125 Taxes on investment goods

5126 Taxes on specific services

5127 Other taxes on international trade and transactions

5128 Other taxes on specific goods and services

5130 Unallocable as between 5110 and 5120

5200 Taxes on use of goods, or on permission to use goods or perform activities

5210 Recurrent taxes

5211 Paid by households in respect of motor vehicles

5212 Paid by others in respect of motor vehicles

5213 Other recurrent taxes

5220 Non-recurrent taxes

5300 Unallocable as between 5100 and 5200

6. 6000 Other taxes

6100 Paid solely by business

6200 Paid by other than business or unidentifiable

A.2. Coverage

General criteria

1. In the OECD classification the term "taxes" is confined to compulsory unrequited payments to general government. Taxes are unrequited in the sense that benefits provided by government to taxpayers are not normally in proportion to their payments.

2. The term "tax" does not include fines, penalties and compulsory loans paid to government. Borderline cases between tax and non-tax revenues in relation to certain fees and charges are discussed in §11–14.

3. General government consists of the central administration, agencies whose operations are under its effective control, state and local governments and their administrations, certain social security schemes and autonomous governmental entities, excluding public enterprises. This definition of government follows that of the 2008 *System of National Accounts* (SNA).[2] In that publication, the general government sector and its sub-sectors are defined in Chapter 4, paragraphs 4.117 to 4.165.

4. Extra-budgetary units are part of the general government system. These are general government entities with individual budgets that are not fully covered by the main or general budget. These entities operate under the authority or control of a central, state, or local government. Extra-budgetary entities may have their own revenue sources, which may be supplemented by grants (transfers) from the general budget or from other sources. Even though their budgets may be subject to approval by the legislature, similar to that of budgetary accounts, they have discretion over the volume and composition of their spending. Such entities may be established to carry out specific government functions, such as road construction, or the nonmarket production of health or education services. Budgetary arrangements vary widely across countries, and various terms are used to describe these entities, but they are often referred to as "extra-budgetary funds" or "decentralised agencies".

5. Compulsory payments to supra-national bodies and their agencies are no longer included as taxes as from 1998, with some exceptions. However, custom duties collected by EU member states on behalf of the European Union are still identified as memorandum items and included in overall tax revenue amounts in the country tables of the country in which they are collected (See §99). In countries where the church forms part of general government church taxes are included, provided they meet the criteria set out in §1 above. As the data refer to receipts of general government, levies paid to non-government bodies, welfare agencies or social insurance schemes outside general government, trade unions or trade associations, even where such levies are compulsory, are excluded. Compulsory payments to general government earmarked for such bodies are, however, included, provided that the government is not simply acting in an agency capacity.[3] Profits from fiscal monopolies are distinguished from those of other public enterprises and are treated as taxes because they reflect the exercise of the taxing power of the state by the use of monopoly powers (see §65–67), as are profits received by the government from the purchase and sale of foreign exchange at different rates (see §74).

6. Taxes paid by governments (e.g., social security contributions and payroll taxes paid by governments in their capacity as an employer, consumption taxes on their purchases or taxes on their property) are not excluded from the data provided. However, where it is possible to identify the amounts of revenue involved,[4] they are shown in Chapter 4.2 of this Report.

7. The relationship between this classification and that of the System of National Accounts (SNA) is set out in Sections A.9 and A.11 below. Because of the differences between the two classifications, the data shown in national accounts are sometimes calculated or classified differently from the practice set out in this guide. These and other differences are mentioned where appropriate (e.g., in §30 below) but it is not possible to refer to all of them. There may also be some differences between this classification and that employed domestically by certain national administrations (e.g., see §12 below), so that OECD and national statistics data may not always be consistent: any such differences, however, are likely to be very slight in terms of amounts of revenues involved.

Social security contributions

8. Compulsory social security contributions, as defined in §39, and paid to general government, are treated here as tax revenues. Being compulsory payments to general government they clearly resemble taxes. They may, however, differ from other taxes in that the receipt of social security benefits depends, in most countries, upon appropriate contributions having been made, although the size of the benefits is not necessarily related to the amount of the contributions. Better comparability between countries is obtained by treating social security contributions as taxes, but they are listed under a separate heading so that they can be distinguished in any analysis.

9. The strict dividing line between tax revenues (compulsory unrequited payments to general government) and non-tax compulsory payments (NTCPs) (payments that are either requited or made to other institutions) is clearly defined. However, within the range of different compulsory payments to governments existing across countries, it is not always straightforward in practice to decide whether specific payments are either taxes or NTCPs. For example, compulsory pension savings that are controlled by general government and that accumulate on an individual account earning a market return or a rate that compensates for inflation would at first sight be categorised as NTCPs as opposed to taxes. However, even these payments might still be "unrequited" and therefore classify as taxes instead of NTCPs (for example if these pension savings are not paid out when the taxpayer dies before reaching the pension age and the funds are then used to provide a minimum pension to all taxpayers that are insured). These issues result in the social security revenue figures reported for most countries being based on the premise that all types of compulsory payments to general government are judged to some extent to have a re-distributional element. It should be noted that this conclusion is based on a typically broad interpretation of the term "unrequited" in the tax definition.

10. Social security contributions which are either voluntary or not payable to general government (see §1) are not treated as taxes, though in some countries, as indicated in the country footnotes, there are difficulties in completely eliminating voluntary contributions and certain compulsory payments to the private sector from the revenue figures. Imputed social security contributions are also not treated as taxes.

Fees, user charges and licence fees

11. Apart from vehicle licence fees, which are universally regarded as taxes, it is not easy to distinguish between those fees and user charges which are to be treated as taxes and those which are not, since, whilst a fee or charge is levied in connection with a specific service or activity, the strength of the link between the fee and the service provided may vary considerably, as may the relation between the amount of the fee and the cost of

providing the service. Where the recipient of a service pays a fee clearly related to the cost of providing the service, the levy may be regarded as requited and under the definition of §1 would not be considered as a tax. In the following cases, however, a levy could be considered as "unrequited":

a) where the charge greatly exceeds the cost of providing the service;

b) where the payer of the levy is not the receiver of the benefit (e.g., a fee collected from slaughterhouses to finance a service which is provided to farmers);

c) where government is not providing a specific service in return for the levy which it receives even though a licence may be issued to the payer (e.g., where the government grants a hunting, fishing or shooting licence which is not accompanied by the right to use a specific area of government land);

d) where benefits are received only by those paying the levy but the benefits received by each individual are not necessarily in proportion to her/his payments (e.g., a milk marketing levy paid by dairy farmers and used to promote the consumption of milk).

12. In marginal cases, however, the application of the criteria set out in §1 can be particularly difficult. The solution adopted – given the desirability of international uniformity and the relatively small amounts of revenue usually involved – is to follow the predominant practice among tax administrations rather than to allow each country to adopt its own view as to whether such levies are regarded as taxes or as non-tax revenue.[5]

13. A list of the main fees and charges in question and their normal[6] treatment in this publication is as follows:

- *Non-tax revenues:* court fees; driving licence fees; harbour fees; passport fees; radio and television licence fees where public authorities provide the service.
- *Taxes within heading 5200:* permission to perform such activities as distributing films; hunting, fishing and shooting; providing entertainment or gambling facilities; selling alcohol or tobacco; permission to own dogs or to use or own motor vehicles or guns; severance taxes.

14. In practice it may not always be possible to isolate tax receipts from non-tax revenue receipts when they are recorded together. If it is estimated that the bulk of the receipts derive from non-tax revenues, the whole amount involved is treated as a non-tax revenue; otherwise, such government receipts are included and classified according to the rules provided in §32 below.

Royalties

15. The ownership of subsoil assets in the form of deposits of minerals or fossil fuels (coal, oil, or natural gas) depends upon the way in which property rights are defined by law and also on international agreements in the case of deposits below international waters. In some cases, either the ground below which the mineral deposits are located, the deposits themselves or both may belong to a local or central government unit.

16. In such cases, these general government units may grant leases to other institutional units that permit them to extract these deposits over a specified period of time in return for a payment or series of payments. These payments are often described as "royalties" but they are essentially rent that accrues to owners of natural resources in return for putting these assets at the disposal of other units for specified periods of time. The rent may take

the form of periodic payments of fixed amounts, irrespective of the rate of extraction, or, more commonly, they may be a function of the quantity, volume, or value of the asset extracted. Enterprises engaged in exploration on government land may make payments to general government units in exchange for the right to undertake test drilling or otherwise investigate the existence and location of subsoil assets. Such payments are also recorded as rents even though no extraction may take place. These payments are therefore classified as non-tax revenues.

17. The same principles apply when other institutional units are granted leases that permit them to fell timber in natural forests on land owned by general government units. These payments are also classified as non-tax revenues.

18. These rents or royalties paid to general government should not be confused with taxes on income and profits, severance taxes, business licenses, or other taxes. If the payments are levied on the profits from the extraction activity, then they should be classified as taxes on incomes, profits and gains (1000). In addition, any severance payments that are imposed on the extraction of minerals and fossil fuels from reserves owned privately or by another government should be classified as taxes. Payments related to the gross value of production should be classified as other taxes on goods and services (5128). Payments for a license or permit to conduct extraction operations should be classified as taxes on use of goods and on permission to use goods or perform activities (5213).

Fines and penalties

19. In principle, fines and penalties charged on overdue taxes or penalties imposed for the attempted evasion of taxes should not be recorded as tax revenues. However, it may not be possible to separate payments of fines or other penalties from the revenues from the taxes to which they relate. In this case the fines and penalties relating to a particular tax are recorded together with the revenues from that tax and fines and penalties paid with revenue from unidentifiable taxes are classified as other taxes in Category 6000. Fines not relating to tax offences (e.g., for parking offences), or not identifiable as relating to tax offences, are also not treated as tax revenues.

A.3. Basis of reporting

Accrual reporting

20. The data reported in this publication for recent years are predominantly recorded on an accrual basis, i.e. recorded at the time that the tax liability was created. Further information is provided in the footnotes to the country table in Chapter 4 of the Report.

21. However, data for earlier years are still predominantly recorded on a cash basis, i.e. at the time at which the payment was received by government. Thus, for example, taxes withheld by employers in one year but paid to the government in the following year and taxes due in one year but actually paid in the following year are both included in the receipts of the second year. Corrective transactions, such as refunds, repayments and drawbacks, are deducted from gross revenues of the period in which they are made.

22. Data on tax revenues are recorded without offsets for the administrative expenses connected with tax collection. Similarly, where the proceeds of tax are used to subsidise particular members of the community, the subsidy is not deducted from the yield of the tax, though the tax may be shown net of subsidies in the national records of some countries.

23. As regards fiscal monopolies (heading 5122), only the amount actually transferred to the government is included in government revenues. However, if any expenditures of fiscal monopolies are considered to be government expenditures (e.g., social expenditures undertaken by fiscal monopolies at the direction of the government) they are added back for the purpose of arriving at tax revenue figures (see §65 below).

The distinction between tax and expenditure provisions[7]

24. Because this publication is concerned only with the revenue side of government operations, no account being taken of the expenditure side, a distinction has to be made between tax and expenditure provisions. Normally there is no difficulty in making this distinction as expenditures are made outside the tax system and the tax accounts and under legislation separate from the tax legislation. In borderline cases, cash flow is used to distinguish between tax provisions and expenditure provisions. Insofar as a provision affects the flow of tax payments from the taxpayer to the government, it is regarded as a tax provision and is taken into account in the data shown in this publication. A provision which does not affect this flow is seen as an expenditure provision and is disregarded in the data recorded in this publication.

25. Tax allowances, exemptions and deductions against the tax base clearly affect the amount of tax paid to the government and are therefore considered as tax provisions. At the other extreme, those subsidies which cannot be offset against tax liability and which are clearly not connected with the assessment process, do not reduce tax revenues as recorded in this publication. Tax credits are amounts deductible from tax payable (as distinct from deductions from the tax base). Two types of tax credits are distinguished, those (referred to here as wastable tax credits) which are limited to the amount of the tax liability and therefore cannot give rise to a payment by the authorities to the taxpayer, and those (referred to as non-wastable tax credits) which are not so limited, so that the excess of the credit over the tax liability can be paid to the taxpayer.[8] A wastable tax credit, like a tax allowance, clearly affects the amount of tax paid to the government, and is therefore considered as a tax provision. The practice followed for non-wastable tax credits[9] is to distinguish between the "tax expenditure component",[10] which is that portion of the credit that is used to reduce or eliminate a taxpayer's liability, and the "transfer component", which is the portion that exceeds the taxpayer's liability and is paid to that taxpayer. Reported tax revenues should be reduced by the amount of the tax expenditure component but not by the amount of the transfer component. In addition, the amounts of the tax expenditure and transfer components should be reported as memorandum items in the country tables. Countries that are unable to distinguish between the tax expenditure and transfer components should indicate whether or not the tax revenues have been reduced by the total of these components, and provide any available estimates of the amounts of the two components. Further information is given in Chapter 1 of the Report, which illustrates the effect of alternative treatments of non-wastable tax credits on tax to GDP.

Calendar and fiscal years

26. National authorities whose fiscal years do not correspond to the calendar year show data, where possible, on a calendar year basis to permit maximum comparability with the data of other countries. There remain a few countries where data refer to fiscal years. For these the GDP data used in the comparative tables also correspond to the fiscal years.

A.4. General classification criteria

The main classification criteria

27. The classification of receipts among the main headings (1000, 2000, 3000, 4000, 5000 and 6000) is generally governed by the base on which the tax is levied: 1000 income, profits and capital gains; 2000 and 3000 earnings, payroll or number of employees; 4000 property; 5000 goods and services; 6000 multiple bases, other bases or unidentifiable bases. Where a tax is calculated on more than one base, the receipts are, where possible, split among the various headings (see §32 and §81). The headings 4000 and 5000 cover not only taxes where the tax base is the property, goods or services themselves but also certain related taxes. Thus, taxes on the transfer of property are included in 4400[11] and taxes on the use of goods or on permission to perform activities in 5200. In headings 4000 and 5000 a distinction is made in certain sub-headings between recurrent and non-recurrent taxes: recurrent taxes are defined as those levied at regular intervals (usually annually) and non-recurrent taxes are levied once and for all (see also §47 to §50, §53, §54 and §79 for particular applications of this distinction).

28. Earmarking of a tax for specific purposes does not affect the classification of tax receipts. However, as explained in §39 on the classification of social security contributions, the conferment of an entitlement to social benefits is crucial to the definition of the 2000 main heading.

29. The way that a tax is levied or collected (e.g., by use of stamps) does not affect classification.

Classification of taxpayers

30. In certain sub-headings distinctions are made between different categories of taxpayers. These distinctions vary from tax to tax:

a) Between individuals and corporations in relation to income and net wealth taxes

The basic distinction is that corporation income taxes, as distinct from individual income taxes, are levied on the corporation as an entity, not on the individuals who own it, and without regard to the personal circumstances of these individuals. The same distinction applies to net wealth taxes on corporations and those on individuals. Taxes paid on the profits of partnerships and the income of institutions, such as life insurance or pension funds, are classified according to the same rule. They are classified as corporate taxes (1200) if they are charged on the partnership or institution as an entity without regard to the personal circumstances of the owners. Otherwise, they are treated as individual taxes (1100). Usually, there is different legislation for the corporation taxes and for the individual taxes.[12] The distinction made here between individuals and corporations does not follow the sector classification between households, enterprises, and so on of the System of National Accounts (SNA) for income and outlay accounts. The SNA classification requires certain unincorporated businesses[13] to be excluded from the household sector and included with non-financial enterprises and financial institutions. The tax on the profits of these businesses, however, cannot always be separated from the tax on the other income of their owners, or can be separated only on an arbitrary basis. No attempt at this separation is made here and the whole of the individual income tax is shown together without regard to the nature of the income chargeable.

b) Between households and others in relation to taxes on immovable property

Here the distinction is that adopted by the SNA for the production and consumption expenditure accounts. The distinction is between households as consumers (i.e. excluding non-incorporated business) on the one hand and producers on the other hand. However, taxes on dwellings occupied by households, whether paid by owner-occupiers, tenants or landlords, are classified under households. This follows the common distinction made between taxes on domestic property versus taxes on business property. Some countries are not, however, in a position to make this distinction.

c) Between households and others in relation to motor vehicle licences

Here the distinction is between households as consumers on the one hand and producers on the other, as in the production and consumption expenditure accounts of the SNA.

d) Between business and others in relation to the residual taxes (6000)

The distinction is the same as in c) above between producers on the one hand and households as consumers on the other hand. Taxes which are included under the heading 6000 because they involve more than one tax base or because the tax base does not fall within any of the previous categories but which are identifiable as levyable only on producers and not on households are included under "business". The rest of the taxes which are included under the heading 6000 are shown as "other" or non-identified.

Surcharges

31. Receipts from surcharges in respect of particular taxes are usually classified with the receipts from the relevant tax whether or not the surcharge is temporary. If, however, the surcharge has a characteristic which would render it classifiable in a different heading of the OECD list, receipts from the surcharge are classified under that heading separately from the relevant tax.

Unidentifiable tax receipts and residual sub-headings

32. A number of cases arise where taxes cannot be identified as belonging entirely to a heading or sub-heading of the OECD classification and the following practices are applied in such cases:

a) The heading is known, but it is not known how receipts should be allocated between sub-headings: receipts are classified in the appropriate residual sub-heading (1300, 2400, 4520, 4600, 5130, 5300 or 6200).

b) It is known that the bulk of receipts from a group of taxes (usually local taxes) is derived from taxes within a particular heading or sub-heading, but some of the taxes in the group whose amount cannot be precisely ascertained may be classifiable in other headings or sub-headings: receipts are shown in the heading or sub-heading under which most of the receipts fall.

c) Either the heading nor sub-heading of a tax (usually local) can be identified: the tax is classified in 6200 unless it is known that it is a tax on business in which case it is classified in 6100.

A.5. Commentaries on items of the list

1000 — Taxes on income, profits and capital gains

33. This heading covers taxes levied on the net income or profits (i.e. gross income minus allowable tax reliefs) of individuals and enterprises. Also covered are taxes levied on the capital gains of individuals and enterprises, and gains from gambling.

34. Included in the heading are:

a) taxes levied predominantly on income or profits, though partially on other bases. Taxes on various bases which are not predominantly income or profits are classified according to the principles laid down in §32 and §81;

b) taxes on property, which are levied on a presumed or estimated income as part of an income tax (see also §47(a), (c) and (d));

c) compulsory payments to social security fund contributions that are levied on income but do not confer an entitlement to social benefits. When such contributions do confer an entitlement to social benefits, they are included in heading 2000 (see §39);

d) receipts from integrated scheduler income tax systems are classified as a whole in this heading, even though certain of the scheduler taxes may be based upon gross income and may not take into account the personal circumstances of the taxpayer.

35. The main subdivision of this heading is between levies on individuals (1100) and those on corporate enterprises (1200). Under each subdivision a distinction is made between taxes on income and profits (1110 and 1210), and taxes on capital gains (1120 and 1220). If certain receipts cannot be identified as appropriate to either 1100 or 1200, or if in practice this distinction cannot be made (e.g., because there are no reliable data on the recipients of payments from which withholding taxes are deducted) they are classified in 1300 as not-allocable.

Treatment of credits under imputation systems

36. Under imputation systems of corporate income tax, a company's shareholders are wholly or partly relieved of their liability to income tax on dividends paid by the company out of income or profits liable to corporate income tax. In countries with such systems,[14] part of the tax on the company's profits is available to provide relief against the shareholders' own tax liability. The relief to the shareholder takes the form of a tax credit, the amount of which may be less than, equal to, or more than the shareholder's overall tax liability. If the tax credit exceeds this tax liability the excess may be payable to the shareholder. As this type of tax credit is an integral part of the imputation system of corporate income tax, any payment to the shareholders is treated as a repayment of tax and not as expenditure (compare the treatment of other tax credits described in §25).

37. As the tax credit under imputation systems (even when exceeding tax liability) is to be regarded as a tax provision, the question arises whether it should be deducted from individual income tax receipts (1110) or corporate income tax receipts (1210). In this Report, the full amount of corporate income tax paid is shown under 1210 and no imputed tax is included under 1110. Thus, the full amount of the credit reduces the amount of 1110 whether the credit results in a reduction of personal income tax liability or whether an actual refund is made because the credit exceeds the income tax liability. (Where, however, such tax credits are deducted from corporation tax in respect of dividends paid to corporations the amounts are deducted from the receipts of 1210.)

1120 and 1220 — *Taxes on capital gains*

38. These sub-headings comprise taxes imposed on capital gains, 1120 covering those levied on the gains of individuals and 1220 those levied on the gains of corporate enterprises, where receipts from such taxes can be separately identified. In many countries this is not the case and the receipts from such taxes are then classified with those from the income tax. Heading 1120 also includes taxes on gains from gambling.

2000 — *Social security contributions*

39. Classified here are all compulsory payments that confer an entitlement to receive a (contingent) future social benefit. Such payments are usually earmarked to finance social benefits and are often paid to institutions of general government that provide such benefits. However, such earmarking is not part of the definition of social security contributions and is not required for a tax to be classified here. However, conferment of an entitlement is required for a tax to be classified under this heading. So, levies on income or payroll that are earmarked for social security funds but do not confer an entitlement to benefit are excluded from this heading and shown under personal income taxes (1100) or taxes on payroll and workforce (3000). Taxes on other bases, such as goods and services, which are earmarked for social security benefits are not shown here but are classified according to their respective bases because they generally confer no entitlement to social security benefits.

40. Contributions for the following types of social security benefits would, *inter alia*, be included: unemployment insurance benefits and supplements, accident, injury and sickness benefits, old-age, disability and survivors' pensions, family allowances, reimbursements for medical and hospital expenses or provision of hospital or medical services. Contributions may be levied on both employees and employers.

41. Contributions may be based on earnings or payroll ("on a payroll basis") or on net income after deductions and exemptions for personal circumstances ("on an income tax basis"), and the revenues from the two bases should be separately identified if possible. However, where contributions to a general social security scheme are on a payroll basis, but the contributions of particular groups (such as the self-employed) cannot be assessed on this basis and net income is used as a proxy for gross earnings, the receipts may still be classified as being on a payroll basis. In principle, this heading excludes voluntary contributions paid to social security schemes. When separately identifiable these are shown in the memorandum item on the financing of social security benefits. In practice, however, they cannot always be separately identified from compulsory contributions, in which case they are included in this heading.

42. Contributions to social insurance schemes which are not institutions of general government and to other types of insurance schemes, provident funds, pension funds, friendly societies or other saving schemes are not considered as social security contributions. Provident funds are arrangements under which the contributions of each employee and of the corresponding employer on his/her behalf are kept in a separate account earning interest and withdrawable under specific circumstances. Pension funds are separately organised schemes negotiated between employees and employers and carry provisions for different contributions and benefits, sometimes more directly tied to salary levels and length of service than under social security schemes. When contributions to these schemes are compulsory or quasi-compulsory (e.g., by virtue of agreement with professional and union organisations) they are shown in the memorandum item (refer to Chapter 4.2 of the Report).

43. Contributions by government employees and by governments in respect of their employees, to social security schemes classified within general government are included in this heading. Contributions to separate schemes for government employees, which can be regarded as replacing general social security schemes, are also regarded as taxes.[15] Where, however, a separate scheme is not seen as replacing a general scheme and has been negotiated between the government, in its role as an employer, and its employees, it is not regarded as social security and contributions to it are not regarded as taxes, even though the scheme may have been established by legislation.

44. This heading excludes "imputed" contributions, which correspond to social benefits paid directly by employers to their employees or former employees or to their representatives (e.g., when employers are legally obliged to pay sickness benefits for a certain period).

45. Contributions are divided into those of employees (2100), employers (2200), and self-employed or non-employed (2300), and then further sub-divided according to the basis on which they are levied. Employees are defined for this purpose as all persons engaged in activities of business units, government bodies, private non-profit institutions, or other paid employment, except the proprietors and their unpaid family members in the case of unincorporated businesses. Members of the armed forces are included, irrespective of the duration and type of their service, if they contribute to social security schemes. The contributions of employers are defined as their payments on account of their employees to social security schemes. Where employees or employers are required to continue the payment of social security contributions when the employee becomes unemployed these contributions, data permitting, are shown in 2100 and 2200 respectively. Accordingly, the sub-heading 2300 is confined to contributions paid by the self-employed and by those outside of the labour force (e.g., disabled or retired individuals).

3000 — Taxes on payroll and workforce

46. These consist of taxes payable by enterprises assessed either as a proportion of the wages or salaries paid or as a fixed amount per person employed. They do not include compulsory social security contributions paid by employers or any taxes paid by employees themselves out of their wages or salaries.

4000 — Taxes on property

47. This heading covers recurrent and non-recurrent taxes on the use, ownership or transfer of property. These include taxes on immovable property or net wealth, taxes on the change of ownership of property through inheritance or gift and taxes on financial and capital transactions. The following kinds of tax are excluded from this heading:

a) taxes on capital gains resulting from the sale of a property (1120 or 1220);

b) taxes on the use of goods or on permission to use goods or perform activities (5200); see §76;

c) taxes on immovable property levied on the basis of a presumed net income which take into account the personal circumstances of the taxpayer. They are classified as income taxes along with taxes on income and capital gains derived from property (1100);

d) taxes on the use of property for residence, where the tax is payable by either proprietor or tenant and the amount payable is a function of the user's personal circumstances (pay, dependants, and so on). They are classified as taxes on income (1100);

e) taxes on building in excess of permitted maximum density, taxes on the enlargement, construction or alteration of certain buildings beyond a permitted value and taxes on building construction. They are classified as taxes on permission to perform activities (5200);

f) taxes on the use of one's own property for special trading purposes like selling alcohol, tobacco, meat or for exploitation of land resources (e.g., United States severance taxes). They are classified as taxes on permission to perform activities (5200).

4100 — *Recurrent taxes on immovable property*

48. This sub-heading covers taxes levied regularly in respect of the use or ownership of immovable property.

- these taxes are levied on land and buildings;
- they can be in the form of a percentage of an assessed property value based on a national rental income, sales price, or capitalised yield; or in terms of other characteristics of real property (for example size or location) from which a presumed rent or capital value can be derived;
- such taxes can be levied on proprietors, tenants, or both. They can also be paid by one level of government to another level of government in respect of property under the jurisdiction of the latter;
- debts are not taken into account in the assessment of these taxes, and they differ from taxes on net wealth in this respect.

49. Taxes on immovable property are further sub-divided into those paid by households (4110) and those paid by other entities (4120), according to the criteria set out in §30(*b*) above.

4200 — *Recurrent taxes on net wealth*

50. This sub-heading covers taxes levied regularly (in most cases annually) on net wealth, i.e. taxes on a wide range of movable and immovable property, net of debt. It is sub-divided into taxes paid by individuals (4210) and taxes paid by corporate enterprises (4220) according to the criteria set out in §30(*a*) above. If separate figures exist for receipts paid by institutions, the tax payments involved are added to those paid by corporations.

4300 — *Estate, inheritance and gift taxes*

51. This sub-heading is divided into taxes on estates and inheritances (4310) and taxes on gifts (4320).[16] Estate taxes are charged on the amount of the total estate whereas inheritance taxes are charged on the shares of the individual recipients; in addition the latter may take into account the relationship of the individual recipients to the deceased.

4400 — *Taxes on financial and capital transactions*

52. This sub-heading comprises, *inter alia*, taxes on the issue, transfer, purchase and sale of securities, taxes on cheques, and taxes levied on specific legal transactions such as validation of contracts and the sale of immovable property. The heading does not include:

a) taxes on the use of goods or property or permission to perform certain activities (5200);

b) fees paid to cover court charges, charges for birth, marriage or death certificates, which are normally regarded as non-tax revenues (see §11);

c) taxes on capital gains (1000);

d) recurrent taxes on immovable property (4100);

e) recurrent taxes on net wealth (4200);

f) once-and-for-all levies on property or wealth (4500).

4500 — *Other non-recurrent taxes on property*

53. This sub-heading covers once-and-for-all, as distinct from recurrent, levies on property. It is divided into taxes on net wealth (4510) and other non-recurrent taxes on property (4520). Heading 4510 would include taxes levied to meet emergency expenditures, or for redistribution purposes. Heading 4520 would cover taxes levied to take account of increases in land value due to permission given to develop or provision of additional local facilities by general government, any taxes on the revaluation of capital and once-and-for-all taxes on particular items of property.

4600 — *Other recurrent taxes on property*

54. These rarely exist in OECD member countries, but the heading would include taxes on goods such as cattle, jewellery, windows, and other external signs of wealth.

5000 — *Taxes on goods and services*

55. All taxes and duties levied on the production, extraction, sale, transfer, leasing or delivery of goods, and the rendering of services (5100), or in respect of the use of goods or permission to use goods or to perform activities (5200) are included here. The heading thus covers:

a) multi-stage cumulative taxes;

b) general sales taxes – whether levied at manufacture/production, wholesale or retail level;

c) value-added taxes;

d) excises;

e) taxes levied on the import and export of goods;

f) taxes levied in respect of the use of goods and taxes on permission to use goods, or perform certain activities;

g) taxes on the extraction, processing or production of minerals and other products.

56. Borderline cases between this heading and heading 4000 (taxes on property) and 6100 (other taxes on business) are referred to in §47, §52 and §78. Residual sub-headings (5300) and (5130) cover tax receipts which cannot be allocated between 5100 and 5200 and between 5110 and 5120, respectively; see §32.

5100 — *Taxes on the production, sale, transfer, leasing and delivery of goods and rendering of services*

57. This sub-heading consists of all taxes, levied on transactions in goods and services on the basis of their intrinsic characteristics (e.g., value, weight of tobacco, strength of alcohol, and so on) as distinct from taxes imposed on the use of goods, or permission to use goods or perform activities, which fall under 5200.

5110 — *General taxes on goods and services*

58. This sub-heading includes all taxes, other than import and export duties (5123 and 5124), levied on the production, leasing, transfer, delivery or sales of a wide range of goods and/ or the rendering of a wide range of services, irrespective of whether they are domestically produced or imported and irrespective of the stage of production or distribution at which they are levied. It thus covers value-added taxes, sales taxes and multi-stage cumulative taxes. Receipts from border adjustments in respect of such taxes when goods are imported are added to gross receipts for this category, and repayments of such taxes when goods are exported are deducted. These taxes are subdivided into 5111 value-added taxes, 5112 sales taxes, 5113 turnover and other general taxes on goods and services.

59. Borderline cases arise between this heading and taxes on specific goods (5120) when taxes are levied on a large number of goods, for example, the United Kingdom purchase tax (repealed in 1973) and the Japanese commodity tax (repealed in 1988). In conformity with national views, the former United Kingdom purchase tax is classified as a general tax (5112) and the former Japanese commodity tax as excises (5121).

5111 — *Value-added taxes*

60. All general consumption taxes charged on value-added are classified in this sub-heading, irrespective of the method of deduction and the stages at which the taxes are levied. In practice, all OECD countries with value-added taxes normally allow immediate deduction of taxes on purchases by all but the final consumer and impose tax at all stages. In some countries the heading may include certain taxes, such as those on financial and insurance activities, either because receipts from them cannot be identified separately from those from the value-added tax, or because they are regarded as an integral part of the value-added tax, even though similar taxes in other countries might be classified elsewhere (e.g., 5126 as taxes on services or 4400 as taxes on financial and capital transactions).

5112 — *Sales taxes*

61. All general taxes levied at one stage only, whether at manufacturing or production, wholesale or retail stage are classified here.

5113 — *Turnover and other general taxes on goods and services*

62. These are multi-stage cumulative taxes and taxes where elements of consumption taxes are combined with multistage taxes. These taxes are levied each time a transaction takes place without deduction for taxes paid on inputs. Multi-stage taxes can be combined with elements of value-added or sales taxes.

5120 — *Taxes on specific goods and services*

63. Excises, profits generated and transferred from fiscal monopolies, and customs and imports duties as well as taxes on exports, foreign exchange transactions, investment goods and betting stakes and special taxes on services, which do not form part of a general tax of 5110, are included in this category.

5121 — *Excises*

64. Excises are taxes levied as a product specific unit tax on a predefined limited range of goods. Excises are usually levied at differentiated rates on nonessential or luxury goods, alcoholic beverages, tobacco, and energy. Excises may be imposed at any stage of production

or distribution and are usually assessed as a specific charge per unit based on characteristics by reference to the value, weight, strength, or quantity of the product. Included are special taxes on individual products such as sugar, sugar beets, matches, and chocolates; taxes levied at varying rates on a certain range of goods; and taxes levied on tobacco goods, alcoholic drinks, motor fuels, and hydrocarbon oils. If a tax collected principally on imported goods also applies, or would apply, under the same law to comparable domestically produced goods, then the revenue from this tax is classified as arising from excises rather than from import duties. This principle applies even if there is no comparable domestic production or no possibility of such production. Taxes on the use of utilities such as water, electricity, gas, and energy are regarded as excises rather than taxes on specific services (5126). Excises exclude those taxes that are levied as general taxes on goods and services (5110); profits of fiscal monopolies (5122); customs and other import duties (5123); or taxes on exports (5124).

5122 — *Profits of fiscal monopolies*

65. This sub-heading covers that part of the profits of fiscal monopolies which is transferred to general government or which is used to finance any expenditures considered to be government expenditures (see §23). Amounts are shown when they are transferred to general government or used to make expenditures considered to be government expenditures.

66. Fiscal monopolies reflect the exercise of the taxing power of government by the use of monopoly powers. Fiscal monopolies are non-financial public enterprises exercising a monopoly in most cases over the production or distribution of tobacco, alcoholic beverages, salt, matches, playing cards and petroleum or agricultural products (i.e. on the kind of products which are likely to be, alternatively or additionally, subject to the excises of 5121), to raise the government revenues which in other countries are gathered through taxes on dealings in such commodities by private business units. The government monopoly may be at the production stage or, as in the case of government-owned and controlled liquor stores, at the distribution stage.

67. Fiscal monopolies are distinguished from public utilities such as rail transport, electricity, post offices, and other communications, which may enjoy a monopoly or quasi-monopoly position but where the primary purpose is normally to provide basic services rather than to raise revenue for government. Transfers from such other public enterprises to the government are considered as non-tax revenues. The traditional concept of fiscal monopoly is not generally extended to include state lotteries, the profits of which are usually accordingly regarded as non-tax revenues. However, they can be included as tax revenues if the prime reason for their operation is to raise revenues to finance government expenditure. Fiscal monopoly profits are distinguished from export and import monopoly profits (5127) transferred from marketing boards or other enterprises dealing with international trade.

5123 — *Customs and other import duties*

68. Taxes, stamp duties and surcharges restricted by law to imported products are included here. Also included are levies on imported agricultural products which are imposed in member countries of the European Union and amounts paid by certain of these countries under the Monetary Compensation Accounts (MCA) system.[17] Starting from 1998, customs duties collected by European Union member states on behalf of the European Union are no longer reported under this heading in the country tables (in Chapter 4 of the Report). Excluded here are taxes collected on imports as part of a general tax on goods and services, or an excise applicable to both imported and domestically produced goods.

5124 — *Taxes on exports*

69. In the 1970s, export duties were levied in Australia, Canada and Portugal as a regular measure and they have been used in Finland for counter-cyclical purposes. Some member countries of the European Union pay, as part of the MCA system, a levy on exports (see note 16 to §68). Where these amounts are identifiable, they are shown in this heading. This heading does not include repayments of general consumption taxes or excises or customs duties on exported goods, which should be deducted from the gross receipts under 5110, 5121 or 5123, as appropriate.

5125 — *Taxes on investment goods*

70. This sub-heading covers taxes on investment goods, such as machinery. These taxes may be imposed for a number of years or temporarily for counter-cyclical purposes. Taxes on industrial inputs which are also levied on consumers [e.g., the Swedish energy tax which is classified under (5121)] are not included here.

5126 — *Taxes on specific services*

71. All taxes assessed on the payment for specific services, such as taxes on insurance premiums, banking services, gambling and betting stakes (e.g., from horse races, football pools, lottery tickets), transport, entertainment, restaurant and advertising charges, fall into this category. Taxes levied on the gross income of companies providing the service (e.g., gross insurance premiums or gambling stakes received by the company) are also classified under this heading. Tax revenues from bank levies and payments to deposit insurance and financial stability schemes are provisionally included here for the 2012 edition. The detailed classification is set out in §108.

72. Excluded from this sub-heading are:

a) taxes on services forming part of a general tax on goods and services (5110);

b) taxes on electricity, gas and energy (5121 as excises);

c) taxes on individual gains from gambling (1120 as taxes on capital gains of individuals and non-corporate enterprises) and lump-sum taxes on the transfer of private lotteries or on the permission to set up lotteries (5200);[18]

d) taxes on cheques and on the issue, transfer or redemption of securities (4400 as taxes on financial and capital transactions).

5127 — *Other taxes on international trade and transactions*

73. This sub-heading covers revenue received by the government from the purchase and sale of foreign exchange at different rates. When the government exercises monopoly powers to extract a margin between the purchase and sales price of foreign exchange, other than to cover administrative costs, the revenue derived constitutes a compulsory levy exacted in indeterminate proportions from both purchaser and seller of foreign exchange. It is the common equivalent of an import duty and export duty levied in a single exchange rate system or of a tax on the sale or purchase of foreign exchange. Like the profits of fiscal monopolies and import or export monopolies transferred to government, it represents the exercise of monopoly powers for tax purposes and is included in tax revenues.

74. The sub-heading covers also the profits of export or import monopolies, which do not however exist in OECD countries, taxes on purchase or sale of foreign exchange, and any other taxes levied specifically on international trade or transactions.

5128 — *Other taxes on specific goods and services*

75. This item includes taxes on the extraction of minerals, fossil fuels and other exhaustible resources from deposits owned privately or by another government together with any other unidentifiable receipts from taxes on specific goods and services. Taxes on the extraction of exhaustible resources are usually a fixed amount per unit of quality or weight, but can be a percentage of value. The taxes are recorded when the resources are extracted. Payments from the extraction of exhaustible resources from deposits owned by the government unit receiving the payment are classified as rent.

5200 — *Taxes on use of goods or on permission to use goods or perform activities*

76. This sub-heading covers taxes which are levied in respect of the use of goods as distinct from taxes on the goods themselves. Unlike the latter taxes – reported under 5100 –, they are not assessed on the value of the goods but usually as fixed amounts. Taxes on permission to use goods or to perform activities are also included here, as are pollution taxes not based upon the value of particular goods. It is sometimes difficult to distinguish between compulsory user charges and licence fees which are regarded as taxes and those which are excluded as non-tax revenues. The criteria which are employed are noted in §11–12.

77. Although the sub-heading refers to the "use" of goods, registration of ownership rather than use may be what generates liability to tax, so that the taxes of this heading may apply to the ownership of animals or goods rather than their use (e.g., race horses, dogs and motor vehicles) and may apply even to unusable goods (e.g., unusable motor vehicles or guns).

78. Borderline cases arise with:

a) taxes on the permission to perform business activities which are levied on a combined income, payroll or turnover base and, accordingly, are classified following the rules in §81;

b) taxes on the ownership or use of property of headings 4100, 4200 and 4600. The heading 4100 is confined to taxes on the ownership or tenancy of immovable property and – unlike the taxes of 5200 – they are related to the value of the property. The net wealth taxes and taxes on chattels of 4200 and 4600 respectively are confined to the ownership rather than the use of assets, apply to groups of assets rather than particular goods and again are related to the value of the assets.

5210 — *Recurrent taxes on use of goods and on permission to use goods or perform activities*

79. The principal characteristic of taxes classified here is that they are levied at regular intervals and that they are usually fixed amounts. The most important item in terms of revenue receipts is vehicle licence taxes. This sub-heading also covers taxes on permission to hunt, shoot, fish or to sell certain products and taxes on the ownership of dogs and on the performance of certain services, provided that they meet the criteria set out in §11–12. The sub-divisions of 5210 are user taxes on motor vehicles paid by households (5211) and those paid by others (5212). Sub-heading 5213 covers dog licences and user charges for permission to perform activities such as selling meat or liquor when the levies are on a recurring basis. It also covers recurrent general licences for hunting, shooting and fishing where the right to carry out these activities is not granted as part of a normal commercial transaction (e.g., the granting of the licence is not accompanied by the right to use a specific area which is owned by government).

5220 — Non-recurrent taxes on use of goods and on permission to use goods or perform activities

80. This section covers non-recurrent taxes levied on the use of goods or on permission to use goods or perform activities and taxes levied each time goods are used. It includes taxes levied on the emission or discharge into the environment of noxious gases, liquids or other harmful substances:

- Payments for tradable emission permits issued by governments under cap and trade schemes should be recorded here at the time the emissions occur. No revenue should be recorded for permits that governments issue free of charge. The accrual basis of recording means that there can be a timing difference between the cash being received by government for the permits and the time the emission occurs. In the national accounts, this timing gives rise to a financial liability for government during the period.
- Payments made for the collection and disposal of waste or noxious substances by public authorities should be excluded as they constitute a sale of services to enterprises.

81. Other taxes falling under heading 5200 that are not levied recurrently are also included here. Thus, once-and-for-all payments for permission to sell liquor or tobacco or to set up betting shops are included provided they meet the criteria set out in §11–12.

6000 — Other taxes

82. Taxes levied on a base, or bases, other than those described under headings 1000, 3000, 4000 and 5000, or on bases of which cannot be considered to be related to any one of these headings, are included here. Where taxes are levied on a multiple base and it is possible to estimate the receipts related to each base the separate amounts are included under the appropriate headings. If separate amounts cannot be estimated and it is known that most of the receipts are derived from one base, the whole of the receipts are classified according to that base. Otherwise, they are classified here. Other revenues included here are presumptive taxes not included elsewhere in the classification system, taxes on individuals in the form of a poll tax or capitation tax, stamp taxes not related to financial and capital transactions nor falling exclusively on a single category of transaction, expenditure taxes where personal deductions or exemptions are applied and unidentifiable tax receipts. A subdivision is made between taxes levied wholly or predominantly on business (6100) and those levied on others (6200).

A.6. Conciliation with national accounts

83. This section of the tables provides a re-conciliation between the OECD calculation of total tax revenues and the total of all taxes and social contributions paid to general government as recorded in the country's national accounts. Where the country is a member of the European Union (EU), the comparison is between the OECD calculation of total tax revenues and the sum of tax revenues and social contributions recorded in the combination of the general government and the institutions of the EU sectors of the national accounts.

A.7. Memorandum item on the financing of social security benefits

84. In view of the varying relationship between taxation and social security contributions and the cases referred to in §39 to §45, a memorandum item collects together all payments earmarked for social security-type benefits, other than voluntary payments to the private sector. Data are presented as follows (refer to Chapter 4.2 of the Report):

a) Taxes of 2000 series.

b) Taxes earmarked for social security benefits.

c) Voluntary contributions to the government.

d) Compulsory contributions to the private sector.

Guidance on the breakdown of (a) to (d) above is provided in §39 to §45.

A.8. Memorandum item on identifiable taxes paid by government

85. Identifiable taxes actually paid by government are presented in a memorandum item classified by the main headings of the OECD classification of taxes. In the vast majority of countries, only social security contributions and payroll taxes paid by government can be identified. These are, however, usually the most important taxes paid by governments (refer to Chapter 4.2 of the Report).

A.9. Relation of OECD classification of taxes to national accounting systems

86. A system of national accounts (SNA) seeks to provide a coherent framework for recording and presenting the main flows relating respectively to production, consumption, accumulation and external transactions of a given economic area, usually a country or a major region within a country. Government revenues are an important part of the transactions recorded in SNA. The final version of the 2008 SNA was jointly published by five international organisations: the United Nations, the International Monetary Fund, the European Union, the Organisation for Economic Co-operation and Development, and the World Bank in August 2009. The System is a comprehensive, consistent and flexible set of macroeconomic accounts. It is designed for use in countries with market economies, whatever their stage of economic development, and also in countries in transition to market economies. The important parts of the SNA's conceptual framework and its definitions of the various sectors of the economy have been reflected in the OECD's classification of taxes.

87. There are, however, some differences between the OECD classification of taxes and SNA concepts that are listed below. They arise because the aim of the former is to provide the maximum disaggregation of statistical data on what are generally regarded as taxes by tax administrations:

a) OECD includes compulsory social security contributions paid to general government in total tax revenues. Imputed and voluntary contributions plus those paid to private funds are not treated as taxes (§8 and §10 above);

b) there are different points of view on whether or not some levies and fees are classified as taxes (§11 and §12 above);

c) OECD excludes imputed taxes or subsidies resulting from the operation of official multiple exchange rates or from the central bank paying a rate of interest on required reserves that is different from other market rates;

d) there are differences in the treatment of non-wastable tax credits.

88. As noted in §1 and §2, headings 1000 to 6000 of the OECD list of taxes cover all unrequited payments to general government, other than compulsory loans and fines. Such unrequited payments including fines, but excluding compulsory loans can be obtained from adding together the following figures in the 2008 SNA:

- value-added type taxes (D.211);
- taxes and duties on imports, excluding VAT (D.212);
- export taxes (D.213);
- taxes on products, excluding VAT, import and export taxes (D.214);
- other taxes on production (D.29);
- taxes on income (D.51);
- other current taxes (D.59);
- social contributions (D.61), excluding voluntary contributions;
- capital taxes (D.91).

A.10. The OECD classification of taxes and the International Monetary Fund (GFS) system

89. The coverage and valuation of tax revenues in the GFS system and the 2008 SNA are very similar. Therefore, the differences between the OECD classification and that of the 2008 SNA (see §87 above) also apply to the GFS. In addition the International Monetary Fund subdivides the OECD 5000 heading into section IV (Domestic Taxes on Goods and Services) and section V (Taxes on International Trade and Transactions). This reflects the fact that while the latter usually yield insignificant amounts of revenue in OECD countries, this is not the case in many non-OECD countries.

A.11. Comparison of the OECD classification of taxes with other international classifications

90. The table below describes an item by item comparison of the OECD classification of taxes and the classifications used in the following:

a) System of National Accounts (2008 SNA);

b) European System of Accounts (2010 ESA);

c) IMF *Government Finance Statistics Manual* (GFSM 2014).

91. These comparisons represent those that would be expected to apply in the majority of cases. However in practice some flexibility should be used in their application. This is because in particular cases, countries can adopt varying approaches to the classification of revenues in national accounts.

OECD Classification	2008 SNA	2010 ESA	GFSM2014
1000 Taxes on income, profits and capital gains			
1100 Individuals			
1110 Income and profits	D51-8.61a	D51A	1111
1120 Capital gains	D51-8.61c, d	D51C, D	1111
1200 Corporations			
1210 Income and profits	D51-8.61b	D51B	1112
1220 Capital gains	D51-8.61c	D51C	1112
1300 Unallocable as between 1100 and 1200			1113

OECD Classification	2008 SNA	2010 ESA	GFSM2014
2000 Social security contributions			
2100 Employees	D613-8.85	D613	1211
2200 Employers	D611-8.83	D611	1212
2300 Self-employed, non-employed	D613-8.85	D613	1213
2400 Unallocable as between 2100, 2200 and 2300			1214
3000 Taxes on payroll and workforce	D29-7.97a	D29C	112
4000 Taxes on property			
4100 Recurrent taxes on immovable property			
4110 Households	D59-8.63a	D59A	1131
4120 Other	D29-7.97b	D29A	1131
4200 Recurrent net wealth taxes			
4210 Individual	D59-8.63b	D59A	1132
4220 Corporations	D59-8.63b	D59A	1132
4300 Estate, inheritance and gift taxes			
4310 Estate and inheritance taxes	D91-10.207b	D91A	1133
4320 Gift taxes	D91-10.207b	D91A	1133
4400 Taxes on financial and capital transactions	D59-7.96d; D29-7.97e	D214B, C	114114; 1161
4500 Other non-recurrent taxes on property	D91-10.207a	D91B	1135
4600 Other recurrent taxes on property	D59-8.63c	D59A	1136
5000 Taxes on goods and services			
5100 Taxes on production, sale and transfer of goods and services			
5110 General taxes on goods and services			
5111 Value-added taxes	D211-7.89	D211; D29G	11411
5112 Sales taxes	D2122-7.94a; D214-7.96a	D21224; D214I	11412
5113 Other general taxes on goods and services	D214-7.96a	D214I	11413
5120 Taxes on specific goods and services			
5121 Excises	D2122-7.94b; D214-7.96b	D21223; D214A, B, D	1142
5122 Profits of fiscal monopolies	D214-7.96e	D214J	1143
5123 Customs and other import duties	D2121-7.93	D2121; D21221, 2	1151
5124 On exports	D213-7.95a	D214K	1152-4
5125 On investment goods			
5126 On specific services	D2122-7.94c; D214-7.96c	D21225; D214E, F, G, H; D29F	1144; 1156
5127 Other taxes on international trade and transactions	D2122-7.94d D29-7.95b D29-7.97g D59-8.64d	D21226; D29D; D59E	1153; 1155-6
5128 Other taxes on specific goods and services			1146
5130 Unallocable between 5110 and 5120			
5200 Taxes on use of goods and on permission to use goods or perform activities			
5210 Recurrent taxes on use of goods and on permission to use goods or perform activities			
5211 Motor vehicle taxes households	D59-8.64c	D59D	11451
5212 Motor vehicles taxes others	D29-7.97d	D214D; D29B	11451
5213 Other recurrent taxes on use of goods and on permission to use goods or perform activities	D29-7.97c, d, f D59-8.64c	D29B, E, F; D59D	11452
5220 Non-recurrent taxes on permission to use goods or perform activities			11452
5300 Unallocable as between 5100 and 5200			
6000 Other taxes			
6100 Payable solely by business			1161
6200 Payable by other than business, or unidentifiable	D59-8.64a, b	D59B, C	1162

A.12. Attribution of tax revenues by sub-sectors of general government

92. The OECD classification requires a breakdown of tax revenues by sub-sectors of government. The definition of each sub-sector and the criteria to be used to attribute tax revenues between these sub-sectors are set out below. They follow the guidance of the 2008 SNA and GFSM 2014.

Sub-sectors of general government to be identified

a) Central government

93. The central government sub-sector includes all governmental departments, offices, establishments and other bodies which are agencies or instruments of the central authority whose competence extends over the whole territory, with the exception of the administration of social security funds. Central government therefore has the authority to impose taxes on all resident and non-resident units engaged in economic activities within the country.

b) State, provincial or regional government

94. This sub-sector consists of intermediate units of government exercising a competence at a level below that of central government. It includes all such units operating independently of central government in a part of a country's territory encompassing a number of smaller localities, with the exception of the administration of social security funds. In unitary countries, regional governments may be considered to have a separate existence where they have substantial autonomy to raise a significant proportion of their revenues from sources within their control and their officers are independent of external administrative control in the actual operation of the unit's activities.

95. At present, federal countries comprise the majority of cases where revenues attributed to intermediate units of government are identified separately. Spain is the only unitary country in this position. In the remaining unitary countries, regional revenues are included with those of local governments.

c) Local government

96. This sub-sector includes all other units of government exercising an independent competence in part of the territory of a country, with the exception of the administration of social security funds. It encompasses various urban and/or rural jurisdictions (e.g., local authorities, municipalities, cities, boroughs, districts).

d) Social security funds

97. Social security funds form a separate sub-sector of general government. The social security sub-sector is defined in the 2008 SNA by the following extracts from paragraphs 4.124 to 4.126 and 4.147:

> *"Social security schemes are social insurance schemes covering the community as a whole or large section of the community that are imposed and controlled by government units. The schemes cover a wide variety of programmes, providing benefits in cash or in kind for old age, invalidity or death, survivors, sickness and maternity, work injury, unemployment, family allowance, health care, etc. There is not necessarily a direct link between the amount of the contribution paid by an individual and the benefits he or she may receive." (Paragraph 4.124).*

> *"When social security schemes are separately organised from the other activities of government units and hold their assets and liabilities separately from the latter and engage in financial transactions on their own account they qualify as institutional units that are described as social security funds." (Paragraph 4.125).*

"The amounts raised, and paid out, in social security contributions and benefits may be deliberately varied in order to achieve objectives of government policy that have no direct connection with the concept of social security as a scheme to provide social benefits to members of the community. They may be raised or lowered in order to influence the level of aggregate demand in the economy, for example. Nevertheless, so long as they remain separately constituted funds, they must be treated as separate institutional units in the SNA. (Paragraph 4.126).

"The social security funds sub-sector (of general government) consists of the social security funds operating at all levels of government. Such funds are social insurance schemes covering the community as a whole or large section of the community that are imposed by government units." (Paragraph 4.147).

98. This definition of social security funds is followed in the OECD classification with the two following exceptionswhich are excluded

- schemes imposed by government and operated by bodies outside the general government sector, as defined in §3 of this manual; and
- schemes to which all contributions are voluntary.

Supra-national authorities

99. This sub-sector covers the revenue-raising operations of supra-national authorities within a country. In practice, the only relevant supra-national authority in the OECD area is that of the institutions of the European Union (EU). As from 1998, supra-national authorities are no longer included in the *Revenue Statistics*, to achieve consistency with the SNA definition of general government which excludes them. For example, income taxes and social security contributions collected by European institutions and paid by European civil servants who are resident of EU member countries should not be included. However the specific levies paid by the member states of the EU continue to be included in total tax revenues and they are shown under this heading.

Criteria to be used for the attribution of tax revenues

100. When a government collects taxes and pays them over in whole or in part to other governments, it is necessary to determine whether the revenues should be considered to be those of the collecting government which it distributes to others as grants, or those of the beneficiary governments which the collecting government receives and passes on only as their agent. The criteria to be used in the attribution of revenues are set out in §101 to §104 which replicate paragraphs 3.70 to 3.73 from the 2008 SNA.

101. In general, a tax is attributed to the government unit that:

a) exercises the authority to impose the tax (either as a principal or through the delegated authority of the principal);

b) has final discretion to set and vary the rate of the tax.

102. Where an amount is collected by one government for and on behalf of another government, and the latter government has the authority to impose the tax, and set and vary its rate, then the former is acting as an agent for the latter and the tax is reassigned. Any amount retained by the collecting government as a collection charge should be treated as a payment for a service. Any other amount retained by the collecting government, such as under a tax-sharing arrangement, should be treated as a current grant. If the collecting government was delegated the authority to set and vary the rate, then the amount collected should be treated as tax revenue of this government.

103. Where different governments jointly and equally set the rate of a tax and jointly and equally decide on the distribution of the proceeds, with no individual government having ultimate overriding authority, then the tax revenues are attributed to each government according to its respective share of the proceeds. If an arrangement allows one government unit to exercise ultimate overriding authority, then all of the tax revenue is attributed to that unit.

104. There may also be the circumstance where a tax is imposed under the constitutional or other authority of one government, but other governments individually set the tax rate in their jurisdictions. The proceeds of the tax generated in each respective government's jurisdiction are attributed as tax revenues of that government.

Levies paid by member states of the European Union

105. The levies paid by the member states of the EU take the form of specific levies which include:

a) custom duties and levies on agricultural goods (5123);

b) gross monetary compensation accounts (5123 if relating to imports and 5124 if relating to exports); and

c) steel, coal, sugar and milk levies (5128).

106. The custom duties collected by member states on behalf of the EU are recorded:

- on a gross of collection fee basis;
- using figures adjusted so that duties are shown on a "final destination" as opposed to a "country of first entry" basis where such adjustments can be made. These adjustments concern in particular duties collected at important (sea) ports. Although the EU duties are collected by the authorities of the country of first entry, when possible these duties should be excluded from the revenue of the collecting country and be included in the revenue of the country of final destination.

107. This is the specific EU levy that most clearly conforms to the attribution criterion described in §99 above. Consequently as from 1998, these amounts are footnoted as a memorandum item to EU member state country tables and no longer shown under heading 5123. However the figures are included in the total tax revenue figures on the top line for all the relevant years shown in the tables.

A.13. Provisional classification of revenues from bank levies and payments to deposit insurance and financial stability schemes

108. The OECD have adopted the following interim approach to reporting revenue from bank levies plus deposit insurance and stability fees for the 2012 and subsequent editions of *OECD Revenue Statistics*. It is recommended that the amounts should be recorded under category 5126:

- Compulsory payments of stability fees, bank levies and deposit insurance should generally be treated as tax revenues where the payments are made to general government and allocated to the governments' consolidated or general funds so that the government is free to make immediate use of the money for the purposes that it chooses. This principle would apply regardless of whether the government is promising to make payments to guarantee the banks' customer deposits in some future contingency.

- If the compulsory payments are made to general government and placed in funds that are earmarked to be entirely channelled back to the sector of the economy that comprises the companies that are subject to the payment, they would still generally be treated as tax revenues on the grounds that the funds would be available for the government and would reduce its budget deficit, the fee is unrequited for an individual entity and the amounts raised could be unrelated to any eventual pay out to depositors or expenditure on wider support for the financial sector.
- Payments made to the smaller long-standing schemes for insuring "retail" deposits, where the payment levels are consistent with the costs of insurance, should be classified as fee for service.
- Any payments which involve governments realising the assets of a failed institution or receiving a priority claim on its assets in liquidation in order to fund payments of compensation to customers for their lost deposits would be treated as a fee for a service as opposed to tax revenues.
- Compulsory payments that are made to funds operated outside the government sector and non-state institutions backed by the deposit takers and all payments to voluntary schemes should not be treated as tax revenues.

Notes

1. References in this OECD Interpretative Guide to sections or parts of "this Report" refer to OECD (2018), *Revenue Statistics 2018*, OECD Publishing, Paris.
2. All references to SNA are to the 2008 edition.
3. See section A.12 of this guide for a discussion of the concept of agency capacity.
4. It is usually possible to identify amounts of social security contributions and payroll taxes, but not other taxes paid by government.
5. If, however, a levy which is considered as non-tax revenue by most countries is regarded as a tax – or raises substantial revenue – in one or more countries, the amounts collected are footnoted at the end of the relevant country tables, even though the amounts are not included in total tax revenues.
6. Names, however, can frequently be misleading. For example, though a passport fee would normally be considered a non-tax revenue, if a supplementary levy on passports (as is the case in Portugal) were imposed in order to raise substantial amounts of revenue relative to the cost of providing the passport, the levy would be regarded as a tax under 5200.
7. A more detailed explanation of this distinction can be found in the special feature "Current issues in reporting tax revenues", in the 2001 edition of the *Revenue Statistics*.
8. Sometimes the terms "non-refundable" and "refundable" are used, but it may be considered illogical to talk of "refundable" when nothing has been paid.
9. A different treatment, however, is accorded to non-wastable tax credits under imputation systems of corporate income tax (§36–38).
10. This is not strictly a true tax expenditure in the formal sense. Such tax expenditures require identification of a benchmark tax system for each country or, preferably, a common international benchmark. In practice it has not been possible to reach agreement on a common international benchmark.
11. Unless based on the profit made on a sale, in which case they would be classified as capital gains taxes under 1120 or 1220.
12. In some countries the same legislation applies to both individual and corporate enterprises for particular taxes on income. However, the receipts from such taxes are usually allocable between individuals and enterprises and can therefore be shown in the appropriate sub-heading.
13. For example, "...sufficiently self-contained and independent that they behave in the same way as corporations...(including) keeping a complete set of accounts" (2008 SNA, section 4.44).

14. In Canada – a country also referred to as having an imputation system – the (wastable) tax credit for the shareholder is in respect of domestic corporation tax deemed to have been paid whether or not a corporation tax liability has arisen. As there is no integral connection between the corporation tax liability and the credit given against income tax under such systems, these credits for dividends are treated, along with other tax credits, on the lines described in §25.
15. This may also apply where a scheme for government employees existed prior to the introduction of a general social security scheme.
16. In the 2008 SNA these are regarded as capital transfers and not as taxes (see Section A.8).
17. This is the system by which the European Union adjusts for differences between the exchange rates used to determine prices under the Common Market Agricultural Policy and actual exchange rates. Payments under the system may relate to imports or exports and where these amounts are separately identifiable they are shown under the appropriate heading (5123 or 5124). In this Report, these amounts are shown gross (i.e. without deducting any subsidies paid out under the MCA system).
18. Transfers of profits of State lotteries are regarded as non-tax revenues (see also §67).

Annex B

The OECD Classification of Non-Tax Revenues

Table of contents

B.1. Coverage

The definition of non-tax revenues and the main sub-categories identified in this publication generally correspond to the concepts laid out in the 2014 IMF Government Finance Statistics Manual (GSFM). Non-tax revenues refer to increases in government net worth resulting from transactions other than tax revenues. They exclude funds arising from the repayment of previous lending by governments or from borrowing, or proceeds derived from sales of fixed capital assets, stocks, land and intangible assets or private gifts.

Non-tax revenues are made up of the following elements.

B.2. Grants

The GSFM 2014 states "Grants are transfers receivable by government units from non-resident government units or international organisations without the receipt of any goods, services, or assets in return. Grants are normally receivable in cash, but may also take the form of the receipt of goods or services (in kind)". These transfers are un-refundable and unrequited. Grants encompass reparations and gifts given for particular projects or programmes. The term "grants" is not used to refer to transfers to or from non-governmental units and excludes inter-governmental transfers. The remission of funds collected by one government for another in an agency capacity should not be shown as receipt of a grant by the beneficiary government but as its direct receipt of revenue.

B.3. Property income

This category includes income to government arising from their ownership of property, enterprises, financial assets, or intangible assets when government units place them at the disposal of other units. Sales of non-financial assets such as the sales of lands are not recorded as revenue because disposal of such an asset does not increase the net worth. Similarly, repayments on loans and loan disbursements are not revenue. Property income may take the form of dividends, interest, land rents, royalties, or withdrawals from entrepreneurial income. The main components are:

- Interest and dividends: Interest is the revenue earned by the government unit from a financial asset by putting it at the disposal of another institutional unit. Dividends are the revenue earned by placing equity funds at the disposal of a corporation (resident or non-resident corporation). This category also consists of profits of state-owned enterprises except those classified as fiscal monopolies (see §62-§64 of the OECD Interpretative Guide to tax revenue in Annex A), export and import monopoly profits (see §70-§71 of the same document) or those providing public utilities such as rail transport, electricity, post offices and other communications. In this category are included revenue from public financial institutions such as the central banks' profits, profits transferred or distributed from the operation of monetary authority functions outside the central bank and the profits of state lotteries transferred to the government. Transfers from public utilities enterprises are recorded as non-tax revenue under "sales of goods and services" whereas profits for fiscal, export or import monopolies are classified as tax revenue.
- Rents or royalties: Rent is the revenue generated from natural resources, such as land, mining, or oil resources, when a government unit places these at the disposal of private or foreign entities. The rents received relate to a resource lease-giving agreement for the exploitation and extraction of a natural resource by the lessee in return for a payment. Payments for exploration rights are also treated as rent. Rents should not be confused

with other payments a government may receive related to the exploitation of subsoil and similar assets, such as severance taxes, business licenses, or other taxes (e.g. value added taxes, excises, taxes on exports, etc.). They should also not be taken to mean incomes from the rental of buildings and equipment, which are treated as sales of goods and services. Revenues from rents and royalties are in some cases difficult to establish and depend on the agreement between the government unit and the lessee. For example rents, royalties and taxes such as corporate income taxes and VAT are sometimes encompassed in a single payment to the general government. In such cases the revenue should be classified under the category to which the majority of revenue belongs (see §71 of Annex A for further explanation.)

- Other property income: This includes revenue earned by a government unit placing funds at a disposal of quasi-corporations.[1] Conceptually this source of revenue is equivalent to that of dividends from a corporation but by definition, quasi-corporations cannot distribute income in the form of dividends. This category of "other property income" also includes retained or reinvested earnings, i.e. the percentage of distributable revenue not paid out as dividends, but retained by the corporation or quasi-corporation on foreign investment; and property income from investment income disbursements and unidentified property income.

B.4. Sales of goods and services

Revenue under the category "sales of goods and services" is generally reported on a gross basis, without deduction of costs. Since these costs can represent a significant proportion of revenues, they cannot be regarded in total as funds available for governments to finance their general activities. This contrasts with tax revenues, where the collection costs are usually a small proportion of revenue. This difference implies that it may not be meaningful to sum tax and non-tax revenues as part of a calculation of generally available funds.

The proceeds of sales of non-financial assets such as the sale of buildings or lands are not classified as revenues since their disposal does not increase the net worth.

Sales of goods and services consist of:

- Sales by market establishments.[2]
- Administrative fees for services (i.e. fees for drivers' licences, passports, visas, court fees, harbour fees, fees for birth, marriage or death certificates, patent registrations, radio and television licenses when public authorities provide general broadcasting services).
- Administrative fees that are sales of services associated with a regulatory function of government (such as fees for the inspection of premises before delivering a business licence) and considered to be proportional to the cost of producing the service are included in this category. If the fee in return for the service provided by the government unit is disproportionate, then the fee will be classified as a tax. Specific examples of fees that are considered taxes include fees for permission to perform activities such as hunting, fishing and shooting; and fees for business registration where this is a legal requirement for the business to operate.
- Sales by non-market establishments such as fees at government hospitals, tuition fees at government schools and admission fees to museums and parks.
- Leasing of buildings and equipment.

B.5. Fines, penalties and forfeits

The GSFM 2014 states "Fines and penalties are compulsory transfers imposed by courts of law or bodies for violations of laws or administrative rules. Out-of-court agreements are also included. Forfeits are amounts deposited with a general government unit pending a legal or administrative proceeding, and that will be transferred to the unit upon resolution". For example traffic fines are included here. Fines and penalties charged on overdue taxes or penalties imposed for the evasion of taxes should be recorded in this category and not as taxes. However, if it is not possible to separate the amounts paid in taxes and fines, the whole amount should be classified under the tax to which the fine relates (see §14 of Annex A for further explanation).

B.6. Other social contributions

This category includes the actual and imputed contributions to social insurance schemes operated by governments as employers on behalf of their employees that do not create a future defined liability. This category also includes the sum of the total voluntary contributions.[3] Excluded from this category are any contributions to funds in which the contributions of each participant and of her/his employer on her/his behalf are kept in a separate account earning interest and withdrawable under specified circumstances or any contributions to a pension fund autonomous to the general government. This category is not included in this publication.

B.7. Miscellaneous and unidentified revenue

This category consists of unidentified non-tax revenues or those that do not fit into any of the other categories listed above. It includes revenue such as gifts and transfers from individuals, private non-profit institutions, non-governmental foundations, corporations, or sources other than governments and international organisations. Major non-recurrent payments receivable in compensation for extensive damages or serious injuries not covered by insurance policies are also included, such as payments of compensation for damages caused by major explosions; oil spillages; or payments receivable for damage to property other than payments from an insurance settlement.

Notes

1. Quasi-corporations are unincorporated enterprises that exercise some functions of corporations, but have not been granted separate legal personality by statute.
2. A market establishment is an establishment that charges economically significant prices.
3. The IMF includes these contributions as part of their total of social security contributions.

ORGANISATION FOR ECONOMIC CO-OPERATION AND DEVELOPMENT

The OECD is a unique forum where governments work together to address the economic, social and environmental challenges of globalisation. The OECD is also at the forefront of efforts to understand and to help governments respond to new developments and concerns, such as corporate governance, the information economy and the challenges of an ageing population. The Organisation provides a setting where governments can compare policy experiences, seek answers to common problems, identify good practice and work to co-ordinate domestic and international policies.

The OECD member countries are: Australia, Austria, Belgium, Canada, Chile, the Czech Republic, Denmark, Estonia, Finland, France, Germany, Greece, Hungary, Iceland, Ireland, Israel, Italy, Japan, Korea, Latvia, Luxembourg, Mexico, the Netherlands, New Zealand, Norway, Poland, Portugal, the Slovak Republic, Slovenia, Spain, Sweden, Switzerland, Turkey, the United Kingdom and the United States. The European Union takes part in the work of the OECD.

OECD Publishing disseminates widely the results of the Organisation's statistics gathering and research on economic, social and environmental issues, as well as the conventions, guidelines and standards agreed by its members.

CENTRE FOR TAX POLICY AND ADMINISTRATION

The Centre for Tax Policy and Administration (CTPA) is the focal point for the OECD's work on taxation. The Centre provides technical expertise and support to the Committee on Fiscal Affairs and examines all aspects of taxation other than macro-fiscal policy. Its work covers international and domestic tax issues, direct and indirect taxes, tax policy and tax administration. CTPA also carries out an extensive global programme of dialogue between OECD and non-OECD tax officials through events held annually on the full range of OECD work, bringing together over 100 non-OECD economies. For information on the Centre for Tax Policy and Administration, please visit *www.oecd.org/tax*.

OECD DEVELOPMENT CENTRE

The OECD Development Centre was established in 1962 as an independent platform for knowledge sharing and policy dialogue between OECD member countries and developing economies, allowing these countries to interact on an equal footing. Today, 27 OECD countries and 25 non-OECD countries are members of the Centre. The Centre draws attention to emerging systemic issues likely to have an impact on global development and more specific development challenges faced by today's developing and emerging economies. It uses evidence-based analysis and strategic partnerships to help countries formulate innovative policy solutions to the global challenges of development.

For more information on the Centre, please see *www.oecd.org/dev*.

OECD PUBLISHING, 2, rue André-Pascal, 75775 PARIS CEDEX 16
(23 2018 471 P1) ISBN 978-92-64-30800-8 – 2018

www.ingramcontent.com/pod-product-compliance
Lightning Source LLC
Chambersburg PA
CBHW061219240926
51846CB00006B/1285
* 9 7 8 9 2 6 4 3 0 8 0 0 8 *